FOUNDATION
CENTER
Knowledge to build on.

THE 21ST CENTURY NONPROFIT

Second Edition

Managing in the Age of Governance

Paul B. Firstenberg

Library of Congress Cataloging-in-Publication Data
Firstenberg, Paul B., 1933-
  The 21st century nonprofit / Paul B. Firstenberg, Rick Schoff.
      p. cm.
  Includes bibliographical references and index.
  ISBN 978-1-59542-249-1 (pbk. : alk. paper)
 1. Nonprofit organizations—United States—Management.
2. Organizational change—United States. 3. Strategic planning—United
States. 4. Organizational effectiveness. I. Schoff, Rick. II. Title. III. Title:
Twenty-first century nonprofit.

  HD62.6.F57 2009
  658'.048—dc22

                                                    2009029490

To Rusty, Pebbles, and Lilly,
my wonderful constant companions

Table of Contents

Preface

The first edition of this book was published in 1996. Since that time, there have been a series of developments in managerial practices for operating a nonprofit organization, especially the emphasis on governance reform. This edition focuses on these developments.

As used in this book the term "nonprofit" refers to Internal Revenue Code Section 501(c)(3) organizations, tax-exempt entities dedicated to furthering charity, religion, education, science, arts and culture, and other causes enumerated in the tax code. Contributions to such organizations entitle the donor to a tax deduction.

The book is divided into four sections. Section 1, consisting entirely of new material, zeroes in on the pivotal role played by directors in light of the pressure for governance reform. Section 2, also new material, addresses the roles played today by professional staff, professional advisors, and contributors. It includes discussion of the contemporary human resource perspective. Section 3, which includes revised chapters from the first edition, examines a number of strategic issues. Also, the eruption of the economic crisis in the autumn of 2008 demanded the book address the specific issues that may arise during severe economic downturns and recessions.

Section 4 incorporates material from the first edition dealing with operational issues such as cost reduction, strategies for enhancing performance, and how to depict performance and financial condition. It also includes a chapter on fundraising.

The subjects of revised chapters from the first edition are as relevant today as when these chapters were first written. They are included in this edition in order to present in one volume a reasonably comprehensive examination of the primary challenges facing directors and managers of nonprofit organizations today.

The original edition of this book was a broad review of practices and procedures for improving the productivity of nonprofit organizations. At the time, a number of authorities maintained that nonprofits could be run professionally without undermining their charitable purpose. Acceptance of this viewpoint has grown steadily over the past decade. This book seeks to take up where the original edition left off and detail the more significant changes in management practice that have either taken place since the first edition or are on the near horizon.

This new edition paints a portrait of the leadership of nonprofit organizations at a time when the driving force behind change is the need for sound governance.

Introduction

Accountability, Transparency, and Responsibility

Governance is often thought of as connoting a governmental or institutional response to corporate wrongdoing. This is undoubtedly a consequence of the corporate scandals at the turn of the century and, in response, the passage of national legislation, new security exchange rules, and the actions of the Securities and Exchange Commission and state attorneys general. The concept of governance that underlies this book is much broader. It encompasses all the signal decisions and policies that guide the operation of an organization. These include the determination of the information about the organization, both financial and operational, to be communicated to outside parties, as well as a process for accounting for the results an organization achieves. The disclosure of information evidences the "transparency" of the organization and accounting for results its "accountability," the two primary roots of responsible governance. Governance further charges the officers with "responsibility" for making the decisions and policies that drive the organization. Ultimately, governance is the management of an organization to achieve its objectives in the most efficient and effective manner, in accordance with the highest societal standards and practices.

My experience with charitable nonprofit organizations encompasses work with foundations, universities, service organizations, and the incomparable Sesame Street. During the eighties and nineties I observed numerous modest changes in the way some organizations were managed. In the last few years, however, there has been a more sweeping raising of the expectations of the management of such organizations. One driving force is summed up in the word "accountability." Today, all charitable organizations are subject to increasing pressure to demonstrate that they are in fact fulfilling their announced mission and doing so on a cost-effective basis. Once support for such organizations was wholly dependent on the appeal of their missions. Today one must demonstrate not only a compelling cause but also that the cause is being effectively served. A second driving force is the pressure for "transparency"—to make more known to stakeholders, and indeed the general public, how decisions are made in the organization, who makes them, and how the decision makers are chosen. A third force is the exercise of sustained responsibility by the leadership of the organization. Occasional intervention is not enough; direction of the organization must be unambiguous, ongoing, and consistent. These three performance markers— accountability, transparency, and responsibility—are at the heart of effective governance. The net effect is that the forgiveness of inadequate management of nonprofits is no longer acceptable; professionalism will be the standard.

The raising of expectations for management is prompted by a variety of discrete new factors that distinguish the current pressure for improved performance from prior periods. Nonprofit managers are in general better trained than their predecessors. There are numerous colleges and universities offering graduate programs devoted to equipping the current generation with more sophisticated tools for managing nonprofits. These "new" managers are seeking ways to improve the performance of the organizations they lead. At the same time, the barriers to the movement of professionals between for-profit and nonprofit organizations are giving way, at least for business executives seeking positions in nonprofits. As a consequence, professionals with business experience are moving into executive positions in charitable enterprises and adapting business practices to the nonprofit world.

In addition, the world of public corporations has undergone a series of changes dictated by federal legislation and the actions of securities exchanges. Many of these new requirements are the response to a series of notorious corporate scandals of unprecedented magnitude at the beginning of this century. These changes in the business sector have cast their shadow over the work of nonprofits. Managers of such organizations cannot but be aware of the dramatic new governance requirements imposed on public corporations. Nonprofit board members from the business community are also asking why nonprofit organizations should not be held to at least some of the same standards now imposed on public corporations. The attorneys general of several states have also found reason to take more intense interest in and become more active overseers of the work of the charitable sector.

Finally, the industry itself has taken up the issue of governance. In 2005, for instance, a cross section of leaders from throughout the nonprofit sector published a report to the Congress, as well as to the public, calling for greater accountability and transparency in the management of nonprofit enterprises.[1] Governance has thus become part of the vocabulary of the nonprofit sector and has wrought changes in the way tax-exempt organizations are managed.

The emergence of new governance requirements has impacted all levels of nonprofit organizations: the role and responsibilities of boards of directors, the work of the chief executive and chief financial officer and fundraising officers, the role of accountants and lawyers, and the expectations of both institutional and individual contributors. Thus, the evolving changes in the governance of such organizations will increasingly be in the forefront of the consciousness of board members and executives as they direct organizations toward better performance.

The issues of governance of the nonprofit sector arise in a two-fold context. First, there has been a series of instances in which nonprofit organizations have been marred by scandal. For instance, the Smithsonian case (p. 19) raises questions as to whether governance practices of the nonprofit sector are rigorous enough, especially when seen against the backdrop of corporate scandals.

Second, the Sarbanes-Oxley statute was introduced in 2002. It was the first piece of major legislation to deal with the integrity of financial reporting by public corporations since the Securities Acts of 1933 and 1934. With the exception of document tampering and retaliating against a whistle blower, the statute by its terms does not apply to the nonprofit sector. One of its authors, Paul Sarbanes, then a senator from Maryland, told me the nonprofit sector was not in the sights of the committees that drafted the bill. However, there are provisions of Sarbanes-Oxley that it may be prudent for the nonprofit sector to adopt to strengthen their own governance: for instance, requiring the auditor to deal with the board audit committee rather than simply management, barring auditors from also providing certain consulting services to an audit client, requiring the chief executive to sign financial statements and reports, and causing senior management to review the organization's internal controls for financial reporting. A section of the book (p. 140) will look specifically at the implications of Sarbanes-Oxley for the governance of nonprofit institutions. This section will also review the New York Stock Exchange Listing Requirements to identify those that might prudently be applied to the nonprofit sector.

A prime focus of the book is on the evolving role and responsibilities of the boards of directors. Unlike the corporate sector, there is not an array of third parties, from shareholders to credit analysts, continually evaluating the performance of nonprofit organizations and scrutinizing the financial information they publish. There is no governmental agency, such as the U.S. Securities and Exchange Commission, specifically charged with overseeing that thorough, accurate financial information is disseminated. There are no securities exchanges, like the New York Stock Exchange, which sets governance standards for listed companies. With the exception of occasional action by state attorneys general or the Internal Revenue Service, nonprofit boards bear almost the full weight of responsibility for setting standards for the organization.

Indeed, the principal oversight of nonprofits is by the U.S. Internal Revenue Service in its effort to oversee compliance with those provisions of the tax code that apply to nonprofits. These provisions in general are designed to ensure that nonprofit organizations that enjoy tax benefits pursue charitable purposes and that no part of the earnings of the organization inure to the benefit of a private individual.

True, nonprofits must prepare a publicly available Internal Revenue Service Form 990, which contains information about organizational activities, compensation of the highest-paid officials, and financial data. A number of states also require organizations to file an annual report. However, there is no evidence that the forms or reports are yet carefully vetted by any governmental agency.

In short, there is no effective external oversight of the disclosures made to the public by nonprofits or solid evaluation of the effectiveness with which charitable missions are carried out.

In this environment, by its very nature, the board bears the principal responsibility for seeing that an organization disseminates comprehensive information about its activities (transparency) and demonstrates that it executes its mission with maximum efficiency and effectiveness (accountability).

Accordingly, the book begins with the workings of boards of directors
and their evolving role in establishing and overseeing the governance of
organizations. The areas of responsibility of an active board are described.
Boards set not only the governing rules but also the tone of the organization.
Each board determines its own agenda; the specific actions boards take are
not prescribed by law. Rather, boards are vested by state statutes with the
power to govern an organization, but are not obligated to exercise that power
in any specific way. Therefore, the text sets out what can be read as an ideal
set of actions boards can take to be effective governors, from overseeing
the organization's finances and production of financial information to
challenging the status quo by formulating a set of strategic questions, the
response to which will shape the direction of the organization. Section 1
of the text concludes with an analysis of why some boards are effective and
some are not.

The board remains essentially a policymaking body heavily dependent on
the organization's professional staff and advisers for information and the
identification of issues. Indeed, typically a board can be no more effective
than the quality of the professional staff enables it to be. Boards uniformly
delegate the authority to professional staff to conduct the day-to-day
operations of the organization and to implement the objectives set by the
board. In highly efficient organizations, leadership starts at the top with the
board of directors and flows seamlessly down from the highest- to the lowest-
level staff members. Such organizations speak with one voice. Board and staff
act from a common baseline, inspired by a shared vision, joint participation
in establishing the objectives of the organization, and agreement on how the
effectiveness of its work is to be determined. The book therefore will examine
the roles of the chief executive officer, chief financial officer, development
officer, attorneys, and auditors.

The book also examines the role contributors can play in not simply
funding organizations, but also in pressing the organization to strengthen
its management and operations. The book will argue that individuals and
organizations that provide a significant portion of a charity's funding should
use their leverage to insist the organization publish a full and fair picture of
its activities and finances. In so doing, contributors can put some teeth into
the idea that organizations are accountable to their stakeholders.

Contributors with a business background, or experience in directing
nonprofit organizations, can also influence organizations to enhance their
capacity, especially if funding is targeted toward this objective. Contributors

with expertise in a given field may also help shape the organization's programs. The knowledge and experience of contributors can potentially be as valuable as the funds they advance.[2]

The book also covers more than the typical governance terrain. It will, for example, review the role of strategic planning. At the heart of strategic planning is determining the organization's core appeal to the audiences it is counting on for support and how it differs from that of other organizations. Much of the work burnishing an organization's distinctive appeal lies in the domain of public relations. A chapter in the book explores how "PR" can contribute to building support for an organization.

The book, then, is largely about our evolving expectations of nonprofit management, and the forces driving change. The book will describe how new expectations for nonprofit management are affecting the kind of training and experience people interested in working in nonprofits should acquire.

Finally, it must be noted that this book is the product of much more than the author's labors and experience. In the fall of 2006, I taught a course on Governance of Nonprofit Organizations at the Yale School of Management, and it would remiss not to credit those very bright students with contributing significantly to the ideas and organization of the book. In turn, this past year I taught a graduate course on the Governance of Corporations and Nonprofit Organizations at the Baruch College School of Public Affairs. Again, very able graduate students impacted the material that has been incorporated in the book. I also have had the benefit of contributions of my faculty colleagues, especially Professor Fred Lane, who constantly alerted me to relevant new material, posed ideas to incorporate into the text, and enthusiastically supported the book from day one. Of course, this book, like the earlier ones I have authored, would not have happened without the support and careful editing of the Foundation Center's Rick Schoff.

I am indebted to them all, but especially to my wife Joanne, whose character, generous spirit, and boundless energy infuse my life.

NOTES

1. *Strengthening Transparency, Governance, and Accountability of Charitable Organizations*, Final Report of the Panel on the Nonprofit Sector (2005).
2. The themes here were first advanced in Paul B. Firstenberg, *Philanthropy's Challenge: Building Nonprofit Capacity through Venture Grantmaking* (New York: The Foundation Center, 2003).

Section 1.

The Pivotal Role of Directors

Transforming the Dynamics of Nonprofit Boards: From Passive to Active Agencies

Traditionally, a variety of personal motivations have drawn people to serve as directors of nonprofit organizations—empathy for a charitable cause, the prestige of association with an elite organization, the opportunity for humanitarian leadership, relationships with prominent people, the importance of an organization within a community. Today nominees need to examine their readiness to serve in light of the new level of responsibility directors must accept in the governance of nonprofit institutions. The post-Enron changes in the role and responsibilities of directors of public corporations have cast their shadow over the expectations for nonprofit directors and will heavily influence what is deemed best practice on the part of nonprofit boards.

While for-profit and nonprofit enterprises are structured differently and have different motives, the widely publicized and emulated reforms in the public corporate sector represent such a visible, more explicitly articulated standard of governance that it is hard for nonprofit boards to ignore them, especially as corporate executives also act as nonprofit board members and contributors.[1] Businessperson board members will challenge nonprofits as to why the public corporate standards should not be adopted. At the same time, contributors to such organizations are increasingly pressing such organizations for greater accountability and transparency with respect to the use of their funds. With cases of abuse in the nonprofit sector, and intensifying Congressional oversight of the tax treatment of nonprofits, nonprofit leaders have publicly pressed for reforms modeled on changes in corporate governance.[2]

As a consequence of these pressures, nonprofit governance will be transformed; the foundation of nonprofit governance will be rooted in active rather than passive, well-informed rather than casually informed, directors who are committed to lift the organization to conform to best practices. Ideally the board will act as the ultimate insurer that nonprofit programs actually advance charitable interests, generating definable benefits, as opposed to supporting the organization's own administrative interests.

This chapter describes this transformation, the legal and practice environment that is shaping the obligations of nonprofit directors and the new role and responsibilities they are now challenged to assume. The model is the venture capital investor or private equity fund partner.[3]

The Governance Environment

The first years of this century have been marked by the efforts by securities exchanges and the federal legislature to curb corporate abuses and shore up the system for protecting the public from the dissemination of misleading financial information.

The current environment is a product on the one hand of the *failings* of the system of public corporation governance and the *absence* of such a system in the nonprofit world.

PUBLIC CORPORATION GOVERNANCE REFORMS

Since the 1930s, the integrity of information disseminated to the public has been screened by the combined guardianship of boards of directors, their accountants and attorney advisors, stockholders, banks, credit analysts, state attorneys general, and the SEC. The role of the board is compromised by the inherent conflict between shareholders/owners and managers when the directors—charged with representing the interests of owners but often selected by management—give their loyalty to management.[4]

When the system failed in Enron and other cases, the market exchanges moved to shift power to independent directors and called for the creation of a series of committees that would govern the review of financial statements and internal controls, the nomination of board members, and the compensation of senior managers. The thrust of the reforms was to strengthen the hands of the independent directors in running the corporation.

Sarbanes-Oxley (SOX) went further and interjected the government into the internal processes of a public corporation and its relationship with its auditor; specifically, it required corporations to establish internal controls for financial reporting and then for senior officials to assess how effective the system is in practice. In addition, it requires the auditor to review management's assessment of its internal control system, thereby changing the scope of accounting review by auditors. SOX also barred auditing firms from most forms of consulting with audit clients, seeking to end the incentive the firms may have had to place a higher value on lucrative consulting work than their audit practice and consequently exhibiting less resistance to earnings management by their clients.[5] SOX also ended the exclusive authority of accounting firms to set accounting standards for public corporations, vesting the review power in the Public Company Accounting Oversight Board (PCAOB) appointed by the SEC and empowering it to audit the work of auditing firms, assessing them with fines as well as suspensions from practice. Finally, SOX requires the CEO of a public corporation to sign the company's financial statements, undercutting the "I didn't know or get it" defense to the company's financial condition.[6]

Proposals by various reformers to separate the CEO and board chair role, even to create a "lead director" position, have been slow to gain acceptance. CEO's still very much want to retain control over the agenda of their boards and thus the matters the board addresses.

Despite these reforms, we continue to see occasions of the executive sense of entitlement to personal enrichment. Two examples are the flagrant, widespread backdating of stock options, and lucrative exit pay packages. This has led even some businesspeople to argue that further measures are required to deter such conduct.[7] Others would simply say that perhaps there is no systemic prophylactic for greed. It will always find a way to circumvent what defenses can be devised, because the cost of compliance with such defenses adversely affects the competitive position of American business and capital markets with their global competition.

OVERSIGHT OF NONPROFIT ORGANIZATIONS

In the case of nonprofit organizations, since there is no ownership interest, there is no division of financial interest between agent and owners to contend with. Rather, the tension is between managers—and their stake in their organization's welfare—and charitable beneficiaries. In the best of worlds, managers would be regarded as essentially agents for their organization's charitable beneficiaries with oversight vested in the board of directors. However, there are no structural requirements imposed on an organization by SOX or the exchanges, no new mandates for organization accounting, nor SEC or PCAOB mechanisms.

There is marginal oversight in the form of occasional intervention by state attorneys general, who are empowered to enforce the historic common law trust duties of care and loyalty and state tax-exemption grants, as well as, in several states, the filing with their office of audited annual financial statements. The IRS also has a role in ensuring that tax exemptions are granted for genuine charitable purposes and that exempt organizations are operated for public, not private, benefit. It has also published requirements calling for greater transparency by exempt organizations (see the sidebar "The Revised Form 990"). But the overwhelming burden of overseeing the integrity of charities rests with boards of directors. Government acts, if it acts at all, after the fact, not to prevent wrongful conduct. It is the board that can act before the fact to ensure that the organization is operated to serve its exempt purpose and in a manner that actually advances the welfare of society. The board is also on line to see that senior management receives reasonable but not excessive compensation. It is this *power to prevent* wrongful conduct that makes the board role pivotal.[8]

In addition—and perhaps most critical of all—there is the duty to satisfy the mounting demands for accountability, the objective demonstration of outcomes that justify the mission of the organization and its special tax status. Claims that such outcome analysis is difficult to produce will no longer suffice. The board has no greater obligation than to find the means and methodology to satisfy such demands. Responsibility, then, for the governance of nonprofits lies with the board of directors.

The Passive Director

Traditionally, to be asked to become a board member was perceived more as an honor than a responsibility, thereby setting the tone for the director's performance on the board. Fram analyzes two studies of corporate directors, observing that, "simply stated, the directors in the two studies recognize there are risks to being on boards, but they are more prone to look at the rewards."[1]

A particularly disturbing finding is that "... the type of information needed to help boards avoid disaster is not getting to directors. Managements are not doing an adequate job of delivering vital information on changes to their internal financial controls. And apparently board members are not demanding the information."

Fram observes that, "This adds up to a modest change in board environment at a time when most people assume a great deal is happening." He also cites *New York Times* writer Gretchen Morgenson's observation (May 16, 2004) that "boards seem to be taking a 'business as usual' stance."

My own perception of nonprofit boards is that they are too often not activist, have not learned the business of the organization, and thus continue to be generally passive recipients of often bland reports by management, uncritically accepting the organization's financial status, rarely striking at the heart of a presentation by asking probing questions, or insisting a new direction be examined. There is little realistic evaluation of the organization's strengths and weaknesses or challenge to the status quo. Too frequently, routine prevails and board meetings are conducted in a state of non-noncontentious fellowship.[9]

Fram, it seems to me rightly, concludes: "Both the business and nonprofit worlds have a long way to go to attain broad governance reform."

Changing the Board Dynamics: From Passive to Active

To discharge its modern-day responsibilities, the board must be transformed from a passive to an active agency, significantly changing the nature of board membership.

An active board develops an independent sense of the activities of the organization and how it is perceived by those it serves, helps frame the organization's agenda, conducts the reviews necessary to evaluate the effectiveness and efficiency of operations, and infuses a value system and consciousness into the organization.

The new director's role demands not only the conscientious dedication of time, often at inconvenient moments, but also the determination to learn the story first-hand, to push beyond management briefings, digging beneath the surface of things, to be aware of the state of morale of the staff, and be able to direct attention to the pivotal issues that genuinely shape the direction of the organization. It calls for the art of building support in the face of inertia, conflicting outlooks, and uncertainty about change. It calls for persistence in the face of sharp resistance, of not just going along but the taking a clear position that may fail to prevail. As the price of admission and influence, more and more directors are expected to contribute and raise money annually (with a reciprocal obligation to those whose gift they solicit). This role of a durable, very engaged stakeholder is akin to the role of a private equity investor whose capital and reputational stake encourage working to turn around potential failures rather than withdrawing early.[10]

An effective board can be seen as having two core functions: 1) a fiduciary role in ensuring that compliance with law and best practices preserves the essential integrity of the organization—a role that has become more complex and demanding in the post-Enron era; and 2) a strategic role in helping to guide the organization in building its capabilities to accomplish its mission—a role venture capitalists and private equity investors see as their primary focus.[11] In fact, these are complementary roles and an organization is best served when both command board attention.

In areas critical to the success and continuing viability of the organization, a board so focused will display a genuine leadership role by:

- Assessing the organization's strengths and weaknesses, its capabilities to expand its program, framing the pivotal strategic issues, and prompting the organization to undertake a plan that addresses them and lays out a path to enhance the performance of the organization, including the acquisition of the personnel and capital resources necessary to achieve the plan's goals.

- Ensuring meaningful financial oversight with financial statements and reports[12] prepared with meticulous care, presenting a realistic picture of the organization's financial condition reviewed by an audit committee composed of directors with financial acumen and no ties to staff or the organization's auditor. This also should be read and understood by all board members. The board audit committee should select and draw up the contract with the auditor spelling out the scope of review the accounting the firm is expected to perform and its obligation to promptly inform the committee of any questionable practice. Inquiry should also be made as to how the accounting firm resolves internally questions of interpretation of the applicability of accounting rules to the organization's financial reports.

- Paying close attention to the organization's compensation system, process, and awards, including how it compares with other comparable organizations, and the relationship of remuneration to performance benchmarks. Review here must encompass health care and pension plans, two of the most costly obligations of any organization. The board must determine the balance between making available benefits in the form most appealing to employees and those benefits' affordability. And throughout its review the board wants to gain a clear sense of the equity in all aspects of the organization's compensation structure. The initial review work is best done in the committee format and, if affordable at all, expert advice should guide the committee with respect to both the choice and administration of health and benefit plans.

- Creating a transparent process for nominating and electing board members, pursuant to criteria for membership established by the board that identify the skills and experience that should ideally make up the composition of the board. The process for selection and election should insulate the organization from any one person or clique exercising undue influence over the makeup of the board.

- Establishing the cost effectiveness of the organization's programs through documenting, in reasonable detail, that the maximum available funds are expended on programs, as opposed to administration. The analysis should encompass an independent assessment of the outcomes that result from such expenditures and the costs of delivering them compared to the costs incurred by other organizations in operating comparable programs. How effective and efficient the organization is in deploying its resources is the litmus test of the value of the organization, and publicly available documentation is the heart of accountability and transparency. Nonprofits, under the active supervision of their boards of directors, need to *account* for the extent to which they satisfy these justifications for the tax benefits accorded such organizations. Without demonstration of this accountability the diversion of potential tax revenues for the benefit of private organizations cannot be sustained.[13]

- Setting the agenda of board meetings with input from the executive director and his/her staff. The items brought before the board will directly influence what the board knows and considers about the organization and whether it has the opportunity to affect policy and operating decisions in a timely manner.

An illustration of the harm that can result from an insufficiently engaged board is the American University case. An apparently inattentive board was unaware of the president's spending habits. His salary was $633,000, but in addition he spent nearly $400,000 in university funds on his personal lifestyle. He also failed to pay the income tax due on the expenditures that could not be legitimately defended as university business. The story broke in the newspapers in Washington DC, where the university is located, and an embarrassed board had to discharge the president, seek recovery of monies due the university, and testify, mea culpa, before the chairman of the Senate Finance Committee about the reforms the board adopted in the wake of the scandal.

In contrast to the lax American University board, employing directors to bring about positive change in the academic programs of colleges and universities is the surprising recommendation of former Harvard president Derek Bok. Boards of trustees traditionally avoid any interference with academic programs. Bok, however, urges boards to prompt university leadership to establish a continuous system of evaluating the effectiveness of undergraduate education and to develop innovations in teaching methodologies. In cases in which faculty resistance to such experimentation is strong, in his view, departure from the classic principle that trustees do not interfere in academic matters is warranted. Bok argues that such intervention is necessary and appropriate,

> ... so long as trustees do not try to dictate what courses should be taught and what instructional method employed, but merely to ask for reports on the procedures used to evaluate academic programs and encourage innovation. It is surely within the prerogatives of the board to take an interest in these activities and to urge the president to work with faculties to develop a process designed to ensure continuing improvement in the quality of education.[14]

Bok's view of boards seeking to effect change, even in new arenas, is a harbinger of the future.

THE REVISED FORM 990

In weighing the changes to be made in the governance of an organization, the requirements of the revised Form 990 need to be carefully taken into account. Every tax-exempt nonprofit must file this form annually with the IRS. The form contains a wealth of information about an organization's programs, finances, payroll, and governance and it must be made available to any member of the public who requests it.

In June of 2008, the IRS announced changes in this form that will require significantly increased reporting, not only of financial data but also of internal governance and policy information. Another major change is increased reporting of compensation and benefits for highly paid employees. The whole thrust of the changes is to make the operations of nonprofits more transparent. Organizations that monitor nonprofits are sure to seize upon the additional information called for by the revised form.

The new form calls for disclosure of any business relationship between directors, employees, their families, and the organization. At another level it requires disclosure whether contemporaneous minutes of board meetings are kept and whether Form 990 is shown to the board before it is filed.

The new form also requires organizations to disclose whether they have written policies covering: 1) conflicts of interest; 2) whistle-blower protection; 3) document retention and destruction; 4) objective determination of compensation of the organization's senior professional and other key employees; and 5) tax-exemption ramifications of joint ventures or similar arrangements with taxable entities.

Prior to the new form, organizations were required only to report the five highest-paid individuals, whether or not they were employees. Under the new form the organization must report the compensation of all current directors, trustees, officers, and key employees. There are additional disclosure requirements with respect to third parties and former directors, trustees, and officers. A detailed breakdown of the components of such compensation is required for any individual with total compensation greater than $159,000. The organization must also state whether there is a detailed written policy regarding the reimbursement of expenses.

The new form is complex, with detailed instructions, and further revisions are possible before the final document is issued. Compliance with the requirements of the new form will undoubtedly prove burdensome for many organizations, especially smaller organizations. But the revised form issued on June 30, 2008 is confirmation that greater scrutiny of tax-exempt organizations is well under way and boards would be well advised to take heed.

Making Minimum Expectations Explicit

Holding a board to high standards is aided immeasurably by declaring in writing, preferably in the organization's bylaws, a director's most critical duties. For example, a nonprofit wanted to reduce the size of its board, eliminating a number of directors who no longer contributed financially, whose meeting attendance was erratic, and who when present became carping critics, turning board meetings into divisive struggles accomplishing little. Outside of board meetings they conveyed negative views of the organization to anyone who would give them an ear. But board members could be removed only by a vote of the full board. There was no mechanism for the nomination of board members against preestablished standards. The application of term limits would have eliminated productive and nonproductive members alike, and there were no declared attendance or financial contribution requirements. Here was a case of a board virtually paralyzed by the absence of standards of conduct spelled out in writing in the organization's bylaws or minutes.

The core of structural reform is the creation of audit, nominating, and compensation committees and defining in the bylaws their respective responsibilities. Incorporating into the bylaws any minimal expectations of financial contributions and attendance by board members avoids conflicting memories as to what, if any, requirement has been adopted. A director's responsibility for being fully informed about the organization's strategy, financial condition, compensation practices the cost effectiveness of its programs, and responsibility to act with good will toward the organization should be made explicit. Writing it down turns a hortatory list of good intentions into a code of acceptable conduct.

Directors should be fully aware of their responsibilities from the start of their terms—learning of them after the fact of some breakdown in the organization is too late and undermines the role of the board as empowered to act before the fact, in order to prevent organizational error. Orientation sessions for new directors are surely useful, but the most powerful message will be the black and white of the written word.

Nonprofit bylaws do not typically set out the duties of directors in the manner suggested here. But such bylaws would help, by a process of self-selection, weed out from membership those who in fact would not bring the requisite dedication to the board. When it unfortunately becomes necessary to remove a director involuntarily, such bylaws provide a foundation for doing so. Thus, bylaws with clear statements of director responsibility become important instruments in building the cohesion and effectiveness of an active, dynamic board.

Removing the Underperforming Director

For a board to be fully effective, it cannot be bogged down by dissident members who are unrelentingly and uncompromisingly critical of board deliberations *and* who fail to honor the basic commitments they agreed to when they signed on as board members, especially minimum attendance and financial contributions. An effective board must have room for differences of opinion, but at the same time a board's sense of cohesion cannot be maintained unless board members have a shared understanding of their basic roles and responsibilities. It is this common understanding that gives a board its collective strength and reinforces the willingness of all its members to be alert, informed, and proactive. In a word, constructive behavior becomes a model for the entire board.

When the board's ability to function affirmatively is threatened, it may be necessary to remove one or more members who are not living up to their obligations.

Removing a board member can be a potentially divisive event, creating tension within the board. However, a removal based on a director's failure to meet objective attendance and/or financial requirements can be less disruptive of board harmony than one based on a subjective reaction to a director's performance at board meetings.

To deal with the possible termination of a director, the board has to first establish a process where the performance of all directors is periodically evaluated—a step many organizations seem reluctant to take. But if underperformers are to be weeded out it must be pursuant to a process led by a committee of the most respected or senior board members that reviews the performance of all directors. The committee should of course share its evaluations with individual board members, especially providing directors who are not living up to preestablished expectations the chance to express their side and also the opportunity to make adjustments.

The task of removing directors can be less fraught with tension where the director's term is about to expire and the issue is reappointment. Nonprofits are thus well advised to create term appointments for all directors. For example, a minimum of two or three three-year terms, with one-third of the board up for election, would seem prudent to avoid the burden of having to conduct reviews too frequently.

The concept of term appointments differs from term limits. The latter requires the director to step off the board, at least for a period of time, when the term limit is reached. The drawback is that there may be several invaluable directors whose services the organization can ill afford to lose even for a year, and if there were "term limits" they might be forced off the board for a time. The concept of directorial terms accomplishes the purpose of providing for a review of director performance without running the risk that the board will lose the service of key members.

Forces for Change

The challenge is to motivate board members on a widespread basis to become active and involved leaders. One factor that may sway some is that the best defense against lawsuits and personal criticism is to be fully knowledgeable about the operations of the organization of which you are director. There is no foolproof insurance against complaints or even lawsuits against directors. But the best defense, one that is widely recognized in law, is that "I conscientiously exercised my best judgment," even though it may not have been, in hindsight, the "right" one. In any case, being out of touch as a director offers little excuse, to colleagues or complainants.

What is going to motivate board members to adopt a more proactive stance, especially since it will only increase the demands of the job for which non-foundation directors commonly receive no financial compensation?

A series of factors is likely to move boards in this direction.

First, of most value are the examples of those whose passivity allowed serious wrongful conduct to occur and then were compelled to take steps that would have been wiser to take to prevent the offending conduct. American University officials, in testifying before the Senate Finance Committee, stated: "In the fall of 2004, the Board of Trustees approved the 2005 Internal Audit Plan, which included using a significant portion of internal audit's time to begin Sarbanes-Oxley type review of the university's internal control of financial processes. Although Sarbanes-Oxley essentially does not apply to not-for-profit institutions with two exceptions,[15] the Audit Committee concurred with a recommendation from management that the University should be highly proactive in applying rigorous internal control standards across the enterprise."[16]

American University, having explicitly opened the door for SOX to the nonprofit world, isn't likely to be able to close it again. Other institutions can be expected to follow suit in applying the principles of SOX to the nonprofit world, as recommended by the ABA Coordinating Committee on Nonprofit Governance in their *Guide to Nonprofit Governance in the Wake of Sarbanes-Oxley*, and the Panel on the Nonprofit Sector's *Strengthening Transparency, Governance, and Accountability of Charitable Organizations*, Final Report of the Panel on the Nonprofit Sector, June 2005.

An even more powerful voice in favor of changing the dynamics of the board will be that of business executives who live with the reforms in corporate governance. Despite some frustration with some reforms,[17] they are likely now to perceive nonprofits as warranting the same extensive board scrutiny they are now obligated to apply to public corporations.

Certainly major contributors, individual and institutional donors, can also press boards to take a more active role, especially to ensure that the organization meets tests of accountability and transparency and can defend its cost structure. Indeed, the presence of such active board leadership should be a condition of their funding, and they can also sponsor programs for new board members that outline the new role and responsibilities of such directors. The Ford Foundation in its *Primer for Endowment Grantmakers* (March 12, 2001) writes that one of the key qualifications for an endowment grant is "... an active and diverse board that truly governs the organization." Tuckman and Firstenberg similarly suggest a critical factor in determining eligibility for endowment and venture grants is a board "composed of members who are actively dedicated to the organization and who have demonstrated that they provide effective leadership, ensuring the organization complies [with] best practices."[18] Foundations and educated private contributors, then, have a genuine opportunity to foster a movement toward a new kind of board leadership.

One can also expect the attorneys general of major states to pay more attention to nonprofit transactions. Accordingly, forces are at work to bridge the divide in governance between for-profit and nonprofit enterprises, applying the best practices to both sectors.

NOTES

1. Eugene H. Fram. "Governance Reform: It's Only Just Begun," *Business Horizons* 47/6, November–December 2004): pp. 10–14.

2. *Strengthening Transparency, Governance, and Accountability of Charitable Organizations*, Final Report of the Panel on the Nonprofit Sector (2005); *Guide to Nonprofit Governance in the Wake of Sarbanes-Oxley*, ABA Coordinating Committee on Nonprofit Governance (2005); *The Sarbanes-Oxley Act and Implications for Nonprofit Organizations*, BoardSource (2003).

3. "Venture investors are by no means passive investors; they take a proactive stance in guiding, leading, and nurturing the companies in which they invest." Paul B. Firstenberg, *Philanthropy's Challenge: Building Nonprofit Capacity through Venture Grantmaking* (New York: The Foundation Center, 2003), p. 13. "Private equity funds, while investing at a later stage of a business's evolution than venture capitalists, adopt a similar posture of active and continuous engagement with the companies in which they invest." *Philanthropy's Challenge*, p. 9. "Unlike the owners of public companies, who tend to be too remote and thinly spread to spend time and money closely monitoring a business, private equity firms have big stakes. Because their people's careers are on the line they have a powerful incentive to keep a close eye on things." "Briefing Private Equity," *The Economist*, February 10, 2007, pp. 75–76.

4. Paul B. Firstenberg and Burton G. Malkiel, "The Twenty-First Century Boardroom: Who Will Be in Charge?" *Sloan Management Review* (Fall 1994), p. 38. M. C. Jensen and W. H. Meckling, "Theory of the Firm: Management Behavior, Agency Costs and Ownership Structures," *Journal of Financial Economics* (1976).

5. John C. Coffee, Jr. *Gatekeepers: The Professions and Corporate Governance* (Oxford University Press, 2006).

6. See "The Applicability of SOX and NYSE Reforms of Public Corporations."

7. John P. Bogle, *The Battle for the Soul of Capitalism* (New Haven: Yale University Press, 2005).

8. The role of attorney, serving either as in-house general counsel or outside counsel, could be strengthened by being granted an express mandate from the board of directors to review an organization's compliance not only with the law but also with best practices. Such a role, proposed by a Task Force of the New York City Bar Association, would have to be reinforced by ready access to the board whenever counsel deems it necessary. "New York City Bar Association Task Force Urges Stronger Role for Lawyers in Corporate Governance." Forty-Fourth Street Notes, January 2007 (see "The Role of Lawyers as Gatekeepers"). More support for sound governance could also be provided by the accounting firm that audits an organization's financials. A draft of the audit is usually presented at a meeting with the audit committee together with a draft of a "management letter" setting forth recommendations for improvements in accounting practices. Such a letter and its discussion with the audit committee present an excellent opportunity for an exchange of ideas with the board audit committee on steps that could be taken to strengthen governance practices. (See "The Role of the Auditor in the Wake of Sarbanes-Oxley.)

9. See "The Urban Institute Study of Directors."

10. "Companies with smaller boards ... and larger equity holdings ... outperform their counterparts.... Our results do not suggest that more outside directors lead to improved performance but that outsiders often resign from the board instead of challenging managerial shirking. We conclude that choosing directors for whom board exit will be costly will better reduce agency costs." William O. Brown and Michael T. Maloney, "Exit, Voice and the Role of Directors: Evidence from Acquisition Performance" (1999).

11. Tom Perkins, "The Compliance Board," *Wall Street Journal*, March 2, 2007, p. A17.

12. The basic document all tax-exempt charities must file with the IRS is Form 990; it requires a statement of the " accomplishments" of the four largest programs, measured by expenses, and the combined information for remaining programs, but no review to ensure it has the specificity required or the activities of evaluation of the degree of success or failure—"accomplishments" doesn't really touch on the "quality" of individual programs, or require analysis of "outcomes" of programs against objectives or the organization's overall performance; organizations should prepare real outcome analysis that is available to the public, but also for its own benefit. Review should be conducted at least biannually and with the use of an independent consultant if the organization can afford it or get a grant for it, and the audit committee should approve the scope of review and results and then report to the full board. (See "The Revised Form 990.")

13. Paul B. Firstenberg. *Managing for Profit in the Nonprofit World* (New York: The Foundation Center, 1986), pp. 13–14. Bittker and Rahdent, "The Exemption of Nonprofit Organizations from Federal Income Taxation," *Yale Law Journal*, vol. 85, no. 3, January 1976.

14. Derek Bok, *Our Underachieving Colleges* (Princeton University Press, 2005), p. 334.

15. See "The Applicability of SOX and NYSE Reforms of Public Corporations."

16. American University Report/Meeting Materials for the U.S. Senate Finance Committee, Friday, March 3, 2006, p. 7.

17. R. Glenn Hubbard and John L. Thorton. "Action Plan for Capital Markets," *Wall Street Journal*, November 30, 2006, p. A16.

18. Paul B. Firstenberg and Howard Tuckman. "The Criteria for Endowment and Venture Grants: Increasing Access to Capital by Nonprofits," paper submitted to Arnova, November, 2006. See also "High Engagement Philanthropy: A Bridge to a More Effective Social Sector," Venture Philanthropy Partners & Community Wealth Ventures (2005), p. 18.

2

Reforming Board Practices

The recent criticism of the Smithsonian and Red Cross boards has focused attention on the shortcomings of board performance at two of the country's premier institutions.

The Smithsonian is the nation's largest museum complex with 18 museums (with one more under construction), nine research facilities, and the National Zoo. For seven years, until the end of March, 2008, the institution was led by an executive from the business world who raised more than $1 billion in new support and led the reopening or refurbishing of several marquee museums. He resigned when Congress threatened to reduce his salary. His total compensation for 2007 was $915,698. The flash point was the nature of his expenses, which inflamed several powerful senators (first-class trips to Hawaii and Las Vegas for the executive and his wife; $273,000 for housekeeping services). Calling the Smithsonian an "endangered institution," Senator Feinstein of California complained that, "... the oversight of his spending practices [was] lacking," and the board's response was "lackadaisical." The *Washington Post*, which published a series of reports on the executive's spending, editorialized that the 17-member board was responsible for letting his spending get out of hand. "The Smithsonian is now a billion dollar annual operation. It needs an engaged board," the *Post* declared. The board included the Chief Justice of the U.S. Supreme Court and the Vice President as nonvoting members, as well as six members of Congress.

The Inspector General of the institution charged that the board had been deliberately kept out of the loop of growing problems, including a large maintenance backlog, and that the board was not fully aware of the details of the executive's compensation arrangements. The executive was also criticized for sitting on the board of a company that insures the Smithsonian—a practice now banned by the Smithsonian.

Following the disclosures about the executive's compensation, an independent committee appointed by the board to investigate the governance of the Smithsonian said the board was largely in the dark about the terms of the executive's compensation. It also criticized the vacations allowed the executive. From 2000 to 2006, the report said, he took 70 weeks of vacation—about 10 weeks per year—and spent 64 days serving on outside corporate boards, for which he was paid $5.7 million. Rather than rein him in, the report concluded, the board stood passively by, allowing him to spend the institution's money on personal expenses and to treat the board as irrelevant to decision making. "It appears," the report said, "that the board reported to him rather than [he] reporting to the board."

In reflecting on the whole process, a board member said, *"It is never easy to do this kind of self examination, and we wish we'd been doing it on an ongoing basis."* [Italics added]

The American Red Cross was chartered by the Congress in 1900 and in 1947 Congress mandated a 50-member board structure. This proved very unwieldy at the time of Katrina and its aftermath. The Red Cross has since announced its intention, with the support of the president, to draft legislation cutting back its board to between 12 and 20 members. (Congress must still approve the change.) It also intends that the cabinet secretaries appointed by the president no longer serve on the board but serve on an advisory committee. These appointees have rarely attended board meetings.

The Red Cross board of 50 has been described as "meddlesome," overly influenced by the 35 members elected by local chapters and too big to move quickly and efficiently. Friction with the board is thought to be largely responsible for the departure of two of the organization's recent presidents. Its pre-Katrina charter called for the board chairman to be the agency's "principal officer," which led to confusion with the executive role of the full-time professional CEO.

The failings of the two boards are part of a growing need for the transformation of nonprofit governance; the foundation of governance must be rooted in active rather than passive directors, who are dedicated to adhering to best practices. As congressional critics of the Red Cross and the Smithsonian advocated, boards must be transformed from passive to active agencies focused on a board's two core functions: 1) a fiduciary role in ensuring compliance with the law and best practices to protect the integrity of the institution—a role the Smithsonian board apparently failed to fulfill with sufficient rigor, and 2) a strategic role in helping the organization in building its capabilities to accomplish its mission—a role the Red Cross board, dominated by the interest of local chapters, apparently did not exercise with sufficient diligence and insight.

The Urban Institute Study of Directors

Much of what is said or written about the behavior of directors of nonprofit organizations is based on anecdotal evidence or random observations. In 2005, the Urban Institute undertook the first national representative study of nonprofit governance. Over 5,100 organizations of varied size, location, and mission participated in the survey.[1] The survey was mailed to the organization's chief executive officer.

The study begins by observing that nonprofits, "... are facing pressure to be more accountable and transparent, which has had a profound impact on discussions of board roles and policies." The study makes a point of observing that there is a clear relationship between the public policy environment and nonprofits and that the impact on nonprofits extends beyond legislation directly aimed at such organizations; rather, it encompasses changes in the corporate sector and such dramatic legislation as Sarbanes-Oxley. The study observed that directors who sit on both corporate and nonprofit boards become a channel through which corporate practices are brought to the nonprofit world.

The study further observes, "We have to ask not only whether nonprofit boards have various policies and practices in place to prevent malfeasance, but whether they are actively serving the organization's mission and ensuring that the organization is accomplishing its mission."

The study goes on to say: "Here we find that significant percentages of boards are not very active when it comes to carrying out some basic stewardship responsibilities."

The study says further that "Efforts to strengthen nonprofit governance have insufficiently dealt with the fact that many nonprofits are having difficulty finding board members."

The study contains some striking numbers about the level of board activity:

> There were only two activities that over half (52%) of the respondents said their boards were actively engaged in—financial oversight and setting organizational policy. Where a paid CEO/executive director is employed, 54% were active in evaluating his or her performance.

> Only a minority of boards were active in fundraising (29%), monitoring the organization's programs and services (24%), community relations (31%), and educating the community about the organization (33%). When it came to monitoring the board's own performance, participation dropped to 17%, while planning for the future reached 44%.

These data back up the survey's discouraging conclusion that. "… substantial percentages of boards are simply not actively engaged in various basic governance activities." The problem is compounded by the shortage of people willing to serve as directors in the face of the historically steady growth in the number of nonprofits. The study reports that 70% of nonprofits participating in the survey are having difficulty recruiting board members, posing a challenge to the sector and its future.

The Urban Institute survey makes the case for the conclusions of Chapter 1, "Transforming the Dynamics of Nonprofit Boards: from Passive to Active Agencies." However, the basic issue remains how more qualified people can be motivated to serve as directors of nonprofit organizations, especially devoting the time and energy required to be an active director. The challenge in recruiting directors is made worse, as the UI report observed, by "… how many boards seem not to attend adequately to who and how they recruit."

Subsequent to the foregoing report, Ostrower completed a study of midsize nonprofits with annual expenses of from $500,000 to $5 million.[2] The findings were generally consistent with the earlier study. Ostrower found, for example, that 62 percent of chief executive officers saw their boards as doing a fair or poor job of raising revenue, and 60 percent felt the same about board self-examination.

"Substantial percentages feel their boards are doing a poor or fair job in many areas," Ostrower reported. "Our findings," she declares, " clearly do reveal disturbing levels of CEO dissatisfaction with board performance."

The study, not surprisingly, found that the degree of board engagement is the most important factor influencing CEO ratings. For instance, the percentage of CEOs who felt their boards were doing an excellent job of monitoring programs rose from 2 percent, for those seen as not actively engaged, to 55 percent, for those who are.

TWO ACTUAL BOARD MEETINGS

The board meeting of a national charity was held in one of southern Florida's beachfront resort hotels. Board members, who paid their own transportation and room charges, were invited to bring their wives and a fair number did. A half-dozen of the senior professional staff from New York headquarters were present. Each was scheduled to support a committee of the board, preparing materials for the committee and hopefully briefing the chair before he or she would present the findings of the committee. The chairman of the board was in his initial term as chair. This was the first meeting where he presided and that was held away from the organization's offices.

The meeting was scheduled at a leisurely pace to allow those in attendance to enjoy some of the amenities of the hotel. It was also football season and one board member, the chair of the finance and budget committee, handed off his responsibilities as chair so he could stay in his room to watch a game. Board members wore everything from shorts and a polo shirt to a sport jacket and a sport shirt. Most members did not change for dinner. Although a preliminary agenda was distributed in advance, the chairman of the board and the executive director failed in their efforts to meet in person beforehand and work out a jointly-agreed-upon final agenda and discuss how some of the more controversial issues might be handled. The chair, who arrived just an hour before the start of the meeting, also had not had an opportunity to confer with the committee chairs. He was not by nature a commanding personality or forceful speaker, but he was one of the organization's longest-serving board members and one of its largest contributors.

The meeting got off the ground in a desultory fashion. After about an hour and a half a guest speaker was scheduled to talk about an insurance program that could benefit the charity. Just before the speaker was to appear, a number of board members left the room and drifted into an adjoining conference room. Shortly, the remainder of the board members joined them in what had become an unscheduled, free-wheeling discussion of everything about the organization, from reservations about the leadership of the chairman to criticisms of the performance of the staff. The staff was excluded from the meeting, which took up most of the first day of the board meeting and a good part of the second day, leaving only time for essentially pro forma reviews of the items on the agenda requiring board action. Board members left the long private discussions frustrated since there was no agenda and no direction and no one seemed able to exert control over the unscheduled meeting. In short, the meeting became an opportunity for members to vent their personal grievances, but no basis was established at the meeting for follow-up study or action. In short, it was, in the minds of everyone present, as unsatisfactory a board meeting as they had experienced.

Meanwhile across the street, at a modest hotel without beachfront, another national charity was meeting. All members attending the meeting were present throughout. The meeting followed the agenda, close to the allotted times for different topics. There were no recreational breaks and no spouses. The chairman of the board and executive director had met beforehand, and also with the committee chairs, to come up with an agenda.

On an issue expected to be controversial, the chair assigned two supporters of the measure to call expected dissenters before the start of the meeting. The chair's motion, after spirited debate, carried. Committee chairs delivered their reports crisply, answered questions, and plainly were in command of the subject of their report. Four staff were present: the CEO, CFO, controller, and head of programs. Midway, they were excused for a little over an hour so the board could meet in private. The chair controlled this discussion, which was announced as a chance to comment on the staff leadership. The board was presented with memoranda outlining the objectives given each of the four professionals present and an evaluation of what they had accomplished. The memos had been drafted by the CEO and reviewed and approved, with minor modifications, prior to the meeting by the board chair, vice chair, and chair of the compensation committee. There was no serious dissent during the closed session to the actions proposed in the memoranda. The professionals were briefed later by the board chair and chair of the compensation committee on the board's discussion of their performance. The full board meeting adjourned as scheduled in time for an informal dinner.

The description above of the two meetings reflects actual meetings at which I was present: in the case of one for the full meeting and in the second (the meeting across the street), for part of the meeting, long enough to learn how the meeting was conducted.

Preventive Practice

As seen in the foregoing, it is increasingly incumbent on nonprofit boards to become engaged in the critical affairs of the organization. Members must to be in the loop—aware of what is going on in the organization—through their own information sources and not be dependent solely on formal board briefings. Boards should adopt best practices from the outset, rather than wait until some perceived wrongful conduct is uncovered or misinformation is disseminated. In short, don't take the soundness of your governance practices for granted.

To be proactive, board members can adopt a "preventive practice" approach to governance, conducting periodic audits of the organization's governance structure focused on at least the following nine areas:

1. Are there potential conflicts of interest on the part of board members or staff? Ask directors and officers to disclose any transaction or relationship they have had with the organization, or its vendors or other stakeholders, in which they received a form of compensation.

2. Has the compensation of executives been explicitly approved by a board committee? Is such compensation in line with those of peer organizations, and are the arrangements known to, and understood by, the full board?

3. Are the expenses of senior executives reviewed at the right level and reported to the board?

4. Can the organization objectively document that it is fulfilling its mission on a cost-effective basis?

5. Are financial statements, including a cash flow projection, reviewed carefully by a board audit committee with the financial experience to evaluate them intelligently? Are board members familiar with the statements?

6. Has the organization engaged in a strategic planning process assessing its strengths, weaknesses, opportunities, and threats, and have benchmarks for implementing the plan been established and monitored?

7. Do board members know what is expected of them; are board responsibilities spelled out in writing? Is board member compliance with such terms reviewed by the board or a committee thereof?

8. Is the process by which people are chosen for the board transparent and consistent with preestablished criteria?

9. Does the organization make the annual disclosures required by the revised Form 990, and is the form reviewed by the board?

If there is doubt whether something is appropriate, apply the "media test"—if the media picks up on it, would you feel the story tarnishes the organization's reputation for integrity and responsibility? Do you want to put your reputational capital at risk in this way?

When I discussed these ideas with my graduate students at Baruch College's School of Public Affairs, some of the class expressed concern that volunteers would be reluctant to serve on boards if charged with all the responsibilities described in this text. I agreed some might be deterred, but when the valuable name of an organization is at stake, as it was in the cases discussed earlier, it is an unacceptable risk not to take every prudent step to protect the reputation of the institution. Nonprofits today operate in an environment in which various forces review the performance of such organizations from the media to widely available services like Guidestar and Charity Navigator, which rank charities for contributors.[3]

Adherence to best board practices is the best way to protect the integrity and reputation, or, if you will, the value of an organization's name.

Being a director today is a very serious responsibility and board meetings are a crucial opportunity to carry out this responsibility. The value of board sessions, however, is undercut when members fail to attend meetings, or do not address the critical issues facing the institution, allowing individual member agendas to dominate board meetings or having the meetings be captured by staff presentations. In such cases, the net result is that the board effectively becomes a "passive instrument" of governance rather than an active body taking all practical steps to oversee the efficiency, effectiveness, and integrity of the enterprise.

Boards need to be small enough in size so a sense of board cohesion can emerge; an executive committee structure may work, but a better approach is to establish a limited-size board with a larger advisory committee. The smaller, cohesive board pinpoints the responsibility for creating effective leadership.

The effectiveness of the board can be further weakened if the critical committees—audit, nominating, and compensation—have not been formed and are not actively discharging their responsibilities. Solid, arms-length work by these committees is the foundation of effective governance, with due allowance for small or new organizations, which may not be able to establish such bodies.

RESOLVING DISPUTES

In the case of an organization like the Red Cross, with strong local constituents, there is often no effective mechanism for resolving disputes among parts of the organization in a manner that is ultimately binding on the disputants. Without such a mechanism, conflicts can fracture the organization. Take the case of World ORT.

World ORT is a global confederation of approximately 60 autonomous countries dedicated to supporting secondary education. The member countries nominate the leadership of the world organization, providing from their own leadership the board and officers of the international organization. However, no mechanism exists for settling disputes between countries. A long-running dispute between the London headquarters of World ORT and the Israeli organization ultimately led to Israel's withdrawing from the world organization. No independent arbiters were provided for in World ORT's charter to propose a resolution of conflicts between parties to which all would be committed.

On occasion, the parties to a dispute can agree on a single arbiter; more often they have to turn to the formula of each side picking one from a pre-approved list, and then the two initial nominees picking a third nominee to complete the panel.

Whatever the formula, it is important that an organization build into its charter and bylaws a mechanism for resolving disputes.

An Organizational Retreat

An important step in building an effective board of directors is organizing a retreat for board members and senior executives at which there is a comprehensive review of the organization. The objective is to increase the board's understanding of the organization's operations, aims, strategies, and financial position. The ideal retreat should take place over several days in a facility suitable for such meetings and, beyond the briefings about the organization, it should create an opportunity for board members to bond with each other, enhancing the cohesiveness of the board. At the same time, the retreat should serve to reinforce board members' commitment to the mission and programs of the organization. Board members should leave the retreat feeling they have a much better command of the organization and its objectives *and* a positive sense that their service on the board advances the cause of a socially worthy and important enterprise. The board should come away with a belief in the vision of the organization and a determination to commit the time and energy necessary to help realize that vision.

The potential value of such a retreat has been noted by experienced observers and the concept applies equally to public corporations and nonprofit organizations. Martin Lipton, one of the nation's most influential corporate lawyers, has advised:

THE DIRECTOR AT HIS BEST: THE RIGHT QUESTION AT THE RIGHT TIME

It was 1975. Jim Hill and I were newly elected members of the board of directors of the Vanguard Group of Investment Companies. At the time Vanguard was a relatively modest-size investment company; its explosive growth to become the second-largest mutual fund complex did not take place until several years later. At the time, its ability to grow was hamstrung by the structure of the complex.

At the time Vanguard was an outgrowth of a merger of a group of mutual funds managed out of Philadelphia and an investment counseling firm headquartered in Boston. The two groups had merged under the umbrella of the Boston investment firm with Jack Bogle, from Philadelphia, overseeing the mutual funds. The merger of the two enterprises foundered when Bogle and the Boston firm could not get along and Bogle was fired from the firm. However, Bogle retained his position as president of the funds when the independent directors refused to discharge him. A compromise was then worked out to create Vanguard to provide administrative services to the funds with Jack Bogle as its president. The marketing of the funds, however, was vested in the Boston firm. The Vanguard board was divided between directors loyal to Bogle and directors aligned with the Boston firm. The net result was Vanguard was a house divided, without a strategy or vision. Both Jim and I were frustrated as board meetings too often deteriorated into bickering between the Boston senior partner and Bogle, with directors taking sides.

In this environment Jim Hill and I, as new boys on the block, sought to have a private lunch with Jack Bogle to ascertain his views on the business. The three of us met in a quiet restaurant in New York City's midtown. After an hour or so of listening to the shortcomings of the Boston firm and its role in the funds, Jim Hill interrupted Bogle and asked in his blunt style, "Jack, what do you want Vanguard to be in five years?" Without missing a beat, Bogle responded with an articulate, polished vision—to be the low-cost provider of mutual fund services—a vision that Vanguard subsequently implemented to become the extraordinary enterprise it is today. When Bogle finished Hill remarked, "Well, Jack, go ahead and do it. We can't afford to continue as we are."

Hill's one question—when brought to the attention of the full board—set in motion a process by which over the course of a year the Vanguard board reexamined the company's structure. Eventually the board adopted, by a narrow margin, a plan to vest complete authority over all aspects of the fund business in Vanguard, removing the Boston firm from its marketing role. the firm continued to manage several Vanguard funds. Following the reorganization, Vanguard began its extraordinary rate of growth. At the same time, the Boston firm expanded its counseling business, becoming stronger and more prosperous than ever.

> In addition to regularly scheduled board and committee meetings with ample time to cover business, the board should consider an annual two- to three-day retreat with senior executives for a full review of the [organization's] performance, policies, strategies, long-range plans, financial outlook and other critical matters.[4]

To achieve the potential of such a retreat it must be carefully planned and organized, with an agenda that enables all aspects of the organization to be reviewed. Set out below is a model agenda listing the issues to cover. This can be adapted easily by any individual organization to its own needs and objectives.

RETREAT AGENDA

1. *The organization's strategic plan.* The plan needs to encompass a mission statement, identification of strategic issues, strategies for achieving priority objectives, and most critical of all, a vision statement—what the organization wants to become over a defined period of time. Indeed, a primary focus of the retreat should be on defining the vision and the actions necessary to achieve it. There is a risk that an organization that is struggling will devote too much energy in the retreat to reviewing current difficulties and overlook the value of setting out a clear vision for the organization.

2. *Strengths, Weaknesses, Opportunities, and Threats (SWOT) analysis.* This analysis provides the basis for a careful evaluation of the present effectiveness of the organization and the areas where it must improve its operations and build up its capabilities, especially if it is to seize the opportunities that may exist to enhance the impact of its mission.

3. *The cost effectiveness of its programs.* Here one evaluates the extent to which the organization is accomplishing its mission (the heart of accountability), including whether there are objective assessments available of whether programs are in fact having their promised impact. In turn, the costs of delivering such results should be spelled out and compared, to the extent feasible, with costs incurred by other organizations in delivering similar program objectives. Programs which are to be terminated or new initiatives will want special consideration.

4. *The perception of people and institutions outside the organization.* Various people and organizations deal with yours in various ways and will have a view of the effectiveness of your organization, the quality of its programs and its management, and the degree of leadership that your

organization brings to the fields in which it is active. It may not be easy to get candid responses from people questioned along these lines, but an assurance of confidentiality may help prompt such third parties to provide useful insights. One possible source of such observations may be grantmakers and other contributors.

5. *A review of the finances of the organization.* This should include its budget, financial statements, sources and uses of cash flow, Form 990, and the outlook over the next several years for expenses and revenues. Beyond looking at the numbers, the board should review the process by which such data are generated. The board should assess the extent to which financial targets have been met (and if not, why not). The review should include a briefing on the organization's health and retirement benefits and the exposure it may have with respect to health costs given the rising price of health care, and an examination of a defined benefit pension plan.[5]

6. *The return objectives for the endowment fund.* For organizations with an endowment, the board should review their objectives in light of the risks associated with seeking such a return, along with the policy governing the amount of endowment earnings that can be expended currently.

   The board may also want to review how such funds are managed; for example, whether the responsibility is delegated to outside professional managers or shouldered by a committee of the board.

7. *The roles and responsibilities of the board of directors.* For instance, what specific responsibilities does the board have for overseeing the operations of the organization, compliance with laws and regulations standards of good practice, the compensation of senior executives, as well as the strategy shaping the direction of the organization? Is the board organized in conformity with best practices—has it established audit, nominating, and compensation committees? What are the expectations for board members in terms of attendance, financial contributions, and fundraising ? Have the criteria for board membership been defined and, if so, is there an active search for new board members who fit those qualifications?

8. *The board's role in fundraising.* For organizations that are heavily dependent on raising contributions, the role board members must play, if objectives are to be achieved, warrants a separate discussion, perhaps inviting an outside expert to discuss how boards of other organizations have been successful in aiding their fundraising efforts.

Of course, different organizations will have needs for their own form of agenda, but the foregoing can serve as a checklist in developing the retreat program. Perhaps, even more critical than the agenda is that board members commit to devoting the time necessary for an unhurried look at the issues, as well as time to meet in executive sessions to share ideas and impressions. Some time for activity is also important—nothing can shorten the attention span faster than meeting after meeting without a break. And the schedule should allow for informal conversations between directors and staff. Meals provide one such opportunity, but other times might be set aside as well.

Such retreats, even where directors bear their own expense, will cost the organization. Some will not be able to afford a full-scale effort, but even they may consider a slimmed-down version in a modest setting (such as a large conference room in the city where the organization is headquartered).

NOTES

1. Francie Ostrower, *Nonprofit Governance in the United States* (Washington DC: The Urban Institute, 2007).
2. Francie Ostrower, "Boards of Midsize Nonprofits: Their Needs and Challenges" (Washington DC: The Urban Institute, May 2008).
3. For a more detailed discussion of: 1) assessing the cost effectiveness of an organization's program, 2) the extent to which the board is exercising meaningful oversight of the organization's operations, and 3) improving the board's own procedures, see Chapter 4, "Preparing Nonprofit Directors for the Coming Changes in Governance."
4. Martin Lipton, "Some Thoughts for Boards of Directors in 2006." [WHERE DID THIS APPEAR?] December 1, 2005
5. The organization creates a plan to provide a certain level of benefits at an employee's retirement, funding the plan through a combination of employer and employee contributions. In contrast, a defined contribution plan provides that the employer and employee will make certain contributions and at retirement pay out whatever income those contributions have generated.

3

Board Responsibility for Operational Issues

The preceding chapters have created a broad framework for defining the role of boards of directors of nonprofit organizations in this era when reform of governance is driving change in the expectations of nonprofit leaders. This chapter addresses a number of specific areas of operations the board needs to focus on:

- The effectiveness with which the operations are executed by the staff
- The process by which the board approves staff compensation
- Avoiding conflicts of interest
- Oversight of endowment risk and return

The Board's Responsibility for Execution

Joan Ganz Cooney, the founding president of Children's Television Workshop (creator of the famed "Sesame Street" television series) once remarked: "I could leave my office and go down and interview people on the street and hear ten ideas for television shows. But not one of the people could execute their idea." The point she was making can be translated into a board obligation: oversight of an organization requires an assessment not just of the importance of its mission but also of how well it's implementing the mission. In a word, the board needs to address the quality of an organization's execution.

Sometimes boards believe the way to ensure a high level of execution is to step in and actually run one or more departments of an organization. An organization I am familiar with, whose mission is raising funds for schools, was struggling with board members' frustration with their roles. Board meetings had become repetitive in nature, largely taken up with staff reports of their activities, and policy questions were very rarely addressed. A number of board members expressed their uncertainty about the nature of their responsibility, against a backdrop of general concern that the organization was stagnating, especially its fundraising, which had been flat for several years. In response to these concerns, the chairman created a series of corporate vice presidencies for board members, each with specific portfolios of responsibility. The object was to give individual board members responsibility for the oversight of specific departments, thereby tightening the review of staff's performance and hopefully rekindling board enthusiasm for the organization. A departmental review can help illuminate whether the organization is maximizing its potential. For example, could the organization increase its fundraising if the communication staff was more effective?

The chairman's plan envisioned vice presidencies for finance, development, planned giving, communications, and human resources. Each board member named to a vice president's post was to supervise the staff personnel in their area of responsibility and was authorized to make decisions relating to the operation of that area, subject to the approval of the full board. Staff members had a dual reporting responsibility—to the board vice president for their area and to the executive director of the organization.

It quickly became obvious that board members were confused as to whether the role was oversight or actual day-to-day direction of a department. Staff members were likewise confused as to who had the final authority over their actions and activities.

In my view, overseeing the quality of execution is the responsibility of the board and one that board members often fail to observe, precisely because it's difficult to establish the basis for such oversight. The chairman's plan had merit in directing attention to how well the individual departments of an organization were functioning, but it failed because it didn't draw a distinction between board-level oversight and day-to-day management.

The challenge is how to establish appropriate measures of departmental performance that a board can review without getting involved in actually running the department. This distinction is analogous to the management of an endowment, where the board's role is in setting certain policies and then reviewing whether or not portfolio managers have created portfolios of investments that achieve targeted returns.

Of course, one of the stumbling blocks to effective board oversight of execution is whether among board members there is the requisite expertise to evaluate the performance of different departments. Thus, in building a board one wants to take into account the need for expertise in various areas. An alternative is to assemble advisory committees made up of experts in different fields who periodically review the performance of different departments. Indeed, many universities appoint such advisory committees to review the work of academic units.

Over time, there can be a tendency to stop questioning whether the organization is adhering to its mission. The adherence to an organization's mission is fundamental, the first level of board oversight. Today, however, accountability also comes very much into play. Does the organization have a set of concrete goals and to what degree does it achieve these goals? Beyond that, is the organization operating with maximum potential efficiency and effectiveness? To answer this question boards must review the performance of the component units of the organization against some agreed-upon performance standards.

The starting point in assessing the quality of execution is reviewing the work of the senior staff executive (e.g., the executive director) against a set of objectives agreed upon by the board and the senior executive. The executive can be required to report on his or her progress in meeting the objectives set at the beginning of the year, and any other objectives that were necessitated by changes in circumstances during the year. In turn, the executive can be required to establish a similar process for his or her senior subordinates and report to the board on their degree of success in achieving these aims. For example, in the case of a development department, this requires going beyond whether the overall target for funds raised was achieved by evaluating the performance of the staff: how many calls to did they make on prospects, on new versus existing prospects, how many follow-up actions, how many calls were converted into gifts, how many donors received continuing communication, etc. Such evaluations can provide a basis for the level of increases in compensation awarded staff professionals, as well as help identify professionals ready for advancement.

Where an organization's staff is too large for a board to review in its entirety, its assessment can be limited to the most senior employees or to employees whose ratings are significantly above or below average. The basic point is that the board needs to convey its concern for the quality of execution.

A challenge that arises when a board delves into evaluating execution is the point at which you discipline executives who are underperforming, particularly dismissing the chief professional from his or her post. William G. Bowen, in his "The Board Book," makes an interesting argument.[1] He refers to the view that corporate CEOs on a long leash get in trouble and that they should be held on a short leash. He goes on to say, "There is a strong argument against assuming that the same guideline should apply in nonprofit settings, especially educational settings." He fairly points out that one difficulty is just how to measure success in a nonprofit setting. He further suggests that patience is often required for a nonprofit to achieve its goals, citing college presidents who accomplished even more during the latter stages of their presidencies than they did in their early days. In addition, he points out the difficulty of recruiting top-flight nonprofit executives, and the time it takes to find highly qualified candidates while the uncertainty inherent in such a process begins to undermine the work of the organization. His conclusion: "… the leash should be at least somewhat longer in most nonprofit settings than it needs to be in much of the for-profit world."

There is undoubtedly some merit to this point of view but there are various measures that can relate an executive's compensation to performance. Future compensation should be adjusted where sub-par performance cannot be excused because of factors beyond an executive's control.[2]

Compensation Review

The aim of a sound compensation structure is to reward employees for performance, for achieving the goals they agreed at the outset to accomplish, and to do so on a basis that is fair and equitable to all employees. Indeed, the objective is to motivate through merit-based compensation all employees to seek to do their best on behalf of the organization's goals.[3] The terms of compensation thus directly impact the character of an enterprise's performance and its values. Oversight of compensation policies is a critical board function. Interestingly, William G. Bowen states, "In my view, the generic problem with compensation in the nonprofit sector—in sharp contrast to the for-profit sector—is that it is too low, not too high."[4]

EXECUTIVE COMPENSATION

For two decades now the corporate world has been struggling with what are the limits of reasonable executive compensation, as high-ranking officials seem to reap endlessly increasing pay. Warren Buffet has said, "In judging whether corporate America is serious about reforming itself, CEO pay remains the acid test." Observations of this character are prompted by the explosive growth in executive compensation that began in the 1980s, which was fueled by large grants of stock options, especially in the years when such options did not have to be expensed by the issuing corporation. At the same time, the increase in compensation of the average worker has not kept pace. The multiple by which executive compensation exceeds worker pay has increased manyfold. There is also some evidence that top executives have been rewarded with lucrative compensation even though the performance of their organization, or its stock price, has been poor.

Aligning compensation with performance and the benefits received by the corporation's owners has been the overriding goal of reformers of the governance of public corporations. Criticism of compensation has come primarily from institutional investors, especially pension funds, and their protests are beginning to have some influence with directors.

The whole issue of executive compensation has now become complicated and indeed inflamed by the public outcry over bonus awards made to executives of companies, such as AIG, receiving massive infusions of public funds to stave off their collapse. The issue, strictly speaking, is what is appropriate executive compensation for companies receiving federally funded bailouts, but the furor spills over into the whole area of what is reasonable and fair compensation for all executives to receive.

With the spotlight on corporate executive compensation, it is inevitable that questions will begin to be asked whether the compensation of nonprofit executives is reasonable and reflects reward for solid performance. While William G. Bowen points out that in general nonprofit compensation is too low, the issue here is heightened by the fact that some nonprofit salaries approach the high six-figure and the seven-figure levels, at least among some colleges and universities, certain hospitals, and institutions like the Smithsonian (its former CEO drew nearly $1 million in salary).

In the foreseeable future, nonprofit institutions are likely to be under similar pressure to justify, in some systematic fashion, the level of compensation awarded highly paid executives and relate that compensation to what they've accomplished. The challenge will likely come from large contributors. At some point the IRS may challenge salaries on the grounds that unreasonable salaries represent a distribution of earnings for private benefit, violating the Tax Code prohibition on the inurement of earnings for the benefit of individuals.

One basic justification for the compensation paid the senior executive officer will depend on how well the executive has met or bettered the goals set for him or her in concert with the board at the outset of a year. The goals should be a road map of what the chief executive ought to address in the coming year. While most of the goals will be quantitative, provision should be made for some qualitative objectives, such as lifting employee morale or improving the quality of service provided. Difficult as it may be to assess performance qualitatively, it is part of a comprehensive assessment of the executive's performance.

In addition, the compensation of an executive should be compared with that received by executives in other organizations of comparable size with comparable missions and executive responsibilities. For the compensation and other comparisons to be meaningful, one has to be careful that the similarities between the organizations outweigh any dissimilarities. Such comparisons can also be misused if they lead to automatically paying executives the same as executives at comparable organizations; the comparison should be just one factor in setting compensation and not a serve as a floor.

COMPENSATING THE STAFF

The compensation structure of a nonprofit should reward performance at every level of employee. Giving every employee the same percentage raise doesn't reward extraordinary performance and implies that ordinary performance is acceptable. Managers need to differentiate between their employees who have achieved the objectives set for them and those who have come up short. The message should be clear: outstanding performance is the institutional goal and compensation awards will be distributed accordingly.

At the same time, making staff feel they are being fairly compensated to the best of the organization's ability is important to the morale of the enterprise. To this end, the organization should be at pains to explain to the staff how compensation is administered, and a one-on-one review of the employee's actual performance versus objectives is an obligation of every supervisor with respect to those who report to him or her. The objectives projected and the goals actually achieved should be in writing, as part of the process. It is also very useful if the supervisor can pinpoint where an employee underperformed and specify how his or her performance could be improved in the coming year. Putting these comments in writing will not only avoid arguments later as to what was said but it provides a clear guide to how the employee can improve. A supervisor can offer criticisms,—indeed should if an employee is to improve,—but while candor is essential, the tone should be constructive, not punitive. These sessions can be pivotal in enabling employees to reach their potential within an organization, and supervisors should devote the time and preparation necessary to make the dialogue beneficial. Also, board members on the compensation committee should satisfy themselves that a carefully constructed and administered process does exist for supervisors to review their employees' performance.

EXECUTIVE PERQUISITES

Perquisites are essentially tangible benefits awarded to an executive that are not treated as income to the executive, and thus not subject to income tax. They are treated as expenses of the institution. Business executives may enjoy free use of a jet plane and personal pilot, car and driver, country club membership, memberships in cultural institutions such as ballet or symphony, etc. The perquisites available to senior nonprofit executives are far more limited. The test of their legitimacy is whether the perquisite primarily serves the interest of the individual or the institution. Some examples:

- A university president may require a larger home than for just his family in order to be able to hold university events. The university can either increase the president's salary, reimbursing him for the additional tax, or make the home available to the president at an affordable price or even without charge.

- The time an officer can save by being driven can be substantial over driving himself, time the official can devote to his employer's business.

- For a flight in excess of a certain length, first-class travel is provided to senior officials. Getting them to their destination in reasonably good physical shape will enable them to perform better.

Almost sure to become public are instances in which the chief executive officer has charged the institution for expenses that were not legitimate organizational expenses, but rather personal expenses for which the executive was not entitled to reimbursement. In the case of American University, some $300,000 in such expenses were uncovered. In the case of the Smithsonian, a substantial amount of such expenses were identified. In both cases, this led to the dismissal of the CEO.

American University is located in Washington DC. When the American University situation was uncovered it drew the immediate attention of the United States Senate Finance Committee. The university was compelled to testify before the committee on the reforms it was to adopt in its governance process. The president of George Washington University, also situated in Washington DC, saw the issue raised by the American University case and immediately retained an outside firm to review all of his expenditures charged to the university. The review concluded that, if anything, he had undercharged the university. However, his action sets a precedent it would be prudent for other institutions to follow where there is substantial reimbursement by the institution of expenditures by a senior executive. At a minimum, there has to be a system where such expenditures by a senior officer are reviewed both by the finance department and by an officer of a higher rank. In the case of the chief executive, of course, there is no higher-ranking officer and it falls to the board or an agent appointed by the directors to conduct a review of such expenditures.

American University advised the Senate Finance Committee that its board audit committee had directed the chief financial officer to provide the chairs of the board of trustees and of the audit committee a quarterly report on the travel and entertainment expenses for the president and each vice president. A potential difficulty with this approach is that it puts the burden on trustees to review a series of individual transactions, the validity of which as reimbursable may not be obvious but turn on the specific facts and circumstances. This can be a time-consuming task. It may facilitate such review to hire, as George Washington University did, an outsider to conduct such a review and in turn raise any questionable transactions with the audit committee and board chair.

All reimbursement of expenses by officers on behalf of the institution are not per se questionable. Most officials are careful to seek appropriate reimbursement, but there will be cases where different people can reach different judgments. For example, the president of a university may be accompanied by a spouse to a meeting with other presidents to confer about common problems. Presidents being accompanied by their spouses has been the custom for years. Assume the spouses participate only in the social functions of the conference, which is held at a deluxe resort. Should the spouse's expenses be reimbursed? In such instances, it is prudent for the president to get the prior approval of the chair of the audit committee or the compensation committee if one has been established.

The Compensation Committee

Under the rules of the New York Stock Exchange (NYSE), companies listed on the must have a compensation committee composed entirely of independent directors that reviews and approves the corporate goals and objectives relevant to CEO compensation, evaluates the CEO's performance in light of those goals, and makes recommendations to the board with respect to the compensation of other executive officers. The NYSE rules call for the committee to draw up a charter of its responsibilities, criteria for membership, and a process for evaluating its work.

The American Bar Association Coordinating Committee on Nonprofit Governance has recommended nonprofit organizations consider the creation of such a committee.[5] Rotation of committee members can expose the full board to the issues firsthand, and also avoid the establishment of a committee that becomes locked into one point of view.

Given the importance of an organization's compensation structure to the welfare of the organization, nonprofit boards should seize this issue as one of its paramount responsibilities and create a mechanism to carry out the same tasks as required of compensation committees by the NYSE rules. The establishment of a compensation review system for executives presents a unique opportunity for the board to shape the performance of the organization. It also provides the best opportunity to prevent excessive compensation and/or unjustifiable perquisites or improper reimbursement of expenses before they become embedded in the operation of the organization and become a target for criticism by contributors, the media, and Congress. Accordingly, attention to compensation issues should be high on the board's list of priorities.

Conflicts of Interest

One of the most important fiduciary duties of the board of directors is to see that appropriate steps are taken to deal with actual or potential conflicts of interest.

Long ago the common law established the principle that directors owe a duty of loyalty to the organizations on whose boards they sit. In simple terms this means a director cannot personally benefit from dealing with the organization to the organization's detriment. To put it another way, a director cannot exploit his relationship with the organization on whose board he sits for his personal gain. The same standard applies, of course, to employees.

The wave of corporate scandals during 2000–2002 drew attention to a series of conflicts of interest. Then, in the fall of 2007, New York Attorney General Andrew Cuomo began investigations centered on conflicts of interest between college and university financial aid programs and student loan providers. Investigations are also under way into potential conflicts between study-abroad administrators and travel providers for practices similar to those uncovered in the student loan area. These cases draw renewed focus on the problem of conflicts of interest in nonprofits.

There are to two basic governing rules and regulations aimed at barring conflicts of interest.

The New York Stock Exchange rules call upon listed companies to adopt and disclose a Code of Business Ethics for directors, officers, and employees. It further requires the Code to address "conflicts of interest." It states that such a conflict occurs "... when an individual's private interest interferes in any way—or even appears to interfere—with the interests of the corporation as a whole." It adds that conflicts can arise when an employee, officer, or director takes actions or has interests that may make it difficult "to perform his or her company work objectively and effectively," or such person receives "improper personal benefits" as a result of his or her position. Loans to, or guarantees of the obligations of such persons "are of special concern." While this rule is directed at listed public corporations, it provides a useful standard for nonprofit organizations.

Nonprofit organizations are also subject to the provisions of the Internal Revenue Code that provide intermediate sanctions when private persons improperly benefit from transactions with an exempt organization. The section (4958) was added to the Code in 1995 as an alternative remedy to revocation of the organization's tax-exempt status. The Code imposes an excess benefits tax, otherwise known as "intermediate sanctions," on "disqualified persons" (a person in a position to exercise substantial influence over the affairs of an organization), their relatives, and controlled companies, who enter into favorable transactions with a charity. Favorable transactions occur when the amount paid by the exempt organization to the disqualified person exceeds the fair market value of the services provided to, or the property transferred to or acquired from, the exempt organization by the disqualified person. The tax rate is 25 percent of the excess benefit amount. An additional 200 percent tax is imposed if the violation is not corrected. There is also a 10 percent tax imposed on the organization manager who knowingly approved the excess benefit transaction.

Congress, in drafting the sanctions legislation, intended to create a rebuttable presumption of reasonableness, or "safe harbor." Under this provision, compensation is presumed to be reasonable and a property transfer is presumed to be at fair market value if: 1) the compensation arrangement or terms of transfer are approved, in advance, by an authorized body of the exempt organization, composed entirely of individuals without a conflict of interest; 2) the board or committee obtained and relied upon appropriate data as to comparability in making its determination; and 3) the board or committee adequately documented the basis for its determination, concurrent with making the decision. The disqualified person or organization manager has the initial burden of proving that the compensation was reasonable. If the three criteria are met, the burden of proof shifts to the IRS, which must prove, by sufficient contrary evidence, that the compensation was not reasonable or the transfer was not at fair market value.

Similar to the excess benefits tax on public charities and social welfare organizations are the excise taxes on self-dealing between a private foundation and a disqualified person, i.e., a foundation insider. Self-dealing includes any transaction between a disqualified person and the foundation, except for certain enumerated exceptions set forth in the Code and Treasury Regulations, including fair compensation for services rendered to the organization.

The challenge to directors and executives is what steps they can take, in light of the foregoing rules and regulations, to prevent conflicts from occurring. The first action is to create a committee of the board to oversee conflict matters, including writing a conflicts policy. Then the committee should make sure that the policy is reviewed by all directors and employees. Consistent with such a policy, directors and employees should certify in writing whether or not they have received any benefits (other than normal compensation for employees) from their role in or their relationship with the organization.

The committee should also be prepared to hear arguments that a true conflict does or does not exist in a given case, or any other issues relating to specific situations. Some conflict cases will be blatantly obvious once the facts are developed—for example, directors selling goods and services on a noncompetitive basis to the organization on whose board they sit at prices that cannot be shown to be market level. Some will be less clear that a prohibited conflict exists. Take the hypothetical case of two presidents of nonprofit organizations. Both sit on each other's board, President A as chair of the compensation committee and President B as chair of the board, which determines executive compensation directly without the benefit of a committee. Assume the compensation committee, under President A, awards the President B an employment contract that is at the uppermost range of comparable executives. Is the contract vulnerable to challenge because President A may be motivated to act favorably on President B's contract because President B will be influential in determining President A's compensation? The committee charged with conflict-of-interest policies must decide in light of all the available facts and circumstances.

It is possible that in larger organizations different departments may have different conflict policies. For example, within a university one policy might guide faculty researchers on accepting grants from industry; another might cover athletic officials receiving free cars or endorsement contracts. The object here is to determine that the varied policies reflect a consistent standard.

The committee should report on its initial work to the full board and provide periodic updates, as circumstances may warrant. The aim is not only to alert the institution to the dangers inherent in conflicts, but also to get out in front on this issue and act without waiting for a government official to open an investigation into some aspect of the organization's activities.

The Director's Responsibility for Endowment Risk and Return

An endowment is a fund of assets that are invested to produce income to be expended currently and the principal of which is to be reinvested. Gifts to the endowment may be either restricted or unrestricted in form. The former means the funds can only be expended for a designated purpose. The latter allows the funds to be expended for any purpose that benefits the recipient institution. The directors of an organization with an endowment bear special responsibility for setting the policies that govern the investment of the fund, the type of management employed to invest fund assets, the rate at which the earnings of the fund may be expended, and, of course, whether the fund's performance matches the return objectives set for it. In essence, oversight of the endowment is one of the core fiduciary duties of directors.

The difference between skillful management of an endowment fund generating superior results, compared to a fund producing mediocre returns, can be critical to the welfare of the endowed organization. Take a fund of $200 million. Assume in one case it earns a 15 percent annual total return. That translates to a $30 million gain in the value of the fund. Contrast the same fund earning 5 percent, which produces a $10 million gain. The point is that the stakes in endowment management are very high and behoove a board not only to pay close attention but also to bring onto the board one or more directors with a professional understanding of investments and the management of endowment funds.

Virtually all nonprofits with an endowment appoint a committee of the board of directors to oversee its investment. However, the structure of the oversight varies widely. The history of the management of the Princeton University endowment since the 1970s provides a good illustration of the different styles of oversight. In the 1970s, Princeton's endowment was overseen by a committee of three trustees; one headed a major pension fund, one headed a bank, and one was chief executive of an insurance company. The committee was aided in its work by a professional money management firm. The decision as to which individual securities to buy or sell was made by the committee; in fact, as a practical matter, the buy and sell decisions were often made by the pension head because he was the only investment professional of the three trustees and his colleagues on the committee deferred to him.

After considerable debate and analysis of various methods of trustee portfolio oversight, the Princeton board concluded that the selection of securities to buy and sell should be made by professional managers expert in the different classes of investment. The role of the board investment committee should be to set certain critical policies and to evaluate the performance of the fund. The study done for the board of other institutions showed that the endowments that did not achieve their objectives were, in general, ones at which trustees had failed to exercise adequate control over strategic decisions. For instance, too little direction was given with respect to the composition of the portfolio or its risk level. The study found that the failure of a nonprofit to attain its endowment investment objectives generally could be explained by either a policy or strategic decision by trustees that proved incorrect, or the leaving of such critical decisions by default to the professionals hired to buy and sell securities. In addition, the Princeton board was concerned about the degree to which its portfolio decisions could be influenced by the investment decisions made by the pension fund managed by one of its investment committee in cases in which the endowment invested in the same transaction as the pension fund.

Today Princeton's endowment is managed by a separate corporation that employs investment professionals with diversified expertise, acting under the supervision of a board made up of people with strong investment backgrounds, some of whom also sit on the university board and some who sit just on the corporation board. Under this approach, the university has achieved remarkable investment results.

In the case of Princeton, its outstanding past results, as in the case of most endowments, have been badly marred by the losses sustained in the economic meltdown. Many institutional portfolios have suffered as much as 40 percent or more declines in value. History says eventually the market will revive and at least a good part of such losses will be recouped. No one, however, seems confident enough to predict when this will happen.

Establishing Three Basic Policies

The board of directors, acting on the advice of the investment committee, should be responsible for establishing and monitoring three basic policy and strategic decisions:

1. Setting the risk level for the portfolio in light of the organization's financial needs.

2. Determining the composition of the portfolio; i.e., the basic asset classes to be held.

3. Establishing a spending policy.

SETTING THE RISK LEVEL

One of the immutable investment laws is that investors earn higher long-term rates of return by accepting greater risk. The task of the investment committee is to recommend to the full board a targeted rate of return to be generated by the endowment fund at a level of risk the institution can live with.

The term "risk" in the investment world means the likely variability of future returns. A portfolio whose future returns are not expected to vary greatly is said to carry little risk. A portfolio whose future returns are likely to fluctuate widely from year to year is said to be risky. An investment portfolio, structured to achieve a stable and dependable 9 percent return is less risky than another fund that earns 18 percent in one year in a rising market, but zero the next when the market falls.

In essence, portfolio risk is the fluctuation in returns from one time period to another. The concept of "risk level" references a comparison of the variability of one portfolio relative to another. Thus a portfolio of common stocks, whose value will fluctuate with market conditions, has a higher risk level than a fund of short-term treasury bills whose value tends to remain fairly constant. But the return earned by the stock fund will over time be much greater than the return generated by a T-bill portfolio.

Different organizations will have different tolerances for risk or variability of returns. A reasonable degree of predictability in returns and the funds available for current expenses is important from a planning perspective. Programs and activities cannot be readily turned off and on according to the level of investment return. Indeed, for a good number of nonprofits, the availability of a stable, constant return may be essential to the operations of the organization and thus they will accept a lower rate of return in order to limit the variability of returns. At the same time, too low a return, although quite stable, may provide insufficient funds to sustain the programs of the institution, which is then required to scale back its operations. The task of the investment committee is to balance the organization's need for the highest return with its need for relatively stable returns.

The fearsome loss of value in the current economic downturn is quite likely to move directors to favor in the future conservative risk targets.

DETERMINING PORTFOLIO COMPOSITION

With risk and return objectives set, the investment committee next selects the types of assets it wishes the portfolio to hold: U.S. or foreign stocks, various forms of interest-bearing debt securities, real estate, currencies, private equity firms, and direct investment in businesses (limited to the larger funds that have the capacity to undertake such an investment). Each class of assets will have its own risk/return characteristics, and ideally the various investments will not all react to the same degree to the same variables and trends. When this is the case the portfolio is diversified, which is a way to reduce risk without sacrificing return. However, diversification cannot reduce all risk; even a well-diversified portfolio will fluctuate over time in response to general market trends.

The investment committee may shift the portfolio's asset mix in response to its outlook for different assets. For example, commercial or residential real estate may be considered overbuilt in most parts of the country, and thus not offering attractive returns, or stocks may seem out of favor as various industries experience a downturn. However, there is a line to be drawn between the role of selecting the mix of assets and picking the individual investments. The former is the responsibility of the directors, the latter is the responsibility of the investment professionals employed to make individual investment decisions.

The argument against having trustees select the individual investments in the portfolio, rather than delegating selection to professional managers under appropriate guidelines, rests on a number of concerns, even in the case where there is an active investment professional on the board:

1. The types of securities one invests in and the general policy guidelines governing investments will contribute more to return than the individual securities that are selected. There is the risk that preoccupation with day-to-day operations will distract directors from the critical policy decisions.

2. Vesting responsibility for selection of individual investments in one or more directors can create an awkward situation if certain investments perform poorly and one wants to remove the individual responsible for their selection.

3. Merging the operational and policymaking roles can deprive the organization of the detachment from operations that is vital to the setting of sound policy.

4. Conflicts of interest might arise if the selection of securities for the endowment is made by a director who also manages a private fund. If the two funds were to work together, questions could be raised whether the endowment was being deployed to benefit the private fund.

SPENDING POLICY

The spending of endowment funds made available to Princeton University was limited initially to the dividends and interest payments received on the investment of the fund. However, the university went to court in the 1950s to establish that the "income" of the fund could include not only interest, rents, and dividends, but also capital gains, whether or not realized. The idea was that the "total return" earned annually by the fund was available for spending currently. In turn, the university adopted a spending formula that limited the amount actually spent currently to a portion of the total return. The balance was to be reinvested in order that the value of the endowment would keep pace with the growth in expenses and thus retain its purchasing power. The idea is that the endowment should be invested to maximize its return, consistent with the level of risk set for the fund, and not to produce a certain form in income (namely interest, rents, and dividends). The goal is to insulate investment decisions from current spending requirements. For example, if an institution needs to spend more than dividends and interest received in a given year, it should sell a portion of its stocks to realize a portion of the capital appreciation rather than invest in high-yielding securities, if the latter are not considered the best way to maximize the return on the endowment. At the same time, the ability of the endowment to maintain its value to an institution depends in large measure on its ability to maintain the purchasing power of its financial capital. Spending funds at a rate to meet all of today's expenses simply means that the endowment funds, subject to investment results, may not grow at a rate that is adequate to meet the greater costs in future years.

A total return formula allows the institution to decide consciously how much of the return from the portfolio—regardless of whether it is earned in the form of current income or capital gains—is to be spent for current expenses and how much is to be reinvested in order to offset future gains in expenses. Since returns will fluctuate from year to year, provision has to be made to enable the amount of spending under the total return formula to be modified when actual results vary significantly from projected returns.

THE TERMS OF MAJOR GIFTS

The acceptance of gifts to an institution for the endowment (or for other purposes) is ultimately for the board of directors to determine. They may choose to delegate the power to accept gifts to management. However, the current lawsuit against Princeton by the heirs of a very large gift cautions that boards should review the recommendation of management whether or not to accept gifts of at least a certain size, especially the terms on which they are made, including whether the terms are sufficiently flexible to permit the use of the funds to be adapted to changing times and circumstances.

The dispute in question centers on whether Princeton University adhered to the wishes of the donor who gave the university $35 million in 1961 to support its graduate school of public affairs. The donation is now worth $880 million. The heirs, children of the donor, contend today, decades after the gift was made, that the money was intended to prepare students for work in the federal government, especially international affairs. They assert that few graduates now pursue such careers and the university uses the money for other purposes. The heirs are seeking that the money be taken away from the university and given to a foundation that they would control. Princeton maintains that the heirs' interpretation is unduly narrow and that the gift was made to support the Woodrow Wilson School's graduate program.

As of June 30, 2008, the endowment created by the Robertson gift had grown to more than $900 million. In December of 2008, the case was settled out of court. The critical terms of the settlement enabled the University to retain control and use of the endowment. In turn, it required the University to transfer over a period of years $50 million to a new foundation to be created by the heirs to prepare students for careers in public service. It also obligated the University to reimburse the heirs for some $40 million of their legal expenses.

The case is a warning to all institutions to scrutinize carefully the terms of major gifts, especially when funds are to be expended over a long period of time when conditions could become quite different from those that existed at the time of the gift.

NOTES

1. William G. Bowen, *The Board Book* (New York: W.W.Norton & Co., 2008), pp. 100–102.

2. For a more detailed description of the process of evaluating a nonprofit CEO, see "Board Evaluation of CEOs in a Nonprofit Setting," Bowen, pp. 88–90.

3. Merit salary policy essentially provides that employees of the same rank or seniority will receive different levels of compensation according to the quality of their job performance. For example, if the average raise for a unit is projected to be 6 percent, some employees may receive 8 percent and some 4 percent, according to the quality of their job performance. The alternative is a flat compensation system in which all employee receive the same percentage raise. For a further discussion of compensation policy, see the chapters on the executive director and "Maximizing Your Human Resources."

4. "Guide to Nonprofit Corporate Governance in the Wake of Sarbanes-Oxley." ABA Committee on Nonprofit Governance (2005), p. 17.

4

Preparing Nonprofit Directors for the Coming Changes in Governance

Reform of nonprofits is in the air. It has been propelled by the passage of the Sarbanes-Oxley legislation introducing sweeping reforms in corporate governance. Following the passage of the legislation in 2002, the Senate Finance Committee, under the chairmanship of Senator Charles Grassley (R-Iowa), a frequent critic of nonprofits, held a series of hearings on potential changes in the regulation of nonprofits that resulted principally in increasing the penalties for the violation of certain provisions of the tax code. At the same time, the leaders of the industry produced a report acknowledging the need for change and proposing a package of specific reforms to the Congress and the nonprofit sector.[1] The American Bar Association Coordinating Committee on Nonprofit Governance also issued a report recommending reforms nonprofits should adopt in the wake of Sarbanes-Oxley.[2]

These developments would seem to carry a clear message: tax-exempt organizations should move to get their own house in order before changes are legislated. Nonprofit directors thus need to consider the steps a board can take to be ahead of the curve.

The initial step is the formation of a small committee of leading board members to conduct a comprehensive examination of the organization; when the organization can afford it, an outside firm should be retained to assist the committee.

The committee members should have no conflicts of interest and ideally at least one member should be a CPA. Of course, not every organization will have the capability to conduct an ideal review, but it ought to do as much as practical. The committee would be advised to begin its work by addressing the critical issue of the organization's effectiveness.

Establishing the Cost Effectiveness of an Organization's Programs

The review should address the litmus test for supporting an organization—namely, establishing that the organization is in fact accomplishing the mission that justifies its tax exemption and the grant of deductions to contributors for their donations to the organization. There can be no justification for such status unless the organization generates a public benefit.

The process begins by verifying that the organization can document that funds it receives are expended—less reasonable administrative costs—for exempt purposes. In addition, ideally the organization should provide independent assessments that the programs it funds are in fact achieving their objectives. Not every organization may be able to fund such an independent outcome analysis, but nevertheless it should use its best efforts to establish the results of its programs.

The next step is to identify the amount of the organization's costs and to compare the organization's ratio of expenses to revenues with the ratio of comparable organizations. The object is to assess whether the organization's costs are reasonable in light of the expenditures of other organizations in the same field. This analysis provides a basis for judgment of the organization's cost effectiveness in executing its program.

The outcome and cost-effectiveness analyses provide bottom-line measures of performance. How the organization scores here, perhaps more than any other measure, will largely determine its standing in the eyes of regulators, contributors, and the public.

Then the committee needs to dig deeper into the operations of the organization than boards typically do and examine the following board practices.

1. Review the operations of the board of directors and assess the extent to which it is exercising meaningful oversight of the organization's operations.

There are a range of issues to be addressed. Are board members educated in the business of the organization? Have audit, compensation, and nominating committees been established from among directors who have no financial interest in the organization or other forms of ties to its directors and managers that could be seen as compromising their independence? Is at least one member of the audit committee a CPA or have financial expertise?

Is the board discharging its fiduciary role by requiring all directors to personally review financial reports, 990 forms, pension and health plans, and executive compensation? Does the board ensure that financial documents are signed by the CEO and senior financial officer? (Sarbanes-Oxley requires this in the case of public corporations.) Does the board ensure that the compensation of key executives is carefully evaluated?

Are there adequate internal controls to support an organization's financial statements? What is the opinion of the organization's outside auditors about the adequacy of such controls? (Sarbanes-Oxley requires the management of public corporations to attest to the adequacy of such controls and auditors to attest to the adequacy of management's opinion.) Does the organization's outside auditor provide services that could compromise the integrity of its audit work? (Sarbanes-Oxley bars auditors of public corporations from providing most forms of consulting services to an audit client.)

Does the board have a written conflicts-of-interest policy that it enforces? Is there a process in place to assure the retention of important papers and documents? (Document protection applies to nonprofits under Sarbanes-Oxley.)

Is the board discharging its strategic role by challenging the status quo, assessing the organization's capabilities and the potential for strengthening them? Is the board playing a critical role in identifying and framing for its examination one or two pivotal issues? Is the board alert to organizational blind spots?

2. Examine whether the organization of the board and its own procedures can be improved.

Review the size of the board and whether it serves the organization; also examine the process by which people are elected as directors and as members of key board committees. Is the electoral process transparent? Does it take into account a broad range of views? Are its decisions the product of careful discussion and analysis?

Is a subgroup of the full board charged with developing criteria for board membership, including selecting the skills or experience the board lacks and then, once criteria are approved by the full board, actively seeking candidates?

Are there published contribution and attendance requirements for directors? Do directors meet these requirements? Are directors expected to be active in fundraising and, if so, are they? If a director is not performing adequately, what is the process for removing him/her?

Does the board, especially the chair, have a good working rapport with its professional CEO? Does the chair, in concert with the CEO, prepare any agenda for board meetings? Is the input of the full board solicited? Do the committee chairs help frame the issues for board discussion? Does the CEO prepare an annual report to the board setting out what has and has not been accomplished? Has the board established performance objectives for the CEO to provide a basis for reviewing his or her compensation?

Has the board established a process to enable employees with knowledge of error or wrongdoing on the part of the organization to come forward without fear of retribution? (The protection of whistle blowers under Sarbanes-Oxley applies to nonprofits.)

Building a Consensus for Change

The committee should prepare a written report of its findings for the full board and, to the extent appropriate, circulate it to the staff. The committee should seek agreement of the full board on the most important changes that need to be made and how to implement them. Consensus may not come easily. Some members may have to be convinced in one-on-one meetings. But it will be worth the time and effort to build support for the committee's principal recommendations.

Selecting Board Members

Establishing criteria for the composition of the board of directors is a necessary step in preparing an organization to deal with the changing environment for nonprofits. The board, with input from the executive director and other staff, should deliberate carefully what skills, experience, and other qualities one wants among board members. Each organization will, of course, have its own requirements. However, some generalizations may be drawn.

William G. Bowen, himself a director of many corporations and former president of Princeton University and the Andrew W. Mellon Foundation, has written:

> In thinking about criteria, it is useful to begin with what I would call "common, core qualifications": integrity, competence, reliability, good judgment, independence of mind, and dedication to the cause. As trite as it may seem to list these seemingly old-fashioned virtues, taking them for granted can be disastrous....[3]

Bowen goes on to quote with approval the observation of a CEO of a Fortune 500 company that directors should have a "... demonstrated history of accomplishments in whatever field.... Tangible accomplishments are far more important than credentials."[4]

As a rule, nonprofits need board members who are taken with their organization's mission. Identifying individuals with a true understanding of the work of the organization and a passion for its mission and objectives can be a real asset.

Ideally, some board members should have enough experience in the organization's field to contribute substantive insights into its operations, particularly alerting fellow board members when there is doubt whether the organization is proceeding on the right track. At a minimum, board members should be able to contribute some special competence or experience to board deliberations.

My favorite example of a board member's expertise making a genuine difference is an event that took place at a meeting of the Vanguard Mutual Fund board on which I served for a dozen years. Vanguard CEO Jack Bogle had a passion for naming funds after nineteenth-century British warships. On this occasion, early in the life of the fund complex, Bogle proposed naming a new fund product after another British warship. A director who was an officer of Nabisco, a brand-conscious company, objected. "Jack," he said, "we ought to be in the business of building the Vanguard brand and every fund should bear that name." That one brief comment changed the way funds were named and indeed set the company on the path of building its brand.

In the case of most organizations the ability to give and/or raise money for the organization is a crucial talent. An allied skill is the ability to effectively represent the organization in various forums, including the ability to speak with commitment and strength before audiences. It is useful if at least one member of the board is prepared to forcefully raise difficult questions for management, boldly challenging their assumptions and analysis.

One will also seek to have different generations represented on a board. Recruiting younger board members can be difficult because they often face the demands of building their careers and raising a family. However, working to give them opportunities to participate can be worth the effort over the years.

In fact, the ideal is to have a board diversified not only by age, but also by gender and ethnicity as well as by profession and even temperament. Such diversification will provide an organization with an invaluable array of different perspectives. It also aligns an organization with the demographic trends in America. Today's minorities will be tomorrow's majorities. You can see it as you look at the composition of the youngest school classes. Minority students under five years old are already a near majority nationally, with white high school graduates projected to make up only 58 percent of graduating classes by 2014.[5] The differential birth rates are such that in the foreseeable future—say by the mid-twenty-first century—members of minorities will constitute a majority of the nation's population.

There is a pool of talented minority individuals who readily meet the criteria discussed here for board membership. As for women, there are a great many qualified candidates who would add a great deal to male-dominated boards. In making such appointments it is important to convey, and mutually believe, one is not selecting a woman or minority candidate as a representative of an interest group but because of the broad-ranging contributions he or she can make to the organization. Otherwise, the cohesion an effective board requires will be undermined.

In the corporate world there has been significant pressure to have the majority of boards of directors made up of "independent" directors. In fact, the New York Stock Exchange rules call for a majority of the board to be independent. The focus on independence in the corporate world is a reaction to the number of employees that traditionally sat on boards. In the nonprofit world placing even one employee on the board is a rare occurrence and thus issues of independence are more nuanced. For example, what if the board chair has a business relationship with another board member, or they are close personal friends and serve on a series of other boards together? The issue is whether a board member will subordinate his or her judgment to that of another board member (or the executive director) because of a relationship outside the board in question. Rather than try to define "independence," why not leave this issue to the nominating committee of the board (or to the board itself, in the case of very small boards).

A related question is how to deal with potential conflicts of interest, a subject dealt with in Chapter 3. These can arise where a board member also has a business relationship with the organization, providing it with goods or services. Again a blanket rule is not as useful as case-by-case judgments by the board or a committee thereof. In a good number of instances board members may provide goods or services to the organization without fee or at a discounted fee. These may give the nonprofit access to a quality of products or services it could not afford or otherwise secure. The challenging situation is when the board member receives compensation for his products or services. Was such a transaction reviewed and approved by the board? Were the goods or services provided on favorable terms? If not, was there some form of competitive bidding? How awkward would it be to break the relationship with a board member if the products or services are not satisfactory? Of course, there is the potential for abuse or a conflict of interest in such relationships, but it would be wiser to make judgments on a case-by-case basis based on the actual facts. However, it is sensible to require that all business relationships between board members and the organization be disclosed and approved before they are consummated.

Attracting qualified board members proves to be difficult for many organizations, and the temptation can exist to sign anyone with a credential who is willing to serve. However, careful due diligence is essential. A productive, insightful, and active board member can make a difference to the fortunes of an organization; equally, a poor choice can not only undermine the effectiveness of the board but damage the organization. There is also the challenge, once an outstanding board member is elected, how to keep him or her in engaged in the work of the board and the organization. This puts the burden on the staff and board chair to present the board with meaningful issues for their decision and to provide genuine opportunities for members to contribute their insights to the organization.[6]

Why Become a Director of a Nonprofit Organization?

In my graduate classes at Baruch College's School of Public Affairs, when I set out the responsibilities of the modern director, several students ask why anyone would want to take on such responsibilities on behalf of a nonprofit organization. At the same time, in my class on creating a new nonprofit enterprise, students quickly come to ask how are they going to recruit board members for their fledgling enterprises. Finding qualified directors for most nonprofits, especially the smaller or newer enterprises, is a challenge.

The ability to attract qualified directors will vary, of course, with the size and stature of the institution. Prominent cultural organizations, colleges and universities, and large foundations generally have little trouble attracting the directors they seek. In the case of universities, which generally recruit alumni trustees, most graduates regard it as a personal honor to be asked to serve by the school they attended. They may also feel they especially benefited from attending the institution and see board service as a way of paying back the benefits received. Where the college or university is a well-recognized institution there is an element of prestige in serving on the board. Major foundations also are generally successful in attracting high-caliber directors, especially foundations that have a large enough endowment to support their administration and programs. That frees directors largely from worrying about finances, or making a gift, and lets them throw their energies and imaginations into the programmatic work of the foundation, work that generally offers a liberating contrast to the daily burdens of their main occupations. There is also an element of prestige in being associated with a major foundation or cultural institution. Indeed, some museums and performing arts organizations hold very important places in the culture of the cities where they are located. Being on such a board is generally reserved for accomplished people of stature. Of course, membership on museum and performing arts boards generally requires a financial contribution, and the more prestigious the institution the larger the required gift.

On the other side of the coin, institutions that are struggling financially or have sub-par management by definition are going to find it difficult to attract board members. People are naturally going to be reluctant to throw themselves into a messy situation that will drain their energies and for which they will not get paid. (Few nonprofits, other than certain foundations, pay their director a fee, in contrast to business corporations, which typically pay directors a fee.)

These specific situations aside, one can draw some general observations about what will motivate a person to become a director of a nonprofit. Based on my experience as a board member at various times on several nonprofits and knowing many directors of other organizations, here are some observations about what can attract people to serve as directors.

- *It matters what the mission of the organization is.* Generally people will be more likely to serve an organization whose causes they find compelling and would like to see advanced.

- *The organization is a well-run institution without severe management or financial problems.* While there inevitably will be pressure to raise more revenues, it makes a difference if those additional revenues are to expand the programs or capacity of the organization rather than pull it out of a hole. People generally want to be associated with an organization that is well regarded and where they can devote their energies to helping the institution enhance its impact rather than dealing with crises stemming from past poor management or just bad luck.

- *They have a personal stake in the success of the institution,* such as parents who serve on the boards of the schools their children attend.

- *Board membership offers an opportunity to apply one's skills and experience to aid the organization.* This offers the possibility of achieving a sense of personal accomplishment.

- *The stature of other board members.* The reality is that a board that already has figures of stature will find it easier to attract new directors. If the existing directors are themselves people with interesting careers or professions, that also will be a positive factor.

- *A friend or professional associate on the board who seeks to recruit you to join the board.* The personal appeal can make a genuine difference.

- *A cohesive board, in which members have respect for each other and act with civility toward one another.* This will be far more appealing than a board that has a reputation for indulging in acrimony and personal criticism or that is bitterly divided over one or more important issues.

- *The opportunity to attain a position of leadership on the board,* such as its chair or chair of one of its influential committees.

Ultimately, you want directors to have an appreciation for the role the board plays as *the* governing body of the organization. By and large the responsibility for the well-being, standards, and end results of a nonprofit lies with the board of directors. Nonprofit boards thus, in a sense, have more unfettered influence over the destiny of the enterprise than corporate boards. Therefore, as a board member it is possible to have a significant impact on an organization.

In recruiting board members, one wants to be straightforward with candidates as to the amount of time board service requires. There is a value, some will argue, in "letterhead directors"—a list of prominent people on the organizational stationary is thought to add prestige or prompt others to support the organization. This may be true in certain cases, but in the end the organization needs a working board prepared to play its role and discharge its responsibilities. This takes time and effort, and it's prudent to spell out in the bylaws or the minutes of a board meeting the specific responsibilities, such as minimum attendance requirements, financial contribution levels, and willingness to devote time to promoting the interests of the organization in the community where they live, including seeking qualified candidates for board seats.

In short, there are a variety of reasons why someone may be willing to serve as a nonprofit director. Directors are most effective when they fully understand and accept the role and responsibilities of a board member, and when they believe that in fulfilling them, they are making a difference to the well-being and performance of the organization.

A candidate's motivations warrant exploration before he or she is asked to serve, in order to assess whether the candidate board member will meet your explicit expectations.

Why Some Boards Work and Some Don't

Nonprofit boards play a pivotal role in the governance of nonprofit organizations. Unlike the corporate world, there is not an extensive legislative structure, such as Sarbanes-Oxley, or rules of stock exchanges that directly impact the practices of boards of directors. That day may come, but at present nonprofit boards are left largely to their own devices in establishing their practices with, at best, the guidance of various studies such as the work of the Panel on the Nonprofit Sector, which was organized by Independent Sector. Indeed, one of the reasons some boards are ineffective may be the absence of a clear set of guidelines from an agency with an official role in the governance of nonprofits.

It is also evident that many nonprofits have difficulty in recruiting board members.[6]

They can feel lucky enough to form a board at all that there is a reluctance to ask board members to do more than they seem willing to do. There is often little pressure to ask such board members to devote the time it takes to create an effective board or, in the case of many nonprofits, to contribute and/or raise money. In fact, one of the principal reasons some boards are ineffective is that so little is asked of them, including the amount of time they devote to their board work. A board has little chance to be effective in discharging its responsibilities if its members do not feel an obligation to act with due diligence, investing the time necessary to carry out their role. Obviously, poor attendance by board members will undermine the work of the board.

Such shortcomings can often be the result of membership being seen as lending one's name to a good cause rather than the acceptance of fiduciary and strategic responsibilities. The motivation with which one joins a board will largely influence the effectiveness with which one serves, and boards would be well advised to probe a potential board member's motivation as part of the selection process.

One of the principal reasons boards prove to be ineffective is that the expectations for the work members will be asked to perform, as well as for any financial contributions, are not spelled out in writing in the organization's documents. People can thus join a board without any awareness of the duties they will be expected to fulfill, and will be reluctant to be anything more than a passive member who is just a quiet attendee at board meetings.

An effective board will be a product of work by the board (or nominating committee) in defining the various backgrounds it seeks on the board. All too often little thought is given to the expertise needed on a board, be it finance, expertise in the field in which the nonprofit operates, strategic planning, marketing, or fundraising. Imagine a major hospital without some directors with strong medical backgrounds, or a university board without any members from the academic community. Sometimes chief executive officers will resist having someone from theirr field or active in the organization's business because they don't want someone with such credentials to challenge them. This is precisely why a board needs to have some membership with expertise in the work of the organization.

A board's effectiveness may also be hindered when one person is essentially the dominant voice, especially if he or she is the founder of the organization or its principal funder. As a practical matter, when all decisions require the assent of one person the board becomes at best an advisory body, not a decision-making one. An effective board will make genuine decisions, not simply ratify the decisions of the board leader or CEO. Indeed, until a board comes together to make an important policy decision as a board, it will not likely be effective as a cohesive entity.

Boards may also be ineffective where members do not have a sense of affinity with each other. A board does not function as a cohesive whole without some sense of relationship between the individual board members. Board meetings with management present are generally not good forums in which board members can develop relationships with each other. Participation, especially with management present, tends to see board members acting as individuals, often with a personal agenda, without having developed a consensus among fellow members. This is one reason it is important that periodically the board meet without any management present, in a setting that enables members to get to know each other and explore their views about the organization. In addition, such meetings provide an opportunity for the board to discuss matters concerning the organization's executives (or a policy issue) with a candor and frankness that can be difficult to achieve if management is always present.

A way of building a sense of a board as a board is to hold periodic retreats during which to review the organization's performance and a vision for its future.[7] Such sessions will not only provide useful insights into the organization's operations and plans, but also provide an opportunity for board members to work together over several days with few distractions. They also get to spend time with the staff in an informal setting.

Another benefit of such retreats is the opportunity to educate board members about the organization's business. One of the reasons boards are not effective is that their knowledge of the business of the organization is in fact superficial, and they don't have the time (or the willingness) to learn about it outside of formal board meetings. Ideally, all board members would have the time to acquire meaningful knowledge of the organization's operations on their own, but the board retreat can be a practical alternative.

A board as a whole can only exercise truly informed leadership when it's rooted in knowledge of the organization's mission, as well as the business activities involved in fulfilling the mission. In the case of certain specialized issues, one or more board members with expertise in that area may take the lead in reviewing the topic, but the board functions best when all members are exposed to the issue and develop a full understanding of what is at stake.

Another way for a board to develop a sense of its role and exercise leadership is to make sure the agendas for board meetings fully reflect their input. Board agendas can serve to chart the direction of the organization and the issues to be examined. In particular, the agenda should set out the policy issues the board believes need to be addressed and not allow the entire meeting to be taken up with staff presentations of their activities. However, too often board meeting agendas are drafted by the staff with little timely input from the board. As a consequence, they do not raise the policy issues that the board should address. Board members will lose interest if they are not called upon to make decisions on important matters; a well-crafted agenda will make sure this is not the case.

Accordingly, the board chair as well as committee chairs should work with their counterparts on the staff to develop the agenda for meetings. The board chair and committee members also need to do their homework before meetings, which includes getting briefed by the staff so they can act with knowledge and authority at board meetings. In addition, certain routine reports can be prepared in writing and circulated in advance, saving meeting time for more pressing matters. It is also possible to organize meetings around what needs to be accomplished, rather than just the standard committee and departmental reports.

Board effectiveness can be undermined when board members see their function as playing operating roles. When a board member takes on staff functions, it not only creates confusion but tends to distract the board member from focusing on policy issues. As noted in the section on endowment management in Chapter 3, one of the main reasons for the underperformance of an endowment is the failure the board investment committee to address the critical policy issues that require board decision, and instead to focus its energies on selecting individual investments.

Of course, the character and personality of board members can be such that they don't get along with each other, whether working on a meeting agenda or resolving issues brought before the board. Members may well disagree on matters from time to time, but for the board to work, even in disagreement there must still be mutual respect among board members. While differences may be forcefully expressed, they need to be kept within the bounds of a reasonable level of civility.

There also seems to be uniform agreement that one test of the effectiveness of a board is whether it has a positive and constructive relationship with the organization's chief staff officer (e.g., the executive director). Boards and chief executive officers can be at loggerheads, which generally results in deadlock. If an organization is to progress, its board and chief of staff need to work in harmony, with mutual respect for their respective roles.

Still, within these bounds, it is important that the board have at least one forceful challenger of management and, if need be, even fellow board members. Such a robust personality is often necessary to open up board meetings to full and candid discussions.

The board itself must, in some instances, have the strength to render unpopular decisions. In the current economic climate of 2008–2009, many necessary decisions produce painful results. The board must adopt a surgical approach to such choices, choosing the course that they believe best serves the institution even though the immediate results may be quite hurtful. Ideal as it would be to be able to make such difficult decisions with the assent of all board members, boards may in some cases have to act on the basis of a narrow margin of favorable votes. A test of the durability of a board is whether it can arrive at such a split decision without fractioning the board over the long term.

Finally, boards need to find a process for periodically evaluating their own effectiveness and identifying ways in which the board can be strengthened. Obviously, a board performance review can annoy certain members who don't feel comfortable with their work being judged, especially by their peers; but the board needs to have a sense of where it is effective and where it is not. Thus a review of its work, done as tactfully as possible, is a necessary practice.

NOTES

1. *Strengthening Transparency, Governance, and Accountability of Charitable Organizations*. Final Report of the Panel on the Nonprofit Sector, 2005.
2. "Guide to Nonprofit Corporate Governance in the Wake of Sarbanes-Oxley." ABA Committee on Nonprofit Governance (2005), p. 17.
3. William G. Bowen, *The Board Book* (New York: W.W. Norton & Co, 2008), p. 137.
4. Ibid.
5. Roberts, "Rise in Minorities is Led by Children, Census Finds." *New York Times*, May 1, 2008, p. A18; Bowen, p.143.
6. Francie Ostrower, *Nonprofit Governance in the United States* (Washington DC: The Urban Institute, 2007).
7. See "An Organizational Retreat" in Chapter 2.

Section 2.

Human Resources

5

Maximizing Your Human Resources

A Philosophy of Human Resource Management

In the first edition of this title I wrote:

> One of the pivotal advances in management practice in the second half of the twentieth century has been learning how to use fully the talents of all of the people in an organization. The idea that people are a resource rather than a cost has transformed the way organizations are run.

> The concept of human resources has displaced the notion…that all wisdom was vested in the senior leaders of the organization and that subordinates' task was to do exactly what they were ordered to do by top management. It is now widely agreed that the task of the senior management is to create an environment in which all employees are stimulated to contribute to how the business is run.

Organizations can adopt various practices to enhance the ability of employees to contribute. Efforts can focus on improving the quality of those hired as well as raising the level of skills of current employees. Candidates for employment can be carefully screened to narrow the choice to the most qualified candidates. Mentoring and comprehensive training can also be utilized to enhance the skills of existing staff. Briefings to convey an understanding of the overall business, as opposed to an employee's specific job, are essential. Merit pay or incentive compensation can reward employees for meeting specific goals, motivating employees to perform at their best.

In addition, a process can be established to hear in confidence employee grievances and to protect whistle blowers from retaliation, as provided for in the Sarbanes-Oxley legislation.

The most critical factor in managing staff is to establish a clear set of expectations. The starting point is for the board and the CEO to collaborate in setting out in writing expectations for his or her performance to avoid any later misunderstandings as to what was agreed upon. In turn, to the extent practical, the CEO's responsibilities can be delegated to subordinates as part of their written package of responsibilities. The idea is to establish throughout the organization goals that are consistent and mutually reinforcing.

The process of defining expectations is rooted in the belief that employees will perform at their capacities when their roles and responsibilities are clearly defined, job descriptions are current, provision is made to reward employees who achieve their goals, and their performance is regularly and constructively evaluated in written appraisals. Indeed, the evaluation of an employee's performance may well, as part of the following year's goals, call for overcoming any shortcomings that are noted. At the root is the philosophy that treating people as an asset, and granting them the autonomy and authority necessary to do their jobs, will produce the most productive work force.

The tone and pace of the organization—its culture—will, in the first instance, be defined by the behavior of the CEO. The hours he or she keeps, the speed with which he or she responds to inquiries, and the manner in which he or she makes decisions will be emulated by others in the organization. The way in which the CEO responds to employees also matters—does it reflect respect for the employee, curiosity about their work, and recognition of them as an individual? The CEO thus models the behavior he or she wants others to employ. The CEO must also offer a well-conceived vision of the organization's future and provide a steady hand and confident demeanor, especially in times when the organization is struggling to achieve its goals.

Naturally, the level of employee compensation will directly impact employee behavior. Compensation of employees should be differentiated according to the level of their contributions using a merit- or performance-based system. The organization needs to establish a transparent process for setting its compensation levels in light of the compensation paid by comparable organizations for similar work. An issue that can arise is whether to include comparable jobs in the for-profit sector where salaries are generally significantly higher than in nonprofit organizations.

In addition, a process must be established that balances such market-driven analysis with the need for internal equity between positions whose value to the organization may be greater than their market value.[1]

Human resource practices must enable an organization not only to recruit the right talent, but also to retain it over time. Employees should be motivated to ensure the organization performs at its highest level, out of a sense of commitment to its vision and mission. Employees, in essence, should be made to believe they are true stakeholders in the organization.

Given the importance of the human resources to the well-being of an organization, a committee of the board of directors should periodically review its administration. (Note that in the corporate sector boards are required by stock exchange rules to have a compensation committee.[2]) In particular, this committee will not only negotiate the compensation of the CEO but review the compensation of the most highly paid executives. The committee should also ensure that the reimbursement of officers for expenses they have incurred on behalf of the organization is appropriately reviewed and approved by an official senior to the officer seeking reimbursement; in the case of the CEO, that calls for a board member to review his or her expenses. In addition, a manual should be prepared that outlines the types of expenses that are reimbursable. Finally, the committee should examine the costs and benefits to employees of the organization's health and pension plans. In the case of organizations that offer a defined benefit pension plan promising a specific level of retirement pay, the committee must examine the investment policies and performance of the pension fund to determine whether the organization can fund such commitments.

The human resources approach outlined here is based on the idea that people want to be successful. At the end of the day, they want to feel they've made a contribution to an organization's achieving its valued mission.

Role of the Human Resources Department

The old-fashioned human resources department ("HR") bore the name "Personnel Department." Its role was essentially providing administrative support and hiring and supervising secretaries. With respect to the professional staff, it prepared the necessary paperwork for new hires. Some departments oversaw the health plan, making sure the staff understood the coverage provided. However, the department played no policymaking role and was typically not involved with the recruiting and hiring of new professional staff. When organizations began to understand the contribution an effective human resources department could make, it became essential to transform the personnel department into a human resources department with different staff and functions.

A modern human resources department plays an active part in shaping the culture of the organization, interacting with all departments, based on its firsthand knowledge of all aspects of the business. Its insights into the business of the organization are essential to enable the department to play an effective role in identifying the staffing needs of the organization and to match personnel to those needs. Depending on the circumstances, the department may be an advocate for either adding staff or reducing staff in certain areas. In either case, its recommendations will carry weight. In addition, it will focus on developing improved methods of identifying and evaluating candidates for positions and incentives to retain talented staff.

A fully functioning human resources department's specific functions include:

- Participating directly in the process of identifying candidates for hire.

- Reviewing job descriptions to ensure they match the tasks actually being performed.

- Reviewing the compensation proposed to be offered by way of a promotion or a new hire, particularly the reliability of information developed about comparable positions, and ensuring that appropriate weight is given to consideration of internal equity.

- Reviewing the annual compensation awards to ensure they comply with organizational policy.

- Reviewing the rationale for proposed promotions as well as calling attention to staff the department believes should be promoted.

- Developing orientation programs and materials for new staff.

- Serving as a confidential outlet for employee grievances.

- Conducting exit interviews of departing employees who, because they are leaving, may be objective and candid in their observations.

- Reviewing the provisions and costs of the organization's health plan and how they compare to plans provided by comparable organizations.

- Encouraging staff to make at least annual appraisals in writing of their subordinates and provide the staff with models of appraisals.

- Arranging for training programs for the staff.

- Working with staff to assist them in developing career paths.

- Creating opportunities to reinforce the culture established by the CEO.

These tasks, by definition, will engage HR in the very essence of the organization's operations and vest it with an influential policy voice. The head of the department also plays a critical role, in conjunction with the CEO, in establishing an organization's work environment. The head's responsiveness to inquiries and assignments, his or her composure in times of unusual stress, pride in the importance of the organization's mission, and the ability to balance discipline with empathy for employees with grievances all will contribute significantly to shaping an organization's culture. For this reason, senior executives may be directed to clock some time in the HR department.

The head of the department must have a status in the organization on a par with other department heads (i.e., a vice presidency) and bring a set of outstanding skills and experiences to the job equal to his or her peers in other parts of the organization.

Of course, many organizations are too small to afford an HR department, but the modern philosophy and principles of human resource management are available to any nonprofit.

The Art of Recruiting

There is an inherent uncertainty in hiring someone from outside the organization to replace a professional who is leaving or to fill a newly created position. As diligent as one may be in reviewing possible candidates, in many cases it's still hard to predict whether there will be a good fit between the candidate and the job, and how well he or she will perform in the organization. No organization is going to have a 100 percent success rate in its recruiting. However, the odds of achieving a good outcome can be measurably increased by the nature of the process employed to select a candidate.

In many ways, a key to successful recruiting is to have on hand an insightful and informative description of the organization, its mission, its unique aspects, and its track record of accomplishing its goals. The description should spell out how the job the enterprise is recruiting for fits into its operations. A carefully drawn job description should define the role and responsibilities of the position and the performance expected from an incumbent, including specific goals to be accomplished. Reporting relationships, formal and informal, need to be detailed. An effective job description will have been put together with the same care and emphasis on the organization's appeal as a fundraising solicitation.

The starting point of a rigorous process is to be sure the job description accurately reflects the nature of the position and the qualifications required to fill it successfully. Often job descriptions resort to generalities: energetic, able to relate well to people, outstanding communicator. These may indeed be desirable qualities but they are almost generic in character. A job description should be specific in describing both the qualities a successful candidate must have and the expectations for the position.

One other preliminary step is to evaluate—if there was a predecessor in the position—the qualities that accounted for his or her success or failure. Where there has been no predecessor, interviewing other organizations that have filled a similar position can be informative. One might also review other searches by the organization to identify what factors seem to have produced a successful new hire and what may have accounted for unfortunate results.

There are a range of options when it comes to first identifying good prospects: an executive recruiting firm can be retained, the position can be advertised in various media, it can be posted with one of the online organizations that list positions for job seekers (for a fee), or one can ask friends and contacts for a lead. Employing an executive recruiting firm relieves the organization of a good deal of work, especially searching for candidates and sifting through prospects until at least three names appear to match the qualifications for the position. These firms generally charge one-third of the first year's compensation, but if the candidate does not work out within six months of being hired, the firm is obligated to begin the search again until a new candidate is selected.

The firms will do some reference checking, especially if this is explicitly made part of the engagement, but the task of actually choosing a candidate, once identified, is the same whether found through the other means mentioned above or by a search firm. However one goes about identifying possible candidates, people called on to assist in the process by meeting candidates should have a clear understanding of the specifics of the job and the qualifications required. Where an executive recruiter is to be used, make sure there is detailed discussion with the person who will do the search to make sure you are on the same page. Some explanation of the type of personnel who fare well in the organization is worthwhile.

A critical part of the process is acquiring the relevant information that sheds light on whether the candidate has the personality, skills, and experience to make a go of the job.

Take, for example, the position of "development officer" for an organization that funds secondary education. The interview process should yield the following information for the benefit of both the organization and the candidate:

- to whom the officer reports

- whether the type of fundraising will be direct solicitation of individuals and/or institutional donors, or planning fundraising events, or managing a planned giving program

- whether the organization has a list of target prospects or the officer must develop his or her own list

- if a good deal of travel is involved or if most of the prospects are situated in one area

- was there a predecessor in this job; why did he or she leave

- is familiarity with planned giving required

- the years and type of prior experience being sought

- the size and number of gifts the candidate has previously secured; how such gifts were secured

- were such gifts from people or institutions who had previously made gifts, or did the candidate develop donors who had no previous association with the organization to which the money was given

- to the extent permissible, the identity of the donors and the approach the candidate used in soliciting the gift

- does the candidate have any prior experience raising funds for secondary schools; what is his or her knowledge of such schools

- what prior experience does the candidate believe will help in this position.

The list of questions could be expanded, but the point is that one wants to get into the specifics of the job with the candidate and see if there is a match in experience and professional skills and shared understanding between candidate and potential employer.

One also wants to encourage candidates to speak freely about why they are interested in a particular job and what they would bring to it. They may color their response because they want the position, but with probing questions one can prompt candidates to provide a realistic assessment of why they are a good fit for the job.

When it comes to checking references, you do not want to be limited to the names the candidate supplies. You can ask candidates if they will give you names of people with whom they've done transactions or people at a previous employer. You can ask the references they give you to suggest other people with whom you can talk about the candidate. Your conversations with references should be specific, inquiring about particular qualities and skills of the candidate. Find out if any reference can support his claim to have raised a number of certain size gifts.

In the case of a search for a CEO, the board needs to do its own due diligence, develop its own outreach, and not rely on the candidate's own references or delegate this function to a search firm. Firsthand contact with references is the best way to gain meaningful insights. Getting meaningful references can be difficult on occasion because former supervisors may be bound by severance agreements to "speak no evil."[3]

The interview process also has to be carefully structured to explore specifics and the nature of the candidate's interest in the position. It makes sense that he or she meet a variety of people beyond the person to whom he or she will report, especially people he or she would come into contact with on the job. Adequate time should be provided to allow for thorough interviews. Some people might gain from a second interview with the candidate; do not hesitate to schedule these. You will also want to check your findings about and impressions of the candidate with others outside the organization, such as the search firm, if one has been hired, or people who gave you the candidate's name.

If the candidate is expected to work with board members of a fundraising committee, interviews with these directors should be established. However, make it clear that the board members are being asked for their opinion only, not to decide whether to hire a particular candidate. The decision to hire is a managerial function.

In certain situations, it may be mutually advantageous to hire the candidate as a consultant for a period of time. That formula allows both the candidate and the organization to get to know each other and see if there is a fit between candidate and the job.

A certain degree of realism should color the search. Candidates that "walk on water" are few and far between. Bill Bowen has observed that in the case of a search for a CEO one is lucky to find two solid candidates that fit the criteria.[4]

Once the candidate is actually hired, the supervisor and employee should develop an action plan that spells out the activities he or she should undertake and establishes clear goals to be accomplished during specific time periods. Once hired, the employee should not be left to fend for himself or herself, so to speak. The person's supervisor and perhaps a veteran staff person should take time to provide support early on, especially to explain how the organization functions in various areas, and to answer questions the new employee may have. Once there's agreement on hiring a candidate, announce it to the entire organization, specifying the position he or she will hold. Introducing the person at staff meetings is another useful way of integrating the person into the organization.

Some organizations will have a formal orientation period for new employees, introducing them to the programs, administration, and benefits of the organization. If such a formal program does not exist it can be arranged informally through meetings with the appropriate personnel.

In short, success in hiring does not stop with the decision to hire. The follow-up can be very important in making the selected candidate a successful employee.

One final thought: if it's your responsibility for making the hire, respect your own instincts. If you "feel" someone isn't right, don't let others talk you out of your view and do not respond to pressure to fill a position. It's better to prolong the search than go with a wrong candidate.

Core Skills

The nonprofit sector is significant in size and growing. Consequently there will be increasing demand for professionals to staff both existing and new organizations. The challenge for nonprofit organizations is recruiting personnel endowed with the set of skills that will make them effective nonprofit leaders. These talents may be thought of as the "core skills" top-flight leaders must possess if they are to realize their full potential.

A special feature of the core skills is their portability—employing a skill in one environment enriches its application in another setting. A financially minded executive overseeing an endowment of securities will apply the test of diversification, seeking to insulate the entire portfolio from being adversely impacted by the same economic event. Transfer the setting to an organization that funds community economic development. When selecting communities to support, the same principle of diversification will apply. The same portability analysis can be applied to the core skill of fundraising. The mounting of a major gift campaign for a university will require constructing a case for inducing institutions and individuals to contribute. The lessons learned from this experience will be instructive in managing a program to raise funds for other types of nonprofit organizations. Accordingly, for a professional seeking to expand his or her career horizons, the ability to employ the following set of core skills will be a decided advantage.

FUNDRAISING

There is widespread agreement that a gift for fundraising is critical. All types of tax-exempt organizations, except endowed foundations, are to some extent dependent on the ability to attract such support—at a reasonable cost—and yet relatively few board members or senior staff are highly skilled or even very active at raising funds.

Fundraising encompasses the ability to secure a range of financial support, from foundation and corporate grants to gifts and legacies of individuals. Each of these categories of fundraising has its own criteria for acceptance, method of solicitation, and associated costs. Accordingly, fundraising expertise includes knowledge of:

- how various institutions (e.g., foundations and corporations) consider applicants for funding

- research techniques to identify potential institutional and individual contributors

- how to maintain a database of prospects and contributors

- organizing fundraising events

- planning and overseeing fundraising campaigns

- tax issues, especially those applicable to planned giving

- the content of fundraising materials

In addition, all forms of fundraising require the ability to make a persuasive case for supporting the organization. Moreover, fundraising inevitably involves interaction between the professional staff and members of the board of directors. These relationships are important for motivating board members to play an active role in fundraising. Building and managing a staff of professional fundraisers is equally important.

To some extent, these skills can be developed through academic course work. Many colleges and universities are now offering programs in fundraising. But the academic approach is best supplemented by actual experience raising money. This experience can be gained by working for a nonprofit organization, but may also be gleaned from the business world. For example, I headed the Prudential Life Insurance Company's sales program to attract institutional investors for its real estate funds. Many of the techniques for raising money in that setting proved directly applicable to fundraising for nonprofit organizations.

FINANCIAL MANAGEMENT

Intelligent financial management is critical to the success of an organization. A not-for-profit enterprise, unlike a business, does not have a financial "bottom line" to be compared to other enterprises' results (e.g., net profit as a percentage of revenues or as a return on assets, or shareholder's equity as well as the ratio of share price to earnings per share). Nonprofit financial goals are to: 1) maximize the effectiveness and efficiency of its programs, and 2) achieve long-term financial stability. To manage a nonprofit enterprise, management and board must receive timely reports that set out how well the organization is meeting these goals and detail the financial condition of the enterprise. This requires that the performance and financial data be organized in a way that informs the day-to-day management of the enterprise. The information should also provide a basis for analyzing the efficiency of the organization, spotlighting where costs may be excessive and where they can be reduced. In many cases this requires disaggregating the financial data in order to identify the variables that have the greatest impact on the organization's financial condition.

In depicting the effectiveness and financial condition of a nonprofit enterprise, the number of critical factors requires a diverse set of skills. In particular, the extent to which the program achieves its objectives must be evaluated in and of itself. In addition, the income and expenses must be analyzed, as well as the condition of the organization's physical assets (i.e., are they properly maintained) and the organization's cash position, especially the cash available to pay current bills. Finally, there are the accounting statements that management must prepare in accordance with generally accepted accounting principles and which are audited by a certified public accountant.[6]

Exercising this broad-based financial management requires a degree of imagination in translating numbers into insights into the performance of a not-for-profit. Many of the underlying skills can be acquired through academic training enriched by actual operating experience.

COMMUNICATIONS

A third core skill, valuable in virtually every context, is mastery of the various modes of communicating with different target audiences. There must be the ability to develop sharp, clear, succinct messages to a range of external audiences—from government officials to media professionals, potential contributors, and other possible supporters, many of whom now get their information primarily through the Internet. At the same time, messages to the internal staff will impact their understanding of the vision of the organization and its goals.

At one time both forms of messages were largely circulated on paper. Today much of such communication is distributed through electronic media. Regardless of the form of delivery, the content of the message has to be honed to have maximum persuasive impact. Whether it's a printed brochure, electronic newsletter, or web site presentation, clarity and consistency of message are vital.

In addition to reaching target audiences through direct communication, there is the art of public relations—developing a program, within the limits of affordability, to gain exposure in print and electronic media and at events for the organization and its cause. A successful public relations effort can be time-consuming and costly. Relations with media professionals have to be built over time in order to establish a reputation for the credibility and integrity of the information you communicate. Also, one has to have an eye for the story that serves media self-interest. Merely pushing stories the organization would like to see disseminated generally does not work.

To create an effective communications program, key executives and board members also have to be educated in speaking techniques, acquiring the ability to be persuasive speakers for their organization.

To lead a nonprofit enterprise, then, a senior executive has to have a sound grasp of communication skills and exercise ultimate oversight of the communications program, which speaks for the organization.

STRATEGIC PLANNING

Strategic planning is a rational process for addressing the most critical strategic issues facing an organization, and ultimately developing a vision of the success the organization seeks to achieve in fulfilling its mission. The entire process takes into account the organization's strengths, weaknesses, opportunities, and threats, seeking to capitalize on its strengths and opportunities, curb its weaknesses, and avoid threats, to the extent feasible (a so-called SWOT analysis). The object of the process is to identify specific strategies that will move the organization from its present state to the condition projected by its vision. The strategic steps may range from change in programs, a drive for greater revenues or reduced costs, and changes in its external relationships or internal structure, to new approaches to marketing its programs and campaigns for financial support.

It is important that the plan be in writing and be accepted by key directors, contributors, and staff. Periodic updates comparing annual results with the plan are important. Training in planning in an academic setting can be quite beneficial, but once more, until one lives the exercise through experience, one's education in strategic planning is not complete.

Armed with these four core skills, and reinforced by a rigorous early training, one can look forward to a range of opportunities that offer the potential for advancement to senior positions as well as the opportunity for vertical moves between organizations in different fields.

Pursuing a Nonprofit Career

"Daring to Lead 2006: A National Study of Nonprofit Executive Leadership," a survey released in 2006 by the Eugene and Agnes E. Meyer Foundation and CompassPoint Nonprofit Services, concluded that three-quarters of nonprofit executive directors were planning to leave their jobs in the next three to five years. The principal contributors to executive burnout were identified as difficulties in the relationships with boards and funders, and the belief that these executives were making a significant financial sacrifice by working for nonprofits.[5]

A different survey, "The Nonprofit Executive Leadership Transition Survey 2004," conducted by two consulting firms, had found that the large Baby Boomer generation (at the time of the survey, in their 40s and 50s) comprised over 70 percent of nonprofit leaders. The summary titled "Change Ahead" predicted two waves of leadership transition: the first happening 2004 through 2010 and the second peaking in 2020.[6]

In 2003, a survey by Baruch College's School of Public Affairs forecast that 45 percent of nonprofit executive directors in New York City would leave their positions within five years, and a sample in the fall of 2007 found the prediction right on target.[7]

The survey Berglein maintains that nonprofits are not unique in their turnover rates, citing that 18 percent of corporate CEOs left their positions in 2000 and 16 percent in 2005.[8]

A report entitled "Ready to Lead? Next Generation Leaders Speak Out" was released in 2008. Two-thirds of the nearly six thousand people surveyed, mostly employed by nonprofits, either held a negative opinion or at best were unsure whether they wanted to be an executive director of a nonprofit organization. (Note, however, that the authors of the report concluded that the positive response of one-third of the survey participants was a sign of the strength of the nonprofit leadership pipeline.)

The survey was conducted by the Annie E. Casey Foundation; Idealist.org, a nonprofit web site for recruiters and job seekers; and the principal researchers of the 2006 survey, the Meyer Foundation and Compass Point.

Forty-two percent of those surveyed were younger than 30, and 19 percent were 50 and over. The vast majority worked for charities or foundations, and 20 percent worked for the government or in business.

The principal reasons given for their responses point up some of the limitations of working in the nonprofit sector:

- 41 percent: don't want fundraising responsibilities

- 40 percent: would have to sacrifice work-life balance

- 27 percent: not the ideal way to have an impact on the community or field of interest

- 26 percent: can't have kind of family life I want

- 25 percent: skills better suited to program work

Many participants also expressed concerns about the level of compensation for what they perceived to be a very demanding role, and a fear that they could not earn enough to retire comfortably.[9] Indeed, two of three executives interviewed in another study believe they made a financial sacrifice to lead nonprofits.

Perhaps underlying many reservations, as Albert Ruesga, coauthor of the 2008 report commented, "The data show the impact of working in an atmosphere of scarcity." That report stated that 69 percent of the survey's respondents said they felt underpaid, and 64 percent had concerns about committing to a career in the nonprofit world. The plain fact of life is that compensation in most nonprofits is a good deal less than one could earn in the private sector, although there are university presidents and heads of major foundations that one would perceive to be reasonably well paid. (A survey by the *Chronicle of Higher Education* showed that in 2006–2007 salaries for a good number of university presidents fell in the range between $500,000 and well over $1 million.[10]) Most nonprofits, however, simply lack the financial resources to match private sector compensation and do not earn the "profits" that would enable them to pay the large bonuses executives in the business world can earn. However, unlike in business, generating profits is not the objective. In fact, by law tax-exempt nonprofits to whom gifts are tax deductible [501(c)3 organizations] cannot pay executives so much that it looks as if paying large salaries to employees was the main objective. (The tax code bars tax-exempt charitable nonprofits from generating earnings that inure to the benefit of private persons.) Salaries must be reasonable in light of what comparable nonprofits pay.

In an ideal world, nonprofit executives as a class would be better compensated. However, when one signs on for a nonprofit position he or she buys into the limitations on compensation and reality dictates either acceptance of such limits or, from the outset, building a private sector career, deferring nonprofit service until one is financially independent. The real choice has to be made at the outset of one's career: does one assemble a resume that appeals to the private sector in terms of the skills and experience one develops and postpone a nonprofit executive role until one can afford nonprofit compensation? Or does one pursue a nonprofit career from the outset with full awareness of the limits on compensation?

True, there are exceptional instances in which one has moved from a nonprofit position to a for-profit position, as indeed I have. But two special factors existed when I made that transition: First, I had prior for-profit experience. Second, in the nonprofit world I had been engaged in a venture that had all the earmarks of a major business undertaking. At Princeton, on behalf of the university, I led the development of a 1,600-acre commercial real estate development, in the course of which I negotiated a transaction with senior Prudential executives. Later in my career I was hired by Prudential, when the company was looking for an executive with my financial and administrative background. While the coincidence of such factors is undoubtedly the exception, if one wants the financial rewards the private sector can provide, one needs to acquire the experiences and skills that sector requires.

The pressure of fundraising is often cited as the reason people have reservations about assuming the role of executive director.[11] However, the fact of tax-exempt life is that most nonprofits need to raise money from individual and/or institutional contributors (the exception is heftily endowed private foundations). Raising money for a nonprofit is inevitably a challenging business. In many instances it requires the participation of board members who, even if they have the personal resources to contribute or contacts to call on others, may be reluctant to participate, especially in making the request of others. (Some members are concerned that if they ask another for a contribution, that person will come back to them for a contribution.)

Getting contributions and assistance from board members is an uncertain business for new or smaller organizations. Moreover, with the exception of major colleges and hospitals and other large nonprofits, few organizations can afford to build a high-caliber development staff. The scarcity of highly qualified talent in the field drives up their price. The result is that the burden of raising funds often falls on the executive director, whose interests may lie in program development, not in raising money. In fact, in a survey of chief executives of colleges and universities, presidents were found to spend more time on fundraising than any other task. In addition, many nonprofits conduct their fundraising on a shoestring, lacking the resources to invest in mounting first-class campaigns. Finally, unlike businesses, few nonprofit institutions provide direct rewards for bringing in funds, and thus the person who raises money does not get the satisfaction of benefiting financially from his or her success in the form of a bonus or commission. (However, there can be a good deal of personal satisfaction in accomplishing fundraising goals essential to an organization's well-being.)

The challenge of dealing effectively with the board of directors is also cited as one of the drawbacks of being executive director. Since working with a board is a requirement of the CEO in business—and admittedly it can be a difficult relationship to manage—what is it, if anything, that makes this task uniquely difficult for nonprofit executive directors, as opposed to being inherent in the role of chief executive? The ineffectiveness of some nonprofit boards makes the job of working with then more difficult. The problems include the difficulty in recruiting board members, spotty attendance of board members, their sometimes lack of insight into the nature of the organization's business, and their passive participation in board matters.

Undoubtedly, some executive directors would like to have the dominance of boards that corporate chiefs at one time enjoyed. However, because of the reforms of corporate activity brought about by Sarbanes-Oxley, and revision of the policies of exchanges, there are fewer instances today of CEOs who control their boards. In other words, there are better and worse nonprofit boards, but the same can be said of business. Working with a board of directors is inherent in being the head of an organization and if one wants to lead, he or she must accept this responsibility with some equanimity.

To be fair, most executive directors work hard. In a more perfect world more executive directors would be well compensated, have professional staffs that took charge of fundraising, and have first-class engaged boards to deal with. In reality, that is not the case for most executive directors. The trade-off then must lie in the personal satisfaction of implementing a mission they believe in deeply and that fully engages their interest. In many cases the connection to a mission-driven organization leads one to feel that their energies are employed in a cause larger than themselves, and that leaving one's mark on their field provides special satisfaction. Working in common cause with colleagues to further the public good can be quite rewarding. At the end of the day, these values must be important enough to a person to offset the difficulties inherent in a nonprofit career.

Dealing with the concerns expressed by survey participants, the report "Ready to Lead? Next Generation Leaders Speak Out" contained a set of recommendations to improve the pipeline for future leaders, boards of directors, funders, and others such as contributors.[12] Executive directors were advised to, "... replace dated power structures." In focus groups, the report said that:

> Many younger people expressed frustration over top-down decision-making, overly hierarchical structures, poor communication, lack of transparency around decision-making, a culture of sacrifice, and resistance to change.... Executives who adapt their organizational cultures [to provide] less traditional hierarchy, while holding everyone accountable for meaningful mission impact, are in the best position to attract and retain the next generation of leadership.

The report also urged executive directors to help staff build strong external networks. It recommended inviting younger staff to attend meetings with funding sources and preparing them to participate in more meaningful ways: to join board committees and make board presentations, to suggest new board members for recruitment, and to be liaisons with key external networks.

The report further urged executive directors to be a "good role model" by "changing the perception" that the job automatically involves an unhealthy life-work balance, and by engaging in succession planning, periodically asking "whether they still are the right person for the job." Executive directors were also advised to recognize "generational differences" and that the different approach of younger people does not necessarily mean a lower level of commitment.

Boards of directors were urged to review not just the executive directors' compensation but the salary and benefits provided the entire organization. The object would be for the board to satisfy itself that the organization is, within the limits of its existing resources, paying the maximum practical salaries needed to attract qualified talent. Moreover, the report suggests that where an organization is constrained from paying reasonable compensation by its limited resources, the board consider raising money to improve the compensation structure. The board should also inquire into whether the executive director is recruiting the best available talent for the organization. It also suggested boards recruit young leaders for some of its positions. I found that young people, because of family and career pressures, are sometimes unable to make the commitments of time, not to mention money, to serve on a board. Creating a young leadership group, outside the formal board structure, may address these issues in a way that enables emerging leadership to have contact with the board and to contribute as their lifestyle permits.

The report also recommended that funders make resources available to an organization to engage in leadership and professional development activities. Too many funding sources state they will not pay for the development of an organization. This should be a priority of funders, especially foundations. In *Philanthropy's Challenge* I urged grantmakers to invest in building the capacity of the organizations they support and be active in helping guide the organization toward this objective.[13]

The report's recommendations are by and large the sensible steps any organization can take to build its future leadership. Beyond such actions, however, there is a fundamental issue that nonprofit organizations need to address: to what extent are they willing to devote time and resources to leadership development? In many organizations the dominant objective is furthering the mission of the organization through the various programs the organization provides. The focus is on programming and raising the funds necessary to support the organization's administration and programs. Unless and until the development of a core of professional staff with the capacity to assume the future leadership of an organization becomes a priority goal, it will not happen. Realistically speaking, this laudable and important objective is beyond the reach of those nonprofits plagued by scarce resources. But growing the capacity of an organization is essential to increasing its impact, and accordingly it should be a goal for all organizations.

Starting Out

The young woman I agreed to meet to discuss her search for her first full-time job was determined to find a position as a fundraiser for a not-for-profit organization in New York City, where her fiancé worked as a young Wall Street trader. She had just graduated with her master's in higher education from one of the country's top-flight universities, where she had worked part-time in the school's development office. She had secured interviews with some university development offices, but without receiving a concrete offer. She was bright, articulate, full of enthusiasm for the career path she was pursuing. We talked about how she liked to engage people on behalf of a cause, and she mentioned that someone had suggested approaching private secondary schools, which were now entering the fundraising business with increasing professionalism. I knew some of these schools and was familiar with some of their fundraising operations (both as a parent and an alumnus) and thought this was a good strategy, as the competition to find a position might be less intense than at the college level. One of the paradoxes of the fundraising businesses is that employers are finding it increasingly difficult to find talented development personnel with experience and a track record, and are taken aback at the prices experienced fundraisers can command. And yet they have no program to open the door to newcomers and train them so that, in time, they may become the kind of senior personnel they are desperately seeking, for which they now commonly hire executive recruiters (who receive a fee of 30 percent of the first year's compensation).

I offered to write letters of introduction to some schools and told the young woman if she knocked on the doors of the city's private secondary schools and colleges long enough, a door would eventually open. "But," I asked, "have you thought about beginning your career in business?" When she replied she hadn't, I set out to explain why I thought it could make good sense for her to consider it as an option, one I often suggest to young people who want a career in nonprofit management.

I then listed some of the things a person wanting a career in fundraising should want to learn when starting out:

- all there is to know about the cause you are going to try to raise money for and how to translate that into an appealing case for funding

- how to undertake research to identify prospects and then learn everything one can about them in order to make an effective solicitation (some organizations are far more sophisticated about research than others)

- how to translate that research data into a strategy for calling on prospects

- how to structure a presentation for the prospect (including the ability to catch their interest in the first 15 seconds—the so-called "elevator speech," what one could say if you were riding up in an elevator with a prospect)

- how a good prospect database helps the follow-up with prospects

- how to craft appealing written messages, whether for a direct-mail piece, an e-mail campaign, web site presentations, or talking points for a telephone call

- how to make "cold calls"

- how to generate PR for your case

- how to organize an event that attracts people and money.

These and other skills are best developed under the watchful eye of an experienced professional who, as part of his or her responsibilities, is charged with training staff in a high-performance environment.

"You might get this kind of disciplined training in a nonprofit," I concluded, "but not all such organizations make it part of their business to offer a structured program run by experienced people whose job it is to make you successful."

"And there is one other reality," I added. "It is far easier to move from a business organization to a nonprofit than the other way around." There is still general skepticism that nonprofit experience adequately prepares you for business, while nonprofits often prize candidates with a business background. The logical question, which came quickly enough, was what kind of business provides that kind of training.

Organizations that are driven in large measure by their sales forces, such as insurance companies, have established training programs. Prudential has two sales forces—one for insurance products and one for investment products, the former oriented toward individuals and the latter toward pension funds and other institutions. Other such firms include international insurance brokerage companies like Aon or Marsh, or broadcast companies that have major sales divisions. Banks with divisions that deal with wealthy individuals are another type of organization focused on individual sales.

I also offered to introduce her to a start-up venture that was developing a new kind of radiation therapy for hospitals and looking for a junior member of its sales team. I said:

> You will find it exciting to be part of a new venture that promises to do so much good. At the same time you learn about a business seeking to raise capital, you'll get a sense of the needs of hospitals. In a few years, if you want to enter the nonprofit sector, you'll be able to add real value to a development staff, especially in the medical field.

A critical factor in starting out is to join an organization that is focused on training newcomers and imposes rigorous discipline on their work. Developing habits of thoroughness and precision in one's work is the most valuable lesson of the first years of employment.

Ultimately, the young woman chose to work for a secondary school with a small development staff overseen by a veteran fundraiser, who took special interest in training those new to fundraising and mentored them with a friendly but very demanding hand.

Networking

I am often asked by my students how I've been able to move from one job to others in quite different fields of endeavor. The short answer is that someone who has seen my work in one area has recommended me for a different position, one I may not have even heard of. For example, I moved from oil industry finance to running the program-related investments program for the Ford Foundation, all because my name was put forward by a friend I had made while working for the U.S. Foreign Aid Program in Washington DC.

The art of networking is, of course, to stay in touch over the years with a wide circle of professional colleagues, college and graduate school classmates, and friends and acquaintances with professional careers. Joining professional associations or volunteering on behalf of various organizations is another avenue. Many colleges and graduate schools also run programs for alumni. Reading professional journals and periodicals can also alert one to opportunities. The object is to always be open to new opportunities, even while concentrating on maximizing your performance in your current position.

NOTES

1. Internal equity relates to situations in which positions are seen of equal value to the organization but are compensated differently because one is in a field where the market provides higher pay. For example, because of the scarcity of development professionals, a vice president for development may earn a good deal more than the head of programming, a position for which there may not be as strong an external demand.

2. See the section, "Compensation Review" in Chapter 3.

3. William Bowen, *The Board Book*. (New York: W.W. Norton & Co, 2008), pp. 114–115.

4. Bowen, p. 111.

5. "Daring to Lead 2006: A National Study of Nonprofit Executive Leadership," p. 5.

6. Annie E. Casey Foundation, "The 2004 Nonprofit Executive Leadership Transitions Survey."

The full report is available at: www.aecf.org/upload/publicationfiles/executive_transition_survey_report2004.pdf.

7. Johanna Berglein, "Leadership Transitions in Nonprofit Organizations: A Background Paper." Center for Nonprofit Strategy and Management, School of Public Affairs, Baruch College, City University of New York, December 6, 2007.

8. Ibid.

9. "Ready to Lead? Next Generation Leaders Speak Out," p. 18. (2008)

10. *Chronicle of Higher Education*, February 27, 2009.

11. Jennifer C. Berkshire, "Potential Charity Leaders See Top Job as Unappealing, New Survey Reveals," *Chronicle of Philanthropy*, March 6, 2008, p. 22.

12. "Ready to Lead?" pp. 25–29.

13. Paul B. Firstenberg, *Philanthropy's Challenge: Building Nonprofit Capacity through Venture Grantmaking* (New York: The Foundation Center, 2003).

6

The Executive Director: One of the Most Challenging Assignments in the Nonprofit World

Defining the Executive Director Role

In certain nonprofit organizations, by virtue of knowledge of the organization's business, its competitive environment, and staff capacity, the most influential leader is the executive director. He or she is typically well informed about the rules and practices that govern nonprofits, is skilled at operating a nonprofit enterprise, and is an articulate voice for the organization. Add to this his or her full-time dedication to the job and length of service—sometimes longer than most board members—and it's easy to see that an executive director can effectively shape the direction of, and establish the standards for, a nonprofit organization.

The executive directoor's ability to lead an organization, however, is heavily influenced by how his or her role is defined. Is the executive director a chief executive with the standing and powers akin to the CEO of a for-profit corporation? Or is the executive director viewed as the senior staff professional, but with his or her operating discretion limited? For instance, the board may have appointed a volunteer chairman or president in whom the ultimate executive power is vested under the organizational charter.

Executive power exercises control of the operations of the organization and all employees are subordinate to this power. Ambiguity as to who may exercise executive power—a board chairman, a volunteer president, or the professional executive director—makes the scope of each party's discretion unclear. Employees may feel they have access to the volunteer chair or president and are not obligated to take their direction from the executive director. For example, until recently, the volunteer chairman of the American Red Cross was the principal executive officer, creating uncertainty about the scope of authority of the professional president. This resulted in both inefficiency in program execution and a high turnover of presidents.

To enjoy the most efficient and effective exercise of executive power, an organization's charter should make it clear that it is vested in the senior professional officer, whether titled executive director or president, who is subject only to the policy direction of the board. Clarity on this point will delineate the division between the board's standard-setting and policymaking role, and the day-to-day supervision of operations by the senior professional officer. Making it clear that executive power is vested in the senior professional will enhance the professional's ability to represent the organization to the outside world and to negotiate transactions with third parties. Substantial contributors, in particular, tend to want to consummate major gifts with the executive who has the power to commit the organization and the duty to supervise the programs supported by their gifts. Generally, colleges and universities wisely vest executive power in the professional president, with the board playing a policy role. That doesn't mean there can't or won't be conflicts between the board and professional president over administration of the school, and the board has the final word. But in well-run institutions the respective roles of president and board are well established.

The moral in all this is that before signing on to become an organization's executive director professionals need to read an organization's charter and bylaws carefully to understand the structure of decision making and, in particular, where executive power is lodged. It is worth hammering out language in an employment agreement that states clearly that the executive power of the organization is vested in the executive director. Something like the language below can be inserted:

> The executive director shall be the principal executive officer and principal spokesperson for the organization. Subject to review by the board, he or she shall have full authority for overseeing the implementation of all of the organization's operations including its aims, policies, programs, communications, fundraising,

finances, and human resources; all employees are subordinate and take their directions solely from the executive director and the executive director shall have complete authority over the hiring or discharge of employees without the duty to obtain the consent of any board member.

To reinforce the authority of the executive director, the conditions under which his or her employment may be terminated should also be spelled out in the employment contract. This includes any compensation payable in such event (e.g., six months wages and benefits following termination). Of course, the board can always discharge the executive director, but depending on the contract language, the executive director may receive certain compensation. For example, if the contract is for two years and the executive director is terminated at the end of one year, he or she may be entitled to a second full year's compensation, depending on the grounds for termination specified in the contract. The most favorable provision from the executive director's point of view is that his or her employment may be terminated only "for cause," with cause limited to acts of "fraud," "conflicts of interest," or "gross negligence." The net of such a provision is that unless the executive director engages in one of the specified acts, termination for cause does not exist and the remaining term of the contract will have to be honored in full. Naturally, the board will seek more flexible grounds for termination, but the executive director wants to make it sufficiently expensive to terminate him or her that the board will be reluctant to cut short the contract term, unless a conflict between board and executive director over the management of the organization is so severe that it's not practical to continue the relationship.

Educating the Board

One of the greatest challenges faced by the executive director can be educating the board about the nature of the organization's activities, its competitive position, its financial condition, its compensation practices, the rules and regulations imposed by the government, and the tax treatment of certain transactions. Indeed, the executive director must be an "educator" of all the organization's constituencies—its board, to be sure, but also its employees and supporters who do not serve on the board. Keeping the broader public informed, including officials at various levels of government, is another obligation of the executive director, one that many executives do not fulfill successfully. How well the aims, operations, and results of nonprofit organizations are communicated can impact the environment in which they operate and the level of support they enjoy. How well the executive director educates the board will impact the scope of actions he or she can undertake.

Executive directors must also be a prime source of intelligence about developments in the field in which the organization is active as well as changes impacting charities in general. The board is entitled to expect the executive director to brief it on such matters, and so the director must devote time to keeping up with the field, just as lawyers, doctors, and other professionals do.

Consider the following case of a failure to educate an organization's leadership. An organization traditionally raised its funding through local events in various cities honoring a prominent person. Its volunteer chapters across the country were deeply committed to this approach. They had engaged in it almost from the beginning and remained committed to it, even as over time it became a less fruitful way to raise money. The executive director wanted to move the organization to be less dependent on event fundraising and engage more in direct solicitation of contributors. Ultimately, he failed to transform the organization's fundraising methods.

He failed to establish allies on the board who would support the new direction and were capable of making such solicitations. He also failed to find allies in chapters who were willing to practice direct solicitation on the local level. His professional fundraising staff was wedded to event fundraising and he failed to lay the foundation with the board for a broad remaking of the professional staff—bringing in professionals who could support a direct solicitation strategy. He failed to overcome the board's resistance to the increased salaries such professionals drew compared to the existing staff members, who lacked the skills to support direct solicitation campaigns. The overarching failure was that the executive director tackled the issue piecemeal without building alliances and educating the organization's constituency about what a comprehensive direct solicitation strategy entailed. He didn't think to present models of comparable organizations that had accomplished the transformation. In short, he underestimated the educational effort required to bring about such a fundamental change.

Establishing Compensation Policy

Another area that warrants the executive director's special focus is the organization's compensation system. It would be a mistake to think that because nonprofits try to further a cause, their personnel aren't interested in their compensation. My experience in both sectors clearly indicates that there is equivalent interest in how one is paid, especially related to how others in the organization and even comparable organizations are compensated. Personnel in the nonprofit sector may accept the more limited earnings of nonprofit enterprises, compared to the potential of much larger rewards in the business world; but they generally seek the highest compensation the organization can offer for their position. And it's no surprise that those who are disappointed with their compensation will complain, especially if they believe they are less well compensated than equivalent personnel in other organizations.

The executive director must focus on the design of the system by which increases in compensation are awarded, to be sure the system serves the purposes of the organization and is regarded by employees as fair and equitable.

Some institutions may go to considerable lengths to convince employees that they have been fairly treated. Princeton University, in the years I served as financial vice president, established a committee composed of the president, deans, and faculty members chosen by their colleagues to review salary awards proposed by the individual academic departments. It was a painstaking, time-consuming process that served its purpose of creating a sense among most faculty that compensation decisions were fair. Variations of such a meticulous process may make sense in certain large organizations with many professional employees. For the most part, however, it is up to the executive director and his or her principal reports to persuade the organization that compensation is fairly administered. In addition, a board committee review of the overall pattern of awards may be an appropriate step, although I have seen few boards undertake such a review.

In a typical organization, on the basis of the recommended budget for the year, the board will establish a percentage of the prior year's salaries to be awarded throughout the organization as salary increases for the coming year. One of the critical judgments the executive director must make is whether the size of the pool for salary increases is appropriate in light of the performance of the organization for the year and the priority of other claims on the budget.

Evaluating Program Effectiveness

Another primary challenge for the executive director is devising a system by which the effectiveness of the organization's programs can be objectively evaluated and documented. In a broader sense, can it be shown that the organization is accomplishing its mission and doing so on a cost-effective basis compared to comparable undertakings? Assembling the data that establish the effectiveness of programs can be difficult and expensive. For instance, assume an organization's mission is to increase the number of young people who enter scientific professions. To achieve this objective it has funded high schools around the country to work with colleges and universities on programs to enhance the science learning of high school students, especially to prepare them for a college-level science curriculum. One can readily document the number of students who take the programs in high schools, but will there be a system for tracking whether they continue to pursue science in college? Even more to the point, will there be a way to track how many students who participated in the high school program actually entered the sciences after college? The executive director, marshalling the available professional and financial resources, is obligated to see that a practical process for evaluating the program is established and even upgraded over time. Creating a valid measurement system goes to the heart of the organization's accountability, and the executive director is responsible for seeing that the best available information is collated and presented to the board.

Framing Issues for the Board: Benefits

The executive director must also be an articulate communicator of the organization's mission and the vision for its future, making sure all board members are on the same page. At the same time, the executive director has a duty to make sure the board focuses on issues that require their judgment but that may not have been addressed.

For example, it's easy for even a dedicated board of busy people to be focused on programs and fundraising and to overlook matters like the reasonableness of the benefit structure. Among the benefit issues that potentially warrant review are:

- Has the board examined whether the pension plan is providing payouts in excess of the percentage of final employee income considered necessary in retirement?

- Would the organization save substantial money if it converted from a defined benefit plan to a defined contribution plan?

- Is the severance plan actually a masked pension plan because it pays departing employees no matter whether they left voluntarily or involuntarily?

- Is the investment strategy for the pension fund consistent with returns contained in the organization's financial projections?

- Is the fund earning enough to support the projected pension payouts, or must the organization supplement investment returns with a greater charge to earnings?

- Should some level of employee contribution be required to reduce the cost of health benefits?

- Should low-salaried workers be required to contribute the same percentage of their salaries as high-income employees?

- Can the organization afford to provide health coverage in retirement, especially for employees who reach the age where they qualify for Medicare?

The foregoing is an illustrative, but not exhaustive list of benefit issues. The executive director cannot be expected to know all the answers or even identify all the issues in the increasingly complex world of benefits, but working with the financial officer and head of human resources, he or she can consult the requisite experts to review the organization's benefit structure and bring to the fore issues the board needs to address.

Cultivating Board Allies

The scope of the executive director's job is quite broad and touches on all issues important to the board and fellow employees. A good many of the issues do not lend themselves to clear-cut answers, but rather call for judgments balancing competing interests (e.g., increasing the salary pool by curtailing other organizational expenses, or vice versa). To be successful in resolving matters without rupturing organizational cohesion calls not only for well-considered judgment, but also a network of allies on the board and among employees. In the first instance, such allies can serve as a sounding board while the executive director explores different approaches, identifying pitfalls or suggesting modifications designed to broaden the base of support for an idea. Such allies can also be helpful in marshalling the support of others. In particular, the executive director has to devote attention and energy to cultivating one or more important board members—the chairman certainly, and perhaps the heads of key board committees. These relationships, cultivated one-on-one over time through the sharing of ideas, information, observations, and confidences, can prove to provide the decisive support the executive director needs on an issue. As one executive director remarked to me, "I don't present an issue to the board for decision unless I have tested out beforehand that I will have the support to prevail."

One other key to the executive director's effectiveness is the extent to which he or she does not catch key board members off guard, presenting an issue they had not expected to be put forward and without briefing them beforehand. One of the tasks of the executive director is thus to make sure board members are well informed and have an opportunity to consider the position they wish to take based on a thorough staff briefing on the subject and a sounding out of some of their trusted colleagues on the board.

No executive director, no matter how well he or she tends to allies, can necessarily expect to win every issue, but careful homework with board allies can prevent even a negative outcome from undermining confidence in and respect for the executive director. Often the wisest tactic, when a favorable outcome does not look possible, is to not press the issue to a decision but to withdraw it for consideration at a later time, or to pass it to a committee to consider it more deliberately than is possible at one board meeting.

The Role of Spokesperson

One important challenge, which some executive directors do not take the time to prepare themselves for, is exercising the role of principal spokesperson for the organization. To a certain extent this is a role that can be shared with a volunteer chairman, but the work of preparing the organization's mission statement to be communicated and structuring the themes to be advanced in communications is the responsibility of the executive director. Thus the director must have a way with words and be a persuasive speaker before various audiences. If these skills don't come naturally there are ample ways to improve them if the executive director is willing to be trained in the art of communication. Generally it is not enough for the executive director to speak with clarity and accuracy. In so many instances, presentation of the organization's work must touch the emotions of the audience, thereby persuasively making the "case" for the organization's mission.

Executive directors must also be prepared to play an active role in raising funds for the organization and securing its important contracts. Good staff work here can be invaluable, but the executive director should play a leadership role in conjunction with board members who have the contacts to open doors to fundraising possibilities.

Consistent with the role of principal spokesperson (voice) of the organization, the executive director must oversee whether the public relations staff is promoting the organization using the appeal they agreed to emphasize. This requires the executive director to maintain a direct reporting relationship with the head of communications and public relations. As often as practical, the executive director should preview all forms of communication before they are made public in order to be satisfied with the substantive message. The executive director will probably have the best sense of who should be identified with various communications and make sure they are not overlooked. For example, a new communications director put out an attractive brochure announcing a new program without being aware that the organization always linked the board chair to such announcements. Fortunately, the executive director saw a proof and was able to make a correction. The chance of error is greatly reduced if the head of communications produces a style book outlining the billing to be followed in the case of different publications and communications.

The executive director should meet regularly with the public relations director to plan various forms of communication, especially to clarify the objective of each communication and the messages to be conveyed. In a busy schedule, loaded with immediate issues, it's easy to neglect public relations planning, but it is an essential component of a well-conceived public relations program.

Oversight of the Hiring Process

The executive director must oversee and approve the process by which candidates for positions with the organization are to be identified and recruited. The executive director may retain the right to approve all hires, at least above a certain level, but to the extent practical he or she should meet with final professional candidates, regardless of whether the power to hire is located elsewhere in particular cases. Such meetings provide a useful opportunity for the executive director to convey to the candidate how he or she sees the position the candidate is considered for and to emphasize his or her own vision of the organization and its most important goals. The director will also want to confirm with the professional doing the hiring that they are on the same page as to what the candidate is to accomplish, and to be sure that the organization's formal hiring process was followed. In the case of select hires the executive director will reserve the right to make the final hiring decision.

Responsibility for Finances

The Sarbanes-Oxley legislation was written for public corporations, but it creates a potential issue for executive directors. The Sarbanes-Oxley Act requires chief executive officers of public corporations to sign their company's financial statements. The object is to preclude CEOs from saying they were unaware of their company's financial condition or certain financial reporting practices. In short, they are expected to be in command of their company's financial information. Signing means one has knowledge of the contents of the document. Should executive directors now sign their organization's financial statements and Forms 990?

Given the object of Sarbanes-Oxley's signature requirement, an astute executive director will sign his or her organization's financial statements and reports to demonstrate that he or she is in command of the organization's finances. Some executive directors defer entirely to their chief financial officer or controller in the presentation of financial data to the board. In my view, this undermines the perception that the executive director is fully in charge of his or her organization. Accordingly, I would recommend an executive director sign financial statements and reports (with genuine knowledge of their contents) and be visibly familiar with the auditor's management letter, which enumerates financial issues the auditor believes the organization should address. Such letters can cover everything from a recommendation that the organization write an accounting manual to creating better controls over the organization's cash. The executive director should also attend the portion of board audit committee meetings where management is present with the auditor. The point is that the executive director should not appear as being bypassed on any financial matter, but rather is in charge in the same way he or she is in charge of the organization's other departments. Thus, the executive director should be a full participant in the presentation of financial information about the organization and, indeed, all financial decisions.

A Balancing Act

Maintaining sufficient common ground among the board, between the board and staff, and within the staff is essential to the creation of a unified organization that speaks with one voice. The executive director must be committed to this objective to be successful. The director must recognize that one of his or her important responsibilities is conflict resolution within the organization. The director must strike a balance between implementing his or her vision and maintaining a common cause. There are cases in which directors have been so bent on a particular course that, in their determination to prevail, they have ignored the strong resistance of an important minority. The resulting friction can lead to fissures in the organization that are hard to repair. Avoiding such outcomes calls for a very high level of governance.

A strong, effective executive director, who nevertheless respects the board's authority and role, creates a healthy balance in an organization. However, in some cases the organization is really run by the executive director with the board very much taking a backseat. Some executive directors become deeply entrenched in an organization to the point where the reputation of the director and the organization merge and the board is in reality subordinate to the executive director. This can be the result of long service by the executive director with a board that constantly turns over, especially a board that is consistently deferential to the executive director, or where the executive director's specialized knowledge exceeds that of any board member or other staff person. This is not a healthy environment.

Executive directors that found an organization can also acquire such special status. Where an executive director is so entrenched it becomes a difficult task for the board to exercise its responsibilities, creating an organizational imbalance. The board can be kept out of the critical decision making loop and fail to exercise restraint over the director's decisions and expenditures or even time devoted to the job. It is not a desirable situation.

In the case of such an entrenched director, it can be difficult to remove him or her absent any blatant misconduct. The removal can be disruptive to staff and contributors alike who identify the organization and the executive director as one. In such instances, where the board feels it must make a change, finding a formula that saves face for the executive director may be the key to effecting a transition that doesn't disrupt the organization.

Take the case of the executive director of a theatrical group in New York City that for years had serviced a subscriber list by reproducing classic plays. The number of subscribers was constant over the years and the executive director was the organizational figure they identified with. The board was not visible to the subscribers. The executive director also served as artistic director of the theater, choosing the works that would be performed and recruiting the casts for the productions. The executive director, in essence, represented the theater to the artistic community. However, the theater was struggling financially, teetering on the edge of insolvency, and there appeared to be increasing resistance among actors to playing in its productions, finding the executive director difficult to work with. The executive director's deputy was a recent business school graduate who had impressed the board with his suggestions for productions and casts, virtually all of which the executive director vetoed. In time the board became convinced that the deputy would be a major improvement over the incumbent executive director. Because the director and theater were so closely aligned in people's minds, the issue was how to remove the incumbent in the way least disruptive to subscribers and the theater community. It turned out the executive director was tiring of his role and was interested in concentrating on the tours the theater ran. With a small raise and a nice title, the executive director agreed to step aside to head the tour program and his deputy took over. This case study describes the Roundabout Theater and today it is one of the most important and creative forces on Broadway, with its own theaters and multiple productions every season. That young deputy was the architect of the theater's growth into a major force.

The Executive Director's Challenge

In this era, then, when governance issues are of growing importance, the executive director must be multi-skilled and be able to multi task, not only able to lead all of the organization's day-to-day operations—from program, fundraising, and finance to compensation and benefits—but also to tactfully move the board to fulfill both its fiduciary and strategic roles. The director should also envision the possibility of future reforms of the nonprofit sector, keeping the organization ahead of the curve. Ultimately, the director must possess the tact and gift for relationship building that will enable him or her to gain the necessary support among staff and board to move the organization forward while maintaining its cohesion.

The executive director's domain, then, is as broad as the scope of the organization. His or her knowledge of and commitment to the mission of the organization, talent for educating colleagues, and high energy level can infuse the organization, motivating staff to perform at its highest potential.

The best executive director, given full authority, will be at once the organization's catalyst and strategic visionary, setting a demanding pace, but also its ethical center, establishing boundaries to the organization's actions, molding a moral enterprise that successfully fulfills its mission.

There's danger that without appropriate support from the board, executive directors can become frustrated and lose enthusiasm for their demanding role, becoming "burned out."

As William G. Bowen observed, this can be the case in particular when executive directors are not given the status of *ex-officio* board members, and they're made to feel like merely paid help, carrying out programs set by the board. Of course, sometimes executive directors are too reluctant to lead, to challenge their boards where appropriate. The need is for what Bowen labels a "healthy partnership," when board and executive director mutually support their respective roles.[1]

NOTE

1. William G. Bowen, *The Board Book* (New York: W.W. Norton & Co., 2008), p. 181.

7

The Effective CFO

The nature of executive responsibility for the financial administration of nonprofit organizations is changing, especially at larger, more complex organizations. The content of the financial role is changing—going far beyond maintaining the books of account. The question becomes whether the more broadly conceived role of chief financial officer adds sufficient value to a nonprofit organization to justify its cost.

The greater demand for accountability in the wake of Enron and other corporate scandals, the enactment of the Sarbanes-Oxley legislation, and the new governance rules at the exchanges have created pressure for a broader role for the corporate CFO. The pressure for performance in a global competitive environment, in turn, has intensified this trend. As a consequence, the role of corporate CFO has gone beyond overseeing the accounting function, raising capital, and managing relations with investors to become a critical strategic voice.

The increased focus in the nonprofit world on accountability for performance, coupled with several high-profile scandals in the sector, have led organizations to ask whether they have the right management skills in place in their financial administration. Today, in major nonprofit organizations, a fully effective financial function calls for a CFO with broad-ranging skills and responsibilities. Indeed, the CFO offers the highest value as a financially oriented strategist.

Traditionally, the function has been focused on the preparation of financial statements drawn in accordance with generally accepted accounting principles, managing receivable and payable accounts, managing payroll, and booking the receipt and disbursement of funds. Reports in an accounting format, however, do not always serve management's need for certain types and forms of information, or are not timely enough to enable management to direct the business most effectively, especially tracking the pace and level of revenues, cost, and cash flow against benchmarks. The CFO has to make sure management receives the type of information it needs to run the organization.

The classic accounting function periodically details budget variances, but not necessarily in the form that relates revenues and expenses to departments and programs (e.g., expenses are grouped by type of item, such as salaries or travel, but are not tied to a specific organizational unit).

The preparation of financial statements and budgets is typically geared to the schedule of periodic meetings of the board or its finance committee, which in some organizations meet as infrequently as twice a year, and rarely as often as quarterly.

The fully effective CFO of a major nonprofit organization will not simply scrub the numbers prepared by the accounting department, but will utilize financial processes and analysis to shape the opportunities, risks, and choices open to an organization.

The financial data produced will be tested not only for its accuracy but also for its realism. In the case of revenues, are the projections of revenue provided by operating departments balanced—do they strike an equilibrium between setting stretch goals for departments to achieve and realistic expectations of what can be accomplished? Not infrequently, nonprofits will find themselves in financial difficulty because of overly optimistic revenue forecasts, especially when those forecasts are developed to offset rising costs rather than represent true market potential. A CFO will scrutinize the forecasts from the perspective of a firsthand understanding of the business of the organization and its mission, and an appreciation of the underlying factors that lead to variance between forecasts and actual results. The CFO will also identify markers to be monitored during the year that will provide early indications of whether forecasts are on track.

To illustrate: a new head of fundraising is hired to break a four-year period of stagnation during which revenues have essentially been flat. The board and the CEO want to set a goal of a 10 percent increase in fundraising in year one. The new development chief has an ambitious program that includes hiring several additional fundraisers, creating a set of initiatives designed to draw attention to the needs of the organization, and cultivating prospects. The development officer estimates that the increase in expenses will be offset by the 10 percent increase in revenues. The CFO will question whether specific new targets for contributions have been identified, and even approached, to the point where it is reasonable to expect contributions from them. He will also ask when it is reasonable to expect the new fundraising hires to be on board and how long it's likely to take them to become familiar with the organization and its fundraising case—in other words, what they can be expected to contribute in year one. He will also ask the new development chief to review—existing staff member by existing staff member—how much additional fundraising is expected of them and the basis for this expectation based on their past history. He will also ask for examples of other comparable organizations that have achieved a 10 percent jump in fundraising after a period of stagnation and what actions they took to achieve this end. In short, he will accept the 10 percent increase as a laudable goal to set out for the development staff but, depending on what he learns, he will insist the budget be built on a more conservative estimate of what, as a practical matter, can be accomplished in year one.

Underlying the CFO's financial judgment will be a broad understanding of the organization's business and its competitive position. An effective CFO will cross the cultural boundaries in nonprofit organizations between administration and program (or in higher education between business administration and academic matters).

The same business-grounded approach will be applied by the CFO to the cost structure of the organization. First, the CFO will test the soundness of cost forecasts and again identify factors that can produce variances. Second, going beyond ensuring the accuracy of cost estimates, the CFO will scrutinize whether the costs are reasonable and necessary or whether a particular function can be provided more efficiently, be consolidated with other functions, or be eliminated altogether without undermining the ability of the organization to discharge its mission. Again a system will be established to track and control costs within budgeted limits.

Indeed, for both revenues and expenses, the CFO will see that an internal control system is established that monitors whether they are in line with budget limitations and, in the case of expenditures, within the amounts authorized. For example, traditional accounting would report on the amount of endowment funds expended during a reporting period. A control system would check whether such spending was consistent with the endowment spending formula approved by the board.

In essence, then, the effective CFO will transform the financial function into a system that most efficiently and accurately produces the information management needs, in the form and timing it requires, to operate the organization in accordance with expectations. He or she will create systems that track regularly whether those expectations are being met. Moreover, the CFO will analyze the organization's financial position, not just at one point in time, but also by how it's likely to evolve over time. The object is to project what the organization's financial position will be at various times in the future, if present trends continue or certain foreseeable changes in the environment occur; in short, the CFO will view the organization's financial position as a continually moving target.

On a broader scale, the CFO will analyze whether certain activities of the organization can be justified or even expanded in terms of their costs, results, and benefits, bringing to bear a full sense of the organization's strengths and weaknesses and its potential to enhance its capabilities. This, coupled with responsibility for a more robust financial reporting and control system, places the CFO in the center of formulating strategy for the organization. The CFO will press for a sharp definition of the organization's competitive niche and its advantages and disadvantages versus competitive organizations. An integral part of the CFO's strategic role will be to satisfy the board and third parties that the organization's resources are being applied for designated purposes in support of its mission and producing the promised gains. The CFO also will be expected to demonstrate that the cost of delivering its mission is at least comparable to organizations with similar missions.

The CFO can also serve as the bridge between the needs and opportunities of the operating departments and the availability of resources to implement their plans and programs. This coordinating of operating needs and ambitions with financial realities and risks enables formulating a coherent strategy that does not passively accept the status quo, but rather establishes realistically achievable goals for enhancing the effective delivery of its programs. The highest value of a CFO to the board, the CEO, and colleagues, is to present a picture of the organization that fairly represents its opportunities and perils and, where appropriate, compels an examination of the capacity of the organization to perform its existing programs more efficiently and effectively, and of the potential for the organization to extend its reach.

The effective CFO thus brings to the formulation of strategy a combination of a depth of understanding of the business of the organization, its strengths and weaknesses, and its financial condition and prospects, making him an invaluable member of the organization's strategic team.

The CFO's role in directing the financial function and as a strategist does not complete the list of position responsibilities. The CFO will also oversee:

- the terms the organization negotiates with customers and vendors

- the application of quantitative and qualitative analysis to proposed new undertakings, identifying the potential risks and rewards

- the prudent management of cash flow

- the raising of debt

- the investment of endowment funds and other reserves

- the pension plan's compliance with applicable laws and regulations, especially whether the funding of a defined benefit plan is sufficient to meet the plan's obligations

- whether adequate provision is made for the maintenance of physical assets.

Not every organization is at a stage of development where it can afford, or even make the best use of, a CFO. Organizations with small budgets or a limited scope of operations may not be able to fully exploit the talents an effective CFO can bring, or afford the cost of such an executive. A high-powered CFO is not appropriate for all nonprofits.

Given the CFO's diverse portfolio, what skills and experience will enable a person to meet the demands of the position? Of course, basic financial skills are a "must have"—the ability to manage the accounting function, craft financial reports that serve management, ensure adequate financial controls are in place, oversee investments, and analyze prospective projects. Of equal importance is a basic business sense; that is, an ability to judge whether different types of operations are working as intended and, if not, why not. In addition, an effective CFO is skilled at translating financial and business insights into strategic concepts. Naturally, people skills are also very important, especially the ability to work with others while treading lightly on their turf, and perhaps their toes. And, finally, the CFO must have a talent for presentation—the ability to present financial and strategic analysis to the board, the CEO, colleagues, and third parties such as funding sources and even regulatory authorities. An effective CFO is quite a package of talent and personality.

- Foundations, universities, and other institutions concerned with the nonprofit sector should develop programs to increase the supply of development officers.

NOTES

1. Holly Hall, "Fundraising Frenzy," *Chronicle of Philanthropy*, August 9, 2007, pp. 19–22.
2. Ibid.
3. See the section in Chapter 2 entitled "The Urban Institute Study of Directors."

9

Professional Services

The Role of the Auditor in the Wake of Sarbanes-Oxley

Reform of accounting practices has become a public issue as an outgrowth of the Enron and other public corporation scandals and the role played by Enron's accounting firm Arthur Andersen. While the focus has been on role of the auditor of public corporations, the legislatively mandated changes in this role have implications for the nonprofit sector.

The story behind the changes begins with the recent history of Arthur Andersen. The accounting and consulting firm of Arthur Andersen was at one time one of the nation's five largest. In 2002, a suit filed against the firm by the federal government led to its collapse as an entity. The lawsuit charged that Andersen's Houston office, serving Enron, shredded documents because it feared an investigation by governmental authorities. No charge was brought challenging any action of the firm in reviewing certain transactions. No charge was made that the firm looked the other way when management's presentation of financial information may not have complied with GAAP accounting. Rather, a jury convicted the firm of document tampering, and that verdict was the nail in the Arthur Andersen firm's coffin. Ironically, after the firm was dissolved, an appeals court set aside the verdict on the grounds that government had not established a criminal intent.

The federal government chose to sue the entire firm rather than just the Houston office, a tactic many have questioned as unfair to the hundreds of Andersen employees who had nothing to do with the Enron account. Andersen's collapse reduced the number of large-scale firms capable of handling the biggest corporations to four.

119

Enron was a very lucrative Andersen client—during 2000, Enron generated $27 million in consulting fees and $25 million in auditing fees for Andersen. The firm was involved in passing on questionable Enron practices, but its active responsibility for any wrongful transaction has never been established. Still, Andersen was present when practices later deemed inappropriate occurred, and it never elected to challenge Enron. The surmise was that Enron was such an important client that Andersen did not want to rock the boat.

The Sarbanes-Oxley legislation took dead aim at the responsibility of accounting firms that have wide exposure to their client's business. Sarbanes-Oxley is undoubtedly the most sweeping legislation directed at public corporations' financial reporting since the Securities Acts of the 1930s. It has changed the way public corporations prepare financial information, the nature of auditing practice, and the responsibility of senior executives for the financial reports issued by their companies. Sarbanes-Oxley—with the exception of the provisions relating to tampering documents and retaliation against a whistle blower[1]—does not by its terms apply to nonprofit organizations. Still, while allowing for the differences in the two sectors, these changes in public corporation governance warrant consideration by nonprofit organizations.

APPLYING SOX TO NONPROFIT ACOUNTING

At the outset, it is relevant to note that the role of the auditor is to review the financial presentations of management to determine whether in the firm's opinion management's financials have been prepared in accordance with generally accepted accounting principles (GAAP). The fair presentation of a nonprofit's financial position and activities prepared in accordance with GAAP is primarily the responsibility of management. The auditing firm conducts an audit and on the basis thereof issues its opinion whether the statements prepared by management comply with GAAP. This is not quite the same as saying management has provided all the information necessary to enable outsiders to appreciate fully the realities of the organization's financial position. Thus, it is a responsibility of management (i.e., senior executives and board members, in this context) to develop fully informative and accurate financial information. For this reason, nonprofits should follow the Sarbanes-Oxley requirement that all financial reports be signed by the senior executives, signifying their knowledge of the content of those reports. The "I didn't know or understand" explanation by board members or senior executives for going along with a financial misstatement or omission will no longer work.

That management is responsible for its financial statements does not exculpate the auditor that wrongly certifies that statements comply with GAAP when they do not. Turning a blind eye to abusive accounting practices by management exposes the auditor to the risk of liability, although as a profession accountants have campaigned vigorously for the adoption of legislation that would limit this exposure. On the contrary, the accounting profession may even have an obligation to tighten its standards of review of management's work. Columbia law professor John Coffee argues that, "...reform of the accounting firm will gain little unless there is substantive reform of accounting principles." One reform, he maintains, that would serve both public corporations and nonprofit organizations, would be to require " ...the auditor to certify not simply compliance with GAAP, but to read the auditor's certification that the issuer's financial statements "fairly present" its financial position to mean these financial statements provide all the disclosures necessary for understanding the [organization's] overall financial position."[2]

The Sarbanes-Oxley legislation also increased accounting firm's responsibility by requiring them to review the adequacy of management's assessment of its internal controls for financial reporting. This added substantial expense to the audit, which has been mitigated somewhat by new rules governing the review of financial controls. The New York State Attorney General states that the "...development and maintenance of the organization's internal controls will help to ensure accountability," but does not duplicate the procedures Sarbanes-Oxley establishes with respect to internal controls. The approach of the NY AG seems to be on the right track: the audit committee in concert with management and the outside auditor should periodically review and determine the extent to which the organization maintains adequate internal controls without calling for written, formal assessments.

The Sarbanes-Oxley legislation also requires the senior partner on an account to be rotated every five years. The requirement may be impractical in the case of very small accounting firms. In the case of large firms and clients it may be a useful practice but can be left to the discretion of the audit committee.

Two factors related to the actions of public corporations and their auditors created the basis for other important provisions of Sarbanes-Oxley.

First, the corporate scandals that shocked people at the beginning of this century invariably involved the dissemination of misleading financial information that directly impacted the company's stock price. Moreover, the stock market decline in 2002 prompted widespread restatement of prior earnings reports. This raised the question whether the accounting profession was being rigorous enough in certifying corporate financial reports. Confidence in the ability of the profession to police itself and set appropriate standards was at a low ebb. The outcome was the creation within Sarbanes-Oxley of the Public Corporation Accounting Oversight Board (PCAOB), appointed by the SEC and empowered both to set accounting standards for public corporations and to oversee the performance of accounting firms. In the nonprofit world, where there is no stock issued, the same incentive to stretch earnings does not exist, certainly not to the same degree. Accordingly, there would not seem to be a basis for creating a nonprofit accounting board similar to the PCAOB, but to rely on state attorneys general becoming more aggressive in policing nonprofit financial statements, which many states require to be filed with the AG along with Form 990, which is also filed with the IRS and is publicly available.

Second, in the last decades of the twentieth century, stock options became the preferred mode of compensation of executives and large-scale option awards were made. This created strong pressure to show steadily rising earnings to drive stock prices well above the price of the stock when the options were granted. And the pressure to sign off on earnings escalation fell directly on auditors. This pressure was compounded by the lucrative large-scale consulting contracts corporations offered their auditing firms. In fact, for many firms consulting revenues exceeded audit fees. In the case of nonprofits, which obviously do not issue stock, there are no option awards to tempt the auditor to accept deceptive earnings in order to please executives with significant amounts of compensation tied to stock options. Also, there is far less risk that large consulting contracts will be awarded auditors to induce them to sign off on escalating earnings. Accordingly, Sarbanes-Oxley's barring auditors from most forms of consulting is a considered response to the public corporation environment, but is not warranted by the nonprofit environment.

This is not to say that nonprofit executives do not have a financial incentive to show strong earnings growth (because their compensation will be influenced by such results), but we're talking about increases in base salary, perhaps a bonus, but nothing to compare to the payoff that can be reaped from hundreds of thousands of stock options.

The bottom line here is that there does not seem to be a basis, at least yet, in the nonprofit world to create a PCAOB or bar auditors from consulting work with clients, although boards of directors would be wise to carefully justify employing their auditors in a consulting role.

Both Sarbanes-Oxley and the New York Stock Exchange did introduce a reform, relating to the relationship between auditing firms and their clients, requiring that the hiring of the auditor and drafting the terms of its engagement be set by the board audit committee instead of by management. This change in practice makes sense for nonprofits. It aligns the selection of auditors and the terms of their work with the responsibility of the board for the financial statements of the organization, compelling board members to become more actively engaged in the process by which financial information is developed and published and ending the possibility of cozy relationships between controllers and the organization's auditor.

Indeed, it is a good thing for auditors to align their loyalties with the board committee and feel obligated to make sure that:

- the committee understands the financial position of the organization

- it is cognizant of all the policy issues inherent in the financial statements (e.g., significant expenditures that have been capitalized instead of being charged to the operating statement)

- it has been briefed on any material weakness the auditor has observed in the organization's financial controls.

One of the inquiries the audit committee should make in connection with the selection of an auditor is how the firm exercises quality control over the work of its diverse partners and associates. One of Andersen's weaknesses was that the firm's central quality control unit, designed to review interpretations of accounting principles by engagement teams, yielded to the Houston office on a number of questionable transactions and thus failed to exercise the independent internal oversight the unit was intended to provide.

A good number of nonprofit organizations, especially small enterprises, lack the management skills to prepare financial statements and therefore need to draw on their accountants to prepare such statements. In these situations it is important that a member of management follow closely the process of putting together such statements and be familiar with what adjustments the accountant may make to the organization's books to comply with GAAP. Where the accountant prepared the statements, it will not issue the standard opinion based on a review of management's work.

MANAGEMENT INFORMATION

Audited financial statements will consist of an operating (or income) statement and balance sheet prepared on an accrual basis. The composition of an operating statement and accrual accounting were discussed in the first edition.[3]

Audited financial statements by themselves are, however, not sufficient to assure financial control of an organization. In the first place, they are prepared after the events have taken place, often months later, making it impossible for management to take timely corrective action. Moreover, the information provided for the financial statements may not be in the form that management needs to control operations. Management needs information highlighting key variables in a form that reveals the underlying financial realities.

Here are four illustrations where simply tracking numbers at their face value can lead to unwanted financial results. Additional tracking systems have to be established to avoid such results:

- Contributions are flowing in at the rate projected in the budget. However, the percentage of such contributions that are in the form of pledges of future contributions rather than current cash is substantially higher than expected.

- The trustees have authorized endowment spending at 5 percent. The revenues received from endowment spending are recorded. However, a review reveals the rate of spending exceeds 5 percent.

- Each department is given a travel budget for the year. At the end of the year it turns out the overall travel budget has been overspent because several departments exceeded their budgets and no central department existed to direct an adjustment be made to other units' spending to compensate for such overruns.

- Total program expenditures are in line with budget projections but in fact certain programs are being underfunded in order to offset overfunding of others, indicating certain programs may not be performing as anticipated.

The challenge to an organization's financial team is to track the performance of key variables in a way that highlights if variables are on track at a time when corrective action is possible, especially those that directly impact the cash position of an organization.

Accordingly, a critical financial document for management is the quarterly (or even monthly) Sources and Uses of Funds Statement, which tracks the inflow and outflow of cash.[4] Ironically, despite the statement's importance, management's analysis is not typically reviewed by an accountant and there are no general principles that govern its preparation. Review of the statement by an auditor would seem a wise precaution against errors.

In sum, the auditor is the second line of defense to management in ensuring the publication of fully informative and accurate information. In its engagement with the audit committee, the auditor can play a vital role in alerting the leadership of the organization to weaknesses in its financial position and in its financial reporting. Indeed, the auditor is the best-positioned outsider to play the role of alerting the board to financial issues at a point in time when corrective action is possible. Preservation of its reputation—the true capital of a professional service firm—should motivate auditing firms to be alert to doing so.

The Role of Lawyers as Gatekeepers

The role of attorneys in governance is complicated by the attorney's well-established duty to faithfully and even zealously represent his or her client and to respect the confidentiality of communications with the client. This duty raises the issue in any instance in which the attorney believes the client may be engaged in wrongdoing.

Section 307 of the Sarbanes-Oxley legislation provides that attorneys practicing before the SEC are required to report evidence of a "material breach of law" by the company they are representing to the company's chief legal counsel or chief executive. If the counsel or officer does not respond appropriately to the evidence, the attorney must report the evidence to the audit committee of the board or another board committee made up entirely of independent directors.

The duties set out in Sarbanes-Oxley were prompted by the question raised after the corporate scandals: where were the attorneys? Why didn't they blow the whistle? Section 307 was clearly a product of the Senate's concern that lawyers were present at the corporate scandals of the day. Then-Senator Corzine, former head of Goldman Sachs and now governor of New Jersey, told the Senate:

> ...executives and accountants work day-by-day with lawyers. They give them advice on almost every transaction. This means that when executives and accountants have been engaged in wrongdoing there have been some other folks at the scene of the crime—generally they are lawyers.[5]

Professor John Coffee of Columbia Law School takes a different slant. He writes that perhaps lawyers assisted others in planning financial fraud:

> ...but the greater danger is that lawyers were nowhere near the scene of the crime, thereby enabling others to orchestrate the fraud. Given Section 307's "up the ladder" reporting obligation, the best law compliance is to ensure lawyers know more about their client's activities. Here, the real problem is the fragmentation of legal services so no lawyer has an integrated view of a client's obligations.[6]

In its May 2007 report on "The Lawyer's Role in Corporate Governance," the New York City Bar Association observed:

> Though not necessarily culpable in actual wrongdoing ... lawyers were often sufficiently familiar with aspects of client conduct later alleged to have been fraudulent to have asked questions about that conduct. They appear to have done so in certain instances. Where questions were not asked or pressed, it is reasonable to believe that more assertive action might have avoided or mitigated wrongdoing in some of those situations.[7]

It continued that this conclusion implies that lawyers could act as "whistle blowers" or "gatekeepers" with respect to past or future wrongdoing, but the association did not recommend that lawyers play this role. It maintained that to impose general whistle blowing or gatekeeping duties on lawyers is "so contrary to their traditional role as confidential advisors" that it would be counterproductive.[8]

It did, however, in line with the American Bar Association, recommend that lawyers report "ongoing impending violations of law likely to cause substantial injury to the client up through the corporate hierarchy," and if the board fails to address a clear violation of law, to make limited disclosures of client confidences to regulatory authorities.[9]

With respect to outside counsel, the Bar Association commented that the role of outside counsel has evolved, "...from a general counseling role to one more focused on specific transactions that require special expertise." This, the association points out, may lead to counsel rendering certain services without a full appreciation of their context.

The association went on to observe another change in the profession:

> …its evolution toward a more competitive, bottom-line orientation with client relationships often in play and critical to the compensation of partners. This environment creates pressure on law firms and lawyers to acquiesce in questionable conduct rather than place the client relationship at risk by pressing unwelcome advice.[10]

One of the most ambiguous areas in defining lawyers' duty to report wrongdoing is when the attorney's initial disclosure to the corporation does not produce adequate remedial action. Sarbanes-Oxley's mandate that if an official "does not respond appropriately," then the attorney must take it to a higher level makes sense on the surface. However, who is to be the judge of what is an "appropriate" response? Does the attorney have to accept a course of action adopted by a company with full knowledge of the evidence of wrongdoing even if he or she disagrees with it? Suppose the attorney presses the issues all the way to a committee of the board and still feels the company is not acting appropriately. Is he or she free or even obliged to present the evidence of wrongdoing to a public official when in good faith the attorney believes the company has not acted "appropriately"?

The SEC has attempted to provide objective criteria of what constitutes a "material violation," but its definition is elaborate, involving a double negative. Coffee defends the effort by saying it is an improvement over the accounting profession's "actual knowledge" while still requiring more than "gossip, hearsay, or innuendo."[11] He is critical, however, of the SEC's definition of what constitutes a reasonable response. He maintains that the SEC gives the term "appropriate response" a particularly complex definition that includes a broad escape clause (i.e., an opinion by another attorney that the corporation has a colorable defense.)

Sarbanes-Oxley and the Bar Association are addressing the role of counsel in connection with public corporations. In such cases there are important public interests at stake: protecting shareholders and the investing public, and maintaining confidence in our capital markets. The not-for-profit sector does not present quite the same set of interests, although there is a public interest in protecting the integrity of the tax code's application to nonprofits and the willingness of the public to support the charitable sector. Accordingly, misconduct in the not-for-profit sector cannot be taken lightly. In turn, this imposes an obligation on attorneys who uncover evidence of a material breach of law to report their findings to senior management and/ or the board. And if the client does not act with respect to such evidence, what is the attorney's duty to pursue the matter to a higher level? As noted, certain bar associations have proposed that if the board fails to address a clear violation of law, the attorney may make limited disclosures of client confidences (such as to regulatory bodies) to prevent substantial injury to the client. Still, this area is uncharted waters.

What to make of all of this? The lawyer whom a company should be able to count on to alert the CEO or board to any even potentially unlawful act may not know enough about what is going on in the company to connect the dots and consequently will fail to send out a warning. This may be a real risk according to Coffee, but the remedy has to be the appointment, with board approval, of an attorney whose responsibilities expressly include sufficient oversight of all the activities of the organization, with the authority to review any activity, so that he or she will be alert to any unlawful activity, certainly any involving the use of legal counsel. In most organizations such an attorney will be known as the "general counsel" and he or she must closely monitor all the legal work done in the organization, either by staff attorneys or outside lawyers. He or she will be expressly charged with unearthing any even potentially unlawful activity and reporting both to the CEO and the chairman of the board of directors.[12] The New York Bar Association maintains the board of directors should review and approve the tenure and compensation of the general counsel, articulate its expectations for the role, and have independent meetings with counsel.[13]

In organizations that are too small, or have too little legal work, to afford a full-time general counsel this role should be assigned to a lawyer in a firm retained by the organization. A large percentage of nonprofit organizations will fall into this category. While an outside attorney will not initially be quite as informed about the organization as an inside general counsel, over time he or she should acquire enough knowledge to be alert to at least any use of lawyers to support or help plan an unlawful activity or to look the other way when a dubious transaction is in progress. In short, if a lawyer is at the scene of the crime, he or she must blow the whistle.

NOTES

1. Sarbanes-Oxley amended the criminal code to: 1) make it a criminal offense to tamper with documents to impair their usefulness or availability or to influence an official proceeding, or 2) to retaliate against a whistle blower for providing a law enforcement officer with truthful information relating to a federal offense.

2. John C. Coffee, Jr. *The Gatekeepers* (Oxford University Press, 2008), pp. 104–170.

3. See Chapter 9 of the first edition. See also Coffee, pages 106–108; Warren Ruppel, *Not-for-Profit Accounting Made Easy*, 2nd ed. (John Wiley & Sons, 2007), pp. 36–42.

4. Ibid.

5. Coffee, p. 217.

6. Ibid., p. 231.

7. New York City Bar Association, *The Record*, "The Lawyer's Role in Corporate Governance" (May 2007), p. 168.

8. Ibid., p. 169.

9. Ibid., p. 170.

10. Ibid., p. 173.

11. Coffee, p. 218.

12. The general counsel of Enron received from the chairman of Enron a whistle blower's letter that tore into Enron's off-book partnerships and accounting. The author of the letter was not identified at this point. The GC took the letter and sent it marked "FYI" to a number of Enron executives and that ended his involvement with the letter. In the future, you can bet general counsel will stay right on top of such letters until the accuracy of their allegations are run down. Kurt Eichenwald, *Conspiracy of Fools* (Broadway Books, 2005), p.488.

13. New York City Bar Association, *The Record*, p. 171.

10

The Role of Contributors

A contributor of a significant portion of an organization's funding is in a unique position to exercise influence over how the enterprise operates. The contributor has the leverage that flows from the organization's need for the funds it can provide. The larger the share of the needed funding provided by a contributor, the more influential the contributor's voice. In many cases a donor will have considerable professional experience to draw upon.

As used in this text, the term "contributors" encompasses all individuals and institutions that provide funding to a nonprofit organization, be it in the form of a gift, grant, or contract for products or services.

Many, even large contributors once shied away from questioning the potential recipient about the viability of its organization, as well as such project-specific questions as what objectives it will set for the use of the money the contributor is considering giving to the organization, whether it has the management personnel to achieve such objectives, how it will track the results achieved by the use of the funds, and what reports it will provide the contributor to account for the program's degree of success or lack thereof. It was once enough to describe a program with laudable objectives. Today, increasingly it is necessary to show the specific objectives the program is intended to achieve and how the degree of success it achieves in meeting these will be tracked and reported. The acid test is whether the recipient organization can objectively document for the contributor whether the funds advanced have achieved their stated objectives and, to the extent there is a shortfall, provide an explanation why.

Evaluating the efficacy of the particular program the contributor is asked to fund is important, but equally critical is evaluating whether the organization has the capacity to successfully implement the programs it designs. A focus on just the program for which funding is sought can overlook the organization's overall strengths and weaknesses, the overall needs of the organization, and the opportunities to bolster the organization's capabilities.

The focus on organizational viability addresses whether the organization has assembled the staff with the requisite skills and has access to the resources required to maintain the health of the enterprise over the long term. This means assessing whether the organization is executing its mission in accordance with goals and objectives established by the board pursuant to a strategic plan adopted by the board. It also means assessing whether the organization has the financial, strategic, and administrative capacity and access to funding that underlies long-term viability.

Program-specific analysis by itself may also overlook the organization's overall competitive position, including whatever its advantage in competition with other organizations may be. The object is to assess not just the competitive strength of an organization, but also whether the organization is more likely to meet the funder's goals than another entity. This leads to inquiring into the organization's distinctiveness in its field and whether it can deliver its programs more cost effectively than other organizations with similar objectives.

Assessment of the organization's capabilities certainly includes a review of its financial condition and outlook. This means a careful reading of the organization's financial statements, which should be audited by an independent auditing firm and reviewed by an audit committee of the board. It is also relevant to inquire whether the chief executive officer and chief financial officer have signed the statements to signify their belief that they fairly present the financial condition of the organization.

Contributors also need to think through whether they have the capability to provide ongoing assistance to the organization's management in the form of an advisor or member of its board of directors. The combination of money and assistance may be the most valuable form of aid the contributor can provide.

In the business world, private equity investors typically play an active role in growing the enterprise. Generally, such investors will take one or two seats on the board, giving them direct knowledge of the degree of the company's progress and the problems it may be encountering. Board participation helps investors to work closely with management in shaping company strategy and in building relationships with key personnel that encourage early alert to management weaknesses or problems the company may be encountering. Such an engaged approach differs sharply from the typical contributor's more arms-length relationship with recipients, relying on formal reports where generally one learns about difficulties with the project or management shortcomings after the fact. Too few contributors seek an effective, working collaboration with organizations they fund.

Ideally more and more major contributors should inquire into the capabilities of the organization they propose to fund and whether the organization is devoting enough resources to strengthen its management where appropriate. To be effective here, contributors need to exhibit a willingness to fund organizational requirements, and indeed to become involved in the direction of the organization, providing valuable assistance and timely insight into looming difficulties.[1]

A focus on organizational capacity requires addressing how to build an organization to increase its impact—a process that requires time—and foregoing many contributors' reluctance to make long-term commitments to an organization or to fund organizational expenses.

There is one important caveat to the call for more accountability for the use of funds. Documenting the extent to which objectives have been achieved, especially if a neutral party is retained to make the evaluation, can be both time-consuming and costly. Where the costs of documentation are material it is appropriate to ask the contributor to fund such costs with respect to the project or program the contributor is financing.

There also are nuances in evaluating the performance of an organization, especially when quantitative data are not available, and in linking cause and effect. The first edition provides an example of how a broad qualitative goal can be broken into specific quantifiable goals. It describes an organization that has the goal of improving the lives of young women who grow up in poverty. The goal does not lend itself to quantification. However, when the broad goal is broken down into specific objectives, as it must be to create concrete programs, those specific objectives can be quantified. One objective might be to reduce by a specified percentage the rate of pregnancy among teenage women who participate in the organization's program in a target community, relative to the rate of pregnancy among teenagers who do not join. The extent to which this specific objective is accomplished and the cost of doing so can be calculated and even compared to the cost to society of dealing with teenagers who give birth.

The first edition cautions that the linkage between cause and effect can be uncertain, and notes the various reasons—other than the organization's program—why teenage pregnancy rates may decline. If the rates do not decline one can conclude that the program is not effective. But demonstrating the positive requires the exercise of the best judgment possible.[2]

Despite the difficulties of evaluating outcomes, contributors perform a service by raising the issue and exploring how meaningful assessments can be developed. Indeed, contributors are one of the few sources of external evaluation of a nonprofit; taking the role seriously is an important contribution in and of itself.

NOTES

1. See Chapter 5, Paul Firstenberg, *Philanthropy's Challenge*, The Foundation Center (2003).

2. Paul B. Firstenberg, *The 21st Century Nonprofit: Remaking the Organization in the Post-Government Era* (New York: The Foundation Center, 1996), p. 93.

Section 3.

Strategic Issues

11

Greater Regulation of Nonprofits

This is the fifth book I have written on the subject of nonprofit organizations. All the books have the same general focus—how to enhance nonprofit performance. The writing reflects the extent to which my work in the nonprofit sector has engaged my interest as well as my sense of the critical role nonprofit organizations play in enriching the life of this country.[1]

Significant numbers of Americans are active in the nonprofit sector as board members, volunteers, contributors, and professional staff. Indeed, it is difficult to imagine what America would be without the contributions of nonprofit organizations. Any sector so important deserves to be as well run as possible. However, none of my prior writing has addressed the issue of whether there is adequate governmental oversight over the operations of nonprofits.

The sector is not without its blemishes.[2] Organizations have failed because of poor management. Some have spent excessively on administration at the expense of program support. Some organizations with large endowments have been unduly restrictive in spending such funds on current needs. Far worse, executives in some organizations have diverted resources for their personal benefit and have flagrantly abused their position.

Gilberman and Gelman warn:

> These types of cases (of wrongdoing) have tarnished the image of NGOs, and their perpetuation over time further erodes public trust.... The third sector can ill afford the consequences of public scandal. Public skepticism will continue to grow, affecting charitable giving and fundraising capability.[3]

Such concerns have prompted suggestions for greater government regulation of nonprofit organizations, especially tax-exempt public charities. Private foundations are already more tightly regulated than public charities.[4]

Doubtless, as has been suggested, a set of regulations could be developed to require an organization's administrative expenses not to exceed a certain percentage of revenues, or at least to calculate such a ratio on its IRS Form 990 filing. Each year boards of directors could be required to certify that they reviewed the compensation and expenses of senior executives and found them reasonable. Loans to executives and board members could be banned. Periodically, organizations could be required to apply to the IRS for renewal of their tax exemption. The provisions of Sarbanes-Oxley legislation dealing with the preparation of financial statements and financial controls of public companies, the creation of an audit committee of the board, and the role of the auditor could be applied to nonprofits as well.

In my view, however, it would be excessive to add to the existing regulation of nonprofits. Such additional regulations would divert already limited resources and management energy from nonprofit programs. In fact, there is a risk that such added regulation would shift organizational energy from innovation to compliance. Moreover, given the breadth of purpose, size, and structure of the now over one million tax-exempt organizations, it would not be easy to draft legislation that would apply fairly to all types of nonprofits.

For example, two organizations may both support education but one has a better ratio of expenses to revenue than the other. But the organization with the better ratio may be older and have a larger inventory of mature legacies. It may also raise its money through direct solicitation of donors while the other, being a newcomer, may have to rely on fundraising dinners, which are typically more expensive than direct solicitation. Holding both to the same expenses-to-revenue ratio would not make sense.

William G. Bowen argues in *The Board Book*:

> ... lawmakers should resist the temptation to respond to every perceived instance of bad behavior by passing a new statute.[5]

Bowen goes on cite a study that ninety-two of the ninety-four abuses mentioned in a recent Senate study were already illegal. Bowen then comments:

It is ironic that much of the pressure for more detailed regulation stems from the Internal Revenue Service's failure to invest enough resources to make sure that existing standards of right behavior are enforced.

Perhaps the right legislative approach is to ensure that the IRS has the resources it needs to do its oversight job and gives the task its appropriate priority.

In addition to the legal constraints referred to by Bowen, there are other factors that constrain improper behavior. Contributors are increasingly pressing nonprofits to demonstrate the cost-effectiveness of their operations and to show that the board is exercising appropriate oversight of the organization. In the case of membership organizations the members can exercise some influence. State attorneys general can—and do from time to time—act. An organization's auditor and attorney may also be able to exercise some constraint. Industry groups can also advance best practices. Judgments as to the proper trade-off between endowment spending for the present and in the future are, at least in the case of the larger endowments held by universities and hospitals, subject to pressure from faculty and staff for more current resources. True, all foundations are required by federal law to annually disburse 5 percent of the value of their endowment assets. But there is a difference between saying the foundations must make a certain level of grants and holding all charities to the same spending rule when they may have quite different considerations in setting a spending policy.

In the end, the principal burden of ensuring an organization operates in a sound manner, consistent with its mission and applicable standards, rests with the board of directors. Here the distinction between passive and active board members can make a very substantial difference in the rigor with which the oversight of the organization's practices is exercised. No other body has the same degree of interest in seeing to it that an organization not only operates within ethical and legal boundaries, but also pursues its mission in an effective and efficient manner. In short, the board needs to assess whether actual outcomes fulfill the hopes that form the basis of the organization's mission.

Despite my view that greater regulation is not warranted, the nonprofit sector has no cause to relax its vigilance. The passage of Sarbanes-Oxley should serve as a warning to nonprofits. The statute was enacted in response to an egregious set of corporate scandals that exploded in proximity to each other. If such were to happen in the nonprofit world, legislation adding to government's oversight is a likely outcome. (For a discussion of how a nonprofit board can prepare itself for the possibility of mandated reforms see Chapter 4, "Preparing Nonprofit Directors for the Coming Changes in Governance.")

Sarbanes-Oxley [SOX] and New York Stock Exchange [NYSE] Reforms of Public Corporations

At the turn of this century there were a series of corporate scandals in financial reporting that shocked the nation. The case that captured more of the headlines than any other was Enron. In the year 2000 the company was regarded as one of the nation's leading companies and was the darling of the stock market, with shares that kept rising even in the aftermath of the burst dot-com bubble. At its height the company was the seventh-largest company by revenue in the United States, with a market value of over $75 billion.

A year later, in December of 2001, the company declared bankruptcy, wiping out the savings of thousands of investors and employees. In the end, 16 executives were convicted of criminal offenses, directors had to come up with their own funds to settle lawsuits against them, and a number of investment banks were held liable for their conduct. In the case of Enron all of the safeguards built into the system to prevent the publication of misleading information failed. The company's auditors, attorneys, and board members, as well as security and credit analysts and bankers, were either complicit in Enron's deceptive practices or failed to expose them. Even the SEC did not conduct a review of Enron's filings during the years immediately leading up to its implosion. Enron was a systemic collapse.

To restore confidence in the integrity of our capital markets, the Congress passed the Sarbanes-Oxley legislation in the summer of 2002 and the New York Stock Exchange (NYSE) adopted new rules for registered companies.

The Sarbanes-Oxley legislation (SOX) is the most sweeping reform of public corporation financial reporting since the passage of the Securities Acts of the early thirties. SOX interposes government-devised procedures and standards into the process by which corporations produce financial information. The object is preventing the issuance of misleading information before it is disseminated to the public. (The Securities Acts regulate the quality of information given the public only after it is disseminated.)

A basic thrust of SOX is fundamentally to change the role of auditing firms. The legislation: 1) subjects accounting standards of public companies to review by a board—the Public Company Accounting Oversight Board (PCAOB)—appointed by the Securities and Exchange Commission, in place of the accounting profession setting its own standards; 2) empowers the PCAOB to review the work of public accounting firms; 3) bars virtually all types of consulting work an auditing firm could do for an audit client (such consulting was often the most lucrative work for such firms); 4) requires rotation of a reviewing or coordinating partner every five years; and 5) enlarges accountants' responsibilities to include evaluation of management's own assessment of its internal controls for financial reporting.

The legislation also regulates the relationship between the public corporation and its auditor by requiring the corporation to establish an audit committee of independent directors with financial background to select the auditor and define the scope of its work and compensation. In turn, the auditor reports to the committee rather than corporate management.

The legislation further imposes on the chief executive officer and chief financial officer the duty to sign the corporation's financial statements and reports signifying the officers' belief, based on their knowledge, that those statements and reports fairly present the financial condition of the corporation and do not contain any untrue statement of a material fact or omit a material fact. The corporation must also disclose in periodic reports to the SEC whether it has adopted a Code of Ethics for senior financial officers and if not, why not.

In addition, each annual report must contain an "internal control" report that contains management's assessment of the effectiveness of the internal control system for financial reporting and the auditor's assessment of management's assessment. These requirements have proved to be the most expensive to comply with and extremely controversial because of their cost and lack of definition. The SEC has been active in attempting to define the scope of such internal controls to provide some relief for small corporations.

Parallel with enactment of SOX, the NYSE adopted a set of reforms that strengthened the authority of the board of directors in dealing with corporate management. The principal changes the Exchange requires are:

1. A majority of the board of directors be "independent" (except in the case of a company whose stock is more than 50 percent owned by one party). Heretofore, many boards were controlled by management or others with business relations with the corporation. The Exchange defines independent as not having a material relationship with the company other than the role of director.

2. Nonmanagement directors must meet regularly in scheduled executive sessions without management present. This may be the most important

of the NYSE reforms because it fosters the board's developing a cohesion that doesn't occur when a board meets only in sessions with management present. As Warren Buffet has observed:

> Why have intelligent and decent directors failed so miserably? ...The answer lies not in inadequate laws ... but rather the "boardroom atmosphere." It is almost impossible for a boardroom populated by well-mannered people to raise questions of whether the CEO should be replaced [or] to question a proposed acquisition that has been endorsed by the CEO.[6]

3. The board must create a nominating committee/governance committee, a compensation committee, and an audit committee composed entirely of independent directors.

4. The nominating committee is to identify individuals qualified to be board members, undercutting the past practice of the CEO picking all board members.

5. The compensation committee is to review and approve corporate goals with respect to CEO compensation and to evaluate CEO performance and determine the CEO's compensation level.

6. The audit committee is to be composed of at least three members who are "financially literate." One committee member must have accounting or related financial management expertise.

Self-Regulation: Applicability of Corporate Reforms to the Nonprofit Sector

The SOX legislation by its terms does not, with the exception of two provisions, apply to the nonprofit sector. The applicable provisions make it a crime to tamper with documents in the face of a government investigation and to retaliate against an employee who provides assistance to a federal agency or Congress. However, a number of authorities have urged the nonprofit sector to consider some of the type of reforms proposed by SOX, including the panel of industry leaders formed by Independent Sector, a leadership forum for charities, foundations, and corporate giving programs.[7] The American Bar Association Coordinating Committee on Nonprofit Governance has also urged nonprofits to consider the reforms set forth in SOX as well as those adopted by the New York Stock Exchange, observing that "Nonprofit organizations have not been immune from their share of scandals...."[8] See, for example, the Smithsonian case discussed in Chapter 2; the financial improprieties that led to the bankruptcy of the Allegheny

Health, Education and Research Foundation; the excessive perks and personal use of corporate assets by the chief executive of the United Way of America parent organization; and the apparent conflicts of interest on the part of trustees of Adelphi University. The American Bar Association Coordinating Committee on Nonprofit Governance further observed: "Like their for-profit counterparts, nonprofit organizations have not been immune to high-profile scandals in which management appeared to have 'run amok' and the board seemed either to acquiesce or been shockingly ignorant of illegal or highly questionable activities."[9]

What then are the corporate reforms that might be adopted by the nonprofit sector, keeping in mind that the sector is filled with both wealthy institutions and small, fragile organizations that may not have the capacity to undertake serious reforms of their practices? Clearly one template will not fit all. However, here we lay out a list of potential reforms in light of the governance failures in the nonprofit world.

A MAJORITY OF THE BOARD OF DIRECTORS SHOULD BE INDEPENDENT DIRECTORS

The focus on independence assumes that directors having other business or personal relationships with management may be open to making decisions influenced by their other relationships or that there may be a perception that such relationship played a role. This kind of exposure is more of an issue in the for-profit sector where boards were often hand-picked by the chief executive officer as a way of asserting his or her dominance over the organization. For the most part, nonprofit boards are made up of independent directors, but there are exceptions (e.g., a board member who, or whose company, provides goods or services to the nonprofit). But nonprofits would be served by establishing as a principle that boards be made up of people who do not have any relationship with management that could compromise their objective judgment.

THE BOARD SHOULD MEET REGULARLY WITHOUT MANAGEMENT PRESENT

In many ways, this may be the most important of the corporate reforms in that it provides an opportunity for the board to develop a cohesion that is not feasible in regular meetings presided over by the CEO and with other management executives present. Such private meetings provide an opportunity for the board to discuss important but sensitive issues such as the performance of the CEO and other key executives. As such, it would be a useful practice for nonprofit boards to develop.

THE ORGANIZATION SHOULD ESTABLISH A BOARD AUDIT COMMITTEE
AND PUBLISH AUDITED FINANCIAL STATEMENTS

A number of states, including New York and California, now require audited financials, to be published and filed with the attorney general if revenues exceed a certain figure. Indeed, most nonprofit organizations of size provide audited financial statements because their constituencies expect them as a sign that its finances are transparent.

The issue that is emerging is whether for mission-driven organizations, as opposed to profit-making businesses, a standard audited financial statement is sufficient. There is a view that there ought to be a formal process that reviews and publishes the extent to which the organization is achieving its mission on a cost-effective basis.

The creation of a board audit committee permits a direct relationship with the auditor and the opportunity to review financial statements that have not been pre-digested by management as well as candidly discuss issues with the auditor, especially the auditor's management letter, which contains the auditor's comments on any shortcomings in the organization's financial operations. The existence of the committee will also diminish any perception that there is a cozy relationship between management, which heretofore chose the auditor, and the auditing firm. The creation of the committee also provides an established channel for important, evolving financial issues to be brought directly to board members, enabling the committee to serve as an early warning system.

The audit committee can also serve as a means of reviewing whether an auditor providing other services to the organization compromises its independence as an auditor.

The corporate reforms call for audit committee members to have or to acquire financial literacy. This is a desirable objective but for a good number of nonprofits, especially the smaller ones, it is not practical to expect this type of background on the part of all members of the audit committee.

AN AUDITOR SHOULD BE PRECLUDED FROM MOST FORMS OF CONSULTING FOR AN AUDIT CLIENT

This provision was included in Sarbanes-Oxley out of concern that auditing firms gained so much consulting revenue from audit clients that this influenced their auditing work.

There is great pressure in public corporations to drive up their short-term stock prices, especially if executives have received large stock option grants; auditing firms anxious to keep lucrative consulting contracts might cast a blind eye to the manipulation of earnings. For example, Enron's Houston auditors in one year earned $27 million in consulting fees and $25 million in auditing fees. Such pressures generally do not exist in the nonprofit world because there are no equity shares and the temptation to acquiesce in earnings manipulation is not typically present. (An exception may be where a nonprofit organization, such as a hospital, is seeking to be acquired by a for-profit firm and the profitability of the nonprofit can affect the terms of the merger.) It would seem sufficient, therefore, for the audit committee to approve any consulting work to be given to the auditor without establishing an absolute bar.

THE ENGAGEMENT PARTNER ON AN ACCOUNT SHOULD BE ROTATED EVERY FIVE YEARS

This provision was part of the overall structure created by SOX to reinforce the auditor's independence from clients as a way of reestablishing the credibility with the investing public of the auditor's review of a client's financial statements. The background of course was the complicity or acquiescence in questionable accounting by auditors in the case of certain public corporations, such as Enron, where huge sums, in the form of option grants, were riding on the earnings of the corporation. That kind of situation does not exist in the nonprofit sector because there are no "ownership" interests in a nonprofit. There are many instances, however, where the extensive experience of a particular auditor with a client is invaluable, especially where there is considerable turnover in the executives of an organization. A flat requirement of rotation every five years would not seem useful in the nonprofit sector and it should be left to the discretion of the audit committee whether to ask for a change in an engagement partner.

THE AUDITOR SHOULD ATTEST TO MANAGEMENT'S ASSESSMENT OF THE ADEQUACY OF ITS INTERNAL CONTROLS FOR FINANCIAL REPORT PURPOSES

As noted earlier, this provision of SOX has proved the most expensive to comply with and has drawn the most criticism of the legislation, especially the absence in the statute of guidelines of how extensive the control system must be. This experience suggests that this requirement not be applied to nonprofits, at the very least until the corporate world comes to terms with it. And even then it is questionable because nonprofits do not operate in a capital market with thousands of investors relying on the accuracy of a corporation's financial statements.

THE SENIOR EXECUTIVES SHOULD CERTIFY THAT THEY BELIEVE THE FINANCIAL STATEMENTS FAIRLY PRESENT THE FINANCIAL CONDITION OF THE ORGANIZATION

Many nonprofits are considering whether to require the CEO and CFO to certify, based on their knowledge, that the financial statements fairly present the financial condition of the organization as a way of holding the senior officers accountable for the accuracy of such financials. Not only are boards seeking such assurance but others the organization deals with, such as contributors, grantmakers, lenders, and government agencies, are likely to welcome such certification, if not insist on it. The requirement of states like California and New York that audited financial statements be published and filed with the attorney general for organizations with certain levels of revenues would dictate such certification is a prudent practice.

AN ORGANIZATION SHOULD HAVE A COMMITTEE DEVOTED TO THE NOMINATION OF BOARD MEMBERS AND OTHER GOVERNANCE ISSUES

Nonprofit organizations are increasingly expected to develop criteria for the selection of board members and a profile of the attributes the board as a whole should have.

Moreover, most nonprofits find recruiting board members to be one of their most significant challenges. Creating a committee that would proactively seek to recruit new board members could well benefit organizations. (In the for-profit sector, consultants are now frequently hired to search for directorial candidates.) Such a committee could serve to persuade potential new board members that joining the board can be a positive experience.

THERE SHOULD BE A COMPENSATION COMMITTEE TO REVIEW AND EVALUATE THE CEO'S PAY

Executive compensation warrants careful scrutiny by the board of directors. Executive compensation has been the issue that has drawn the most fire of critics and where there have been abuses; in particular, boards' failure to review executive expenses to determine they are justified has been a weakness of a good number of boards.

A board committee (or at least one or two board members) should determine the compensation of the chief executive officer and review the compensation of other executive officers as well as assure that compensation decisions are tied to the executives' performance in meeting predetermined goals and objectives and in line with compensation awarded by comparable organizations. The committee should also assure that any "perks" granted are reasonable and in line with those provided by comparable organizations. Further, the committee should review the chief executive officer's expenses to determine that they are reasonable and necessary business expenses. Care should be taken in making comparisons to the compensation of other organizations that the positions being compared are comparable in the scope of their duties and responsibilities and that the organization is comparable in size and the scope of its activities.

BALANCING BENEFITS AND COSTS

The risk is that as appealing as any of these proposed steps may be, they will significantly add to the demands on board members when it is already difficult to recruit people to serve and fulfill the existing, traditional obligations of directors. The proposed steps will also create work for the professional staff that does not directly and immediately benefit the organization's programs. Each nonprofit organization should assess whether the purpose behind a particular reform is applicable to its organization and balance the gains such reforms can provide in the governance of the institution with the costs and burden on directors and staff.

NOTES

1. See pages 9–11 of the first edition.
2. See Margaret Gilberman and Sheldon R. Gelaman, "*A Loss of Credibility: Patterns of Wrongdoing Among Nongovernmental Organizations,*" International Journal of Voluntary and Nonprofit Organizations, vol. 15, No. 4, December 2004.
3. Ibid. p. 376.

4. For a definition of these terms see Paul B. Firstenberg, *Managing for Profit in the Nonprofit World* (New York: The Foundation Center, 1986), pp. 166–168.

5. William G. Bowen, *The Board Book* (New York: W.W. Norton, 2008), p. 37.

6. Quoted in John P. Bogle, *The Battle for the Soul of Capitalism* (New Haven: Yale University Press, 2005), p. 227.

7. Panel on Nonprofits.

8. ABA Coordinating Committee on Nonprofit Governance, "Guide to Nonprofit Corporate Governance in the Wake of Sarbanes-Oxley." American Bar Association (2005), p.v.

9. "Guide to Nonprofit Corporate Governance in the Wake of Sarbanes-Oxley," pp. 20–21.

12

Strategic Planning:
A Governance Tool

One of the most difficult challenges in today's world, where change occurs with unprecedented speed, is establishing, and then continually revisiting, the positioning of an organization so as to enjoy an advantage over its competitors. That is the function of *strategic planning*.

Drafting a strategic plan is one of the most frequently undertaken organizational exercises. However, all too often these plans aren't completed or they wind up on a shelf and are never referred to again. This is typically the result of the failure of members of the board to become actively engaged in the process, leaving it to senior staff and perhaps a consultant to draft a plan that the board passively approves. This is unsatisfactory. A strategic plan is an important governance tool.

Strategic planning is an important element in organizational governance— it establishes the basis for the accountability of the organization, and to the extent the plan is made public—at least to those directly affiliated with the organization—it responds to the growing demand for transparency. Illuminating the rationale for strategies the organization adopts makes these operations more transparent. Perhaps most critical of all, to the extent that the board of directors engages in the process of creating the plan, the board discharges one of its core governance functions.

The usefulness of a strategic plan in guiding an organization toward the achievement of its vision depends not only on how broad the participation is in its creation, but also the extent to which it is used as a living reference. That means periodically revisiting the plan to compare the actual performance of the organization with the strategy called for by the plan. Such a review may lead to changes in the operation of the organization or in the specific responsibilities for implementing the plan or, reluctantly, adjustments to the plan itself. It may be necesary to realign its vision with what is feasible to accomplish under current circumstances and conditions. Changes in the competitive environment or funding streams may also call for plan adjustments. A committee of the board should be assigned, working with staff, to review progress in implementing the plan at least annually.

That changes are dictated by evolving facts and circumstances does not defeat the value of the planning process; indeed it is the initial plan that provides the foundation for evaluating potential changes and it serves as ongoing baseline to measure how well the organization has done in accomplishing its vision, the very heart of the accountability called for by sound governance.

Planning is inherently a participative process and the board—or at least a committee thereof—needs to work right along with senior staff in putting a plan together.

The principal components of a strategic plan are:

> **Vision Statement:** It sets out what supporters of the organization want it to accomplish within a defined time period, what is unique about the organization, and what the beneficiaries of its services really need that the organization could uniquely provide. What does the organization want to become over a defined period of time? The vision needs to be expansive, but also realistic.

> **Mission Statement:** This summarizes an organization's purpose; what it seeks to achieve. It typically includes an organization's core goals, area of service, and intended beneficiaries or recipients of its services.

> **Identification of Strategic Issues:** This list includes the most critical challenges facing an organization in the present day and during the next few years. The planning process shifts the focus from many issues to those that will have the greatest impact on the future of the organization.

> **Strategy:** This describes a set of actions designed to respond to an organization's identified strategic issues. It lays out how best to fulfill the organization's mission and vision. It provides a context in which to determine various managerial issues and a framework to guide responses to opportunities and threats. It sets out specific strategic goals to be achieved within defined time periods. It includes how the organization is to be funded in order to achieve financial equilibrium.

Planning best begins with a strengths, weaknesses, opportunities, and threats analysis (SWOT). Strengths and weaknesses relate to the efficiency and effectiveness with which the organization operates its programs (the heart of accountability), the quality of the management team that directs the organization, the financial condition of the organization, and the outlook for future funding. This form of analysis is set forth in the context of the economic, social, demographic, and political environment in which the organization operates and forecasts whether any changes in the environment are likely to impact the organization. SWOT also identifies existing and potentially new competitors and the advantages or disadvantages the organization offers with respect to those competitors. Other risks facing the organization are identified (e.g., technological change).

To the extent practical, SWOT should also reflect the views of those who deal with the organization, such as individual and institutional contributors, recipients of its services, vendors, media, volunteers, and members of the communities it seeks to serve. Their views on the responsiveness of the mission to the needs of the community and on the effectiveness of the organization in fulfilling its mission are key. One also wants to gain a sense of whether in its dealings with outsiders the organization strikes a positive constructive posture or comes across as uncaring, frustrated, or angry, etc. In short, is the organization valued and admired by the outsiders with whom it has contact?

The aim is to develop strategies that enhance the organization's strengths, mitigate its weaknesses, and position it not only to preserve its present competitive niche but also point to opportunities for expanding the work of the organization in areas in which it would have an edge. The actions may entail adoption of best practices, revising the structure of programs or of staff, seeking new audiences for its work, identifying new sources of funding and/ or cutting expenses, and soliciting new supporters, especially those who may be willing to become dedicated board members.

An important objective is to identify those actions that will enlarge the organization's opportunities, in accordance with its vision, or enable the organization to overcome one or more of its weaknesses. Priority should be assigned to areas where there is a match between opportunities, ranked according to their promise, and the capacity of the organization to efficiently and effectively capitalize on each opportunity. Priority should also be assigned to actions that could eliminate or at least mitigate weaknesses. The ultimate objective of the process is to identify the steps that may enable the organization to move toward fulfilling the vision set for it.

Take, for example, an organization that provides several clinics for the treatment of young children with learning disabilities. Its special expertise is diagnosing the nature of the disability and developing a treatment program. At present it services 75 children in its three locations in adjacent areas within a state. Its vision is to become a regionally recognized leader in the field of disability diagnosis—a position it will not achieve through the operation of its several small clinics. In its planning process it identified that there is an opportunity to move toward achieving its vision if it could offer its services to school systems in one or more states.

Research indicates that many school systems lack the capacity to effectively diagnose learning disabilities and to draft appropriate treatment plans. There are no organizations of any scale offering such services. Here then is a definite opportunity for the organization, building on its strength. An action plan should be devised how to provide such services to school systems and to market them to schools. While a number of other opportunities have been identified, the planning process indicates the school strategy could have a greater impact in fulfilling the organization's vision and more closely draw on the organization's strengths than the other possibilities (e.g., a teacher training program in reading literacy, which the organization would have to create from the beginning). Accordingly, the diagnostic program becomes its number one strategic priority and a goal is established to line up at least two school systems for the program during the next two years.

The Strategic Planning Process

The word "plan" does not adequately convey the idea that strategic planning is not the production of a document but a *process*. Strategic planning is a living, breathing, continual effort to channel an organization's efforts in one or more directions in pursuit of a set of specific objectives, and then to measure regularly the degree to which the organization is successful in meeting those objectives. Variances between objectives and results need to be explained, and either the organization's execution improved or its objectives revised.

One of the virtues, for nonprofits, of engaging in a strategic planning process is that it induces them to look beyond the current year in order to identify possible scenarios that could positively or negatively affect the organization in the future. Too many nonprofits still confine their vision to the current year—which coincides with their major funding cycle—and do not look down the road.

which activities it wishes to pursue and which it doesn't. For the most part, the statement will address the same kind of questions a profit-making business needs to ask itself in its strategic planning exercise. In the profit-making context, the questions are, "Why are we in the business we are in and not another? Why are we in the market we are in and not another?" The same questions apply to a nonprofit.

Identifying Unmet Needs and Comparative Advantage

In defining a not-for-profit mission, attention should first be focused on identifying the particular *unmet societal needs* the organization seeks to fill. This effort is an aspect of strategic planning unique to the not-for-profit world, and precision in defining the particular unmet needs should be coupled with an assessment of the institution's special capability to affect that need.

An organization's mission or aims cannot be defined in a vacuum. In framing an enterprise's mission, it is necessary to determine what the organization's edge—its comparative advantage—is in pursuing its proposed mission. "Comparative advantage" means what an organization does better than competitors, what it does uniquely well, its natural strengths. Determining a comparative advantage entails a realistic appraisal of an organization's strengths and weaknesses and how they compare to those of its competitors. Until an organization develops a clear view of what its strengths are in a highly competitive world, it cannot realistically define its mission.

For example, assume that an organization is concerned with mental health and is experienced in training community mental health professionals. Over time, the organization becomes interested in addressing the problem of chemical dependency. It finds, however, that there are already organizations in its area providing good services to people afflicted with such dependency. But the organization may have the capability to administer an aspect of the problem overlooked by other institutions and agencies: the training of medical professionals in the treatment of chemical dependency. Such a focus will enable the organization to concentrate its energies in an area where it can establish a leadership position.

The point of analyzing comparative advantage is to prompt an organization to invest in its areas of strength and to cut back in areas in which it is competitively weaker. An enterprise needs to build on its principal areas of advantage. Over the long term, investing in carefully selected areas of strength is the key to sustaining superiority.

Other Questions to Consider

Other questions a nonprofit organization may ask itself when defining its mission include the following:

- *What is the cost-effectiveness of meeting the need?* Can society afford the cost of the perceived benefits? The cost-effectiveness of the *Sesame Street* television series is one of its appeals; for the roughly $10 million it costs to deliver 130 new shows each year, the series attracts nine million regular viewers under the age of six as well as millions of other viewers. Children who regularly watch the show gain skills. The size of the series' audience, relative to its production expense, means that the cost of these benefits, on a per viewer basis, is quite small.

- *What is the likelihood of drawing support for the programs in the mission? Is there a market for the programs?* More precisely, is there a demand for the service, *and* is there an effective constituency prepared to support, even fight for, the program?

- *Can the organization have an impact on the problem?* Can the organization raise (or earn) enough funds to launch effective programs in support of its proposed mission? Can people with the requisite talents to mount such programs be recruited at a cost the organization can afford?

- *Will the effort be likely to stimulate replications? Is it a model others will emulate?* One aim of exempt organizations is to be at the cutting edge, to blaze new trails for others to follow.

- *How does the mission contribute to the organization's reputation and image?* An organization that does not improve and does not modify or expand its program to keep abreast of the times, will gain a reputation as a staid entity and will be perceived as dull and lifeless rather than as an imaginative and lively place to work. Ultimately, the perception of an institution's liveliness will affect the quality of people who come to work for it and the level of support it gains.

In examining potential opportunities there are a series of questions that need to be addressed:

- Is this an opportunity to fulfill an unmet societal need?
- Can the organization have an impact on the problem?
- What is the likelihood of drawing support for the program?

- If there are competitors, what, if any, is the organization's comparative advantage?

- Will the program be replicated if it is successful?

- Will the program stimulate interest in the organization among potential contributors, volunteers, professional staff?

Choosing a Mission Concept

The analytical framework we have outlined is useful in helping in the selection of a mission concept, but in the end, rational analysis by itself does not necessarily lead to a clear conclusion. For instance, in the case of a media programming organization, going through the preceding checklist does not compel a choice between a narrow television-based mission concept and a broadened communications-based concept. Ultimately, the choice is determined by the personal values of those charged with determining the organization's mission. What do they believe is most important? What do they have the strongest convictions about? In the case of the media organization, do they care so intensely about television that it is of overriding importance to them, or is their interest centered on mass communication media?

Within the boundaries established by analysis, determining a mission is a statement of personal conviction and of personal commitment.

TRACKING RIVALS' BEHAVIOR

Competition is a fact of life for every nonprofit organization, although not all such organizations realize this. *All* exempt institutions compete at some level, whether for public financial support or, if they are fully endowed, for the best talents, the best projects, and the most attention for their work. Very likely, an institution's plan of action will be affected by the behavior of its rivals. Accordingly, the identity of an organization's effective competitors must be delineated and the actions of such competitors monitored.

It can be a mistake to undertake too narrow an analysis of the competition a nonprofit organization faces. In some fields, the competition faced by a nonprofit may come from the commercial world. For instance, a public broadcasting station has a monopoly only on public television in its geographic broadcast area. It would be foolish to ignore the fierce and indeed often overwhelming competition it faces from commercial broadcast channels and cable systems. Public television must and does take into account in its programming the broadcast schedules of its commercial competitors. For instance, the PBS stations would be foolhardy to air a news documentary on Sunday evening in a time slot competitive with the CBS network news feature series, *60 Minutes*, one of television's most popular shows.

In surveying the competition, an organization should look for ways in which it can gain an edge on rivals, for areas in which it can deploy its strengths to play to its comparative advantage. A university, for example, may find that the colleges in its immediate area are really not its prime competitors for students, and that it can increase its appeal, relative to its real competitors, by offering joint programs with these neighboring institutions. Or a university may find that a major concern of students is getting into graduate professional schools. If it faces stiff competition for undergraduate students from institutions that do not have professional schools, it may advertise the fact that its own professional schools look with favor on applications from the university's undergraduates. Or a small community health services organization, in applying for a government grant in competition with larger organizations without a community affiliation, may tap the political power of its constituency to support its application.

The moral here is simple: do not try to overpower the competition if there is any chance that you can outmaneuver it.

EVALUATING THE EXTERNAL ENVIRONMENT

In addition to analyzing present competition, an organization also ought to look down the road to see how it will fare in its competitive universe in the future. In particular, it needs to keep an eye out for changes in the external environment in which it operates. It cannot expect to predict all future changes, but at least it can be alert to the possibilities of economic, social, or technological change that could either adversely affect the organization or open up new opportunities (e.g., in the case of educational institutions, the push for equality for women). An organization can also consider the possibility that other institutions will shift direction and compete more intensely for the organization's revenue sources and market (e.g., arts channels on cable television seek out the public broadcasting audience).

MAKING REALISTIC MULTIYEAR PROJECTIONS OF EXPENSE AND REVENUE TRENDS

Strategic planning also requires taking one's best shot at developing a multiyear forecast of expenses and revenues and the impact of economic trends on those projections. Failing to do so can have deadly consequences, as the experience of many universities over the last several decades illustrates.

Few universities had even heard of multiyear financial planning until the 1970s, when financial hard times pressed it upon them. Prior to that period, they tended to operate and react according to the opportunities of the moment, without examining longer-range trends. Reacting to demographic and government policies of the 1960s, many universities expanded thoughtlessly, adding buildings and programs for which, within relatively few years, insufficient financing in the form of tuition revenue and government grants was available. At the same time, they did not reinvest enough funds in their endowments to enable these funds to grow at the same pace as inflation-driven expenses. Moreover, in the 1960s, universities gave tenure to large numbers of faculty members on the assumption that growth would be continuous. As a result, there was too little room for new faculty in the 1970s, when the economic slowdown struck.

In short, a good number of universities drifted over time into serious financial difficulty from which they found it acutely painful to extricate themselves. That the future of higher education would be different from the present was foreseen by some. But many universities failed to look ahead, to make an effort to project future developments rather than assuming the present would continue into the future, and to assess the implications of potential new conditions. Had they engaged in such long-range planning, many of these universities might have avoided mortgaging their futures.

A number of nonprofit organizations find their current financial position so precarious that it is understandably hard for them to look beyond meeting next month's payroll to more long-range issues. But the plights of others stems—as in the case of universities—from a false expectation that past trends will continue into the future.

Of course, it is difficult to predict future trends with precision. It is, however, possible to develop an informed sense of what will happen. Look at William Bowen's study in the 1960s for the Carnegie Commission forecasting the impact of rising inflation on expenses in higher education,[2] or his book coauthored with Neil Rudenstine analyzing Ph.D. education.[3]

A nonprofit organization needs to appraise the future availability of support sources realistically in the same way that a business would project the trend of revenues. The point is to try to anticipate the larger trends, even if particular numerical projections do not forecast the future with exactness.

SETTING SPECIFIC GOALS

The result of the processes outlined above should be the development of specific goals for the organization to be accomplished in a given time frame. A "goal" differs from a "statement of mission," in that the latter sets out the basic purpose of the institution, whereas the former constitutes the specific aims the institution will pursue over a given length of time. These aims, when restated in an operational and measurable form, become the institution's objectives.

The following scenario illustrates the different meanings of these planning terms: A small private college in southern Wisconsin defines its continuing mission as the "applied liberal arts education business," with emphasis on career preparation through the liberal arts. Its goal in a given year may be to "increase enrollment," in which case the near-term objective will be "a 15 percent increase in the size of next fall's entering class compared to this year's."

Of course, one can become overly enamored of subtleties of planning language and the degree of precision it is possible to obtain in defining mission, goals, and objectives. However, rarely is the effort to do so wasteful, for it usually leads to new insights about the organization and its opportunities.

Establishing a Financial Bottom Line

One result of the planning process should be the adoption of specific financial as well as program goals. In essence, a nonprofit organization should have its own form of financial bottom line as an explicit institutional goal.

The adoption of a bottom line is an important way to express the connection between institutional financial viability and programmatic objectives. Further, it will serve as a source of constructive tension when pressure builds to increase expenditures.

The bottom line may simply call for budgets to be balanced each year, or it may contemplate a planned, manageable deficit, or it may establish as a goal that a certain amount of resources will not be expended currently but saved for future needs, with a view toward accumulating a certain amount of capital. The point is to have a specific financial objective for the institution and to plan how the institution will achieve this objective.

Establishing Performance Standards and Feedback Mechanisms

The argument is often made that the objectives of many nonprofit institutions are inherently too vague to measure. But such arguments assume that greater precision in stating the goals of a nonprofit organization is somehow impossible. The mere fact that a department is not a "profit center" in a financial sense does not mean that one cannot establish specific objectives and criteria for assessing whether these objectives have been achieved. The problem is one of definition.

The exercise of trying to set measurable goals for departments has an underlying value: to build a performance-oriented discipline within the organization. To establish such a discipline requires a process or structure that regularly informs people as to what is expected of them. Thus, the planning process should be conducted from the bottom up, with departmental objectives first drafted and discussed by various levels of working staff, until major organizational goals emerge for top management and the board to consider. Therefore, every department within an organization should be asked to establish specific objectives it will seek to accomplish within specific time periods. At year's end, both senior management and the board should evaluate the extent to which goals were achieved.

The overall aim of the process is to establish, as part of the institutional culture, the idea of managing for results, with individuals accountable for achieving agreed-on goals, using a given level of resources.

COMPETITIVE POSITIONING

When the planning cycle for a given year has been completed, one crucial result needs to emerge from the process: the organization must now be positioned to become a leader in a niche within the field it seeks to serve. This is known as *competitive positioning.*

Let's look at how the strategic planning process might work at "Ivy University," a hypothetical multidivision private university complete with law, business, engineering, and medical schools and a graduate school of government. First, however, some background information may be in order.

For decades, universities have designed their programs based on their own sense of the educational value of the program's components. Shaping a university to compete more effectively against specific competitors is rarely factored into decision making. In reality, however, higher education is an extremely competitive industry: there are only so many students for all the openings in freshman classes; there are only so many dollars for all of a school's research and other funding needs.

What makes competitive positioning essential are the financial realities facing private universities. The opportunity for saving money through productivity gains is limited, because the operation is very labor-intensive. This fact, coupled with dramatic increases in the cost of technology required for teaching and research, means that university expenses rise faster than prices in the general economy, where productivity gains are more of a factor. An added pressure is the huge investment in financial aid that universities have made to ensure that they can admit talented students from a wide range of economic backgrounds, even as governments are cutting back research funding and scholarship dollars.

For more than two decades, most private universities have sought to contain these financial pressures, but not many have adapted in the fundamental ways that may be necessary for survival. They have cut expenses at the margin, boosted tuition, redoubled fundraising efforts, and kept their fingers crossed. That strategy led to a 300 percent tuition increase at private institutions between 1970 and 1987, an increase 70 percent higher than those at public institutions. During the 1980s, private university fees rose at almost twice the rate of inflation. In the 1990s, demographics promised a smaller pool of undergraduate applicants, calling into question the feasibility of continued steep increases in tuition. Nor can private universities expect to dominate the fundraising field as they once did, since they now face increasing competition from public universities and other nonprofit organizations.

The starting point for confronting these harsh economic realities has to be the way in which choices about spending are made. Universities generally make spending decisions without really examining the long- or short-term impact those decisions may have on the institution's competitive position.

The ingrained reflex is to fund changes by increasing the operating budget, rather than by reallocating resources. The ever-expanding field of knowledge is used to defend ever-growing expenses, the implication being that the existing base is unchallengeable.

If economic reality dictates a fresh way of looking at resource decisions, how does one begin to move a university to do so? First, universities have to recognize that they usually gain at the expense of a rival. The average student, for example, is accepted by several universities. If the student enrolls at Ivy, the other schools may have to settle for another student who is not quite as desirable—or even for no student at all. This is also the case in attracting faculty and funding. But most private universities—unlike most successful businesses—are not accustomed to identifying and evaluating their competitive position.

The following scenario illustrates how knowing one's competitive position can affect decision making within a university. Suppose a survey of undergraduate students who were accepted by Ivy University and by other competing universities showed that Ivy most often lost out in competition to a group of six private schools charging slightly lower tuition.

The presumption, without investigation, would be that this obvious difference between Ivy and its major competitors explains the recruiting advantage enjoyed by Ivy's rivals. But what if market research shows that tuition rates are not the most powerful factor influencing students' choices? Suppose, in fact, that Ivy is perceived—*relative to its competitors*—as an institution at which tenured faculty members spend far more time on research than on teaching, and which makes extensive use of graduate students to staff undergraduate courses? Lowering tuition, then, may not offset Ivy's competitive disadvantage in attracting students; rather, Ivy might be better off maintaining its tuition level and by investing more resources in undergraduate teaching. Clearly, Ivy's strategy can be intelligently formulated only on the basis of a realistic assessment of its competitive position.

To assess its competitive position, an organization must talk to its customers. As an administrator at Ivy, you would need to find out how students, faculty members, funding agencies, and grant givers perceive the university. Compare the university with its peers. Seek outside opinions about the quality of its departments and the employability of its graduates. In short, do what universities so infrequently do: ask about the expectations of various customers and how those expectations can be met or exceeded.

Then, identify the university's most frequent competitors for students, faculty, grants, and gifts. Find out the strengths and weaknesses of the competition, and explore the university's opportunities to exploit others' weaknesses. A university should, in fact, spend as much time studying its competitors as it does reviewing itself. Because the universe of competitors will vary among programs and departments, each academic department or school within the university should also examine its own set of competitors.

As the competitive realities become clear, a university must define the areas in which it wants to be strongest. Can it afford to be the equal of its competitors in all fields? Or should it build strength in a manageable number of areas in which it can enjoy a competitive advantage? Many private universities succumb to the danger of trying to be the best in every field—and end up with mediocrity across the board. In an era of limited resources, investing in a smaller number of areas, and truly excelling in them, is the more practical and more attainable goal.

Success requires not only a sharpened vision of what the university stands for and its place in the market, but also a willingness to make tough budget choices. Putting enough dollars in those academic activities that offer the best prospect of strengthening the institution competitively will very likely mean diverting resources from other long-established programs that are considered of significant educational value.

For example, imagine that Ivy's School of Government, staffed with faculty of modest attainments, offers a graduate program identical in almost every respect to those of the schools with which it competes. But it is often the second or third choice of its applicants. As long as the applicant pool for schools of government is significantly larger than the number of spaces in the competitive universe of schools, Ivy's School of Government will do acceptably well. But if career preferences shift, or there is a severe economic recession, enrollment will drop sharply as competitors attract a larger percentage of the diminished pool of applicants.

Suppose, however, that Ivy's School of Government targets its efforts on a market niche that has been overlooked by its principal competitors—for instance, the training of midlevel officials to help them advance further in their careers. To exploit this opportunity, the school reallocates resources from its master's programs to provide faculty and a curriculum suited to midcareer development. By so doing, Ivy's School of Government has transformed itself into a leader in midcareer development, rather than an also-ran in the race for graduate students. Moreover, the presence of midcareerists at the school constitutes a unique attraction for applicants to its master's programs. In short, by positioning itself adroitly, the School of Government is now more competitive in the higher education market.

In order to become more competitive, Ivy needs to take the following three steps:

1. Ivy must identify a competitive universe for each academic unit—that is, a reasonable number of peers with whom the unit competes for faculty and students.

2. It must rank each of its own academic units according to that unit's competitive position within that universe. A large element of subjective or qualitative judgment is involved, but objective factors can also be examined, including the number of undergraduate majors per faculty member, the amount of research dollars brought in by each faculty member, success in recruiting students against competitive institutions, per-capita instructional costs, success in placement of Ph.D.s trained in the program, and the results of student evaluations of the unit's courses.

3. Ivy must tailor a plan to channel resources to those units with the highest competitive ranking or the greatest potential to gain on their competitors. Within limits, those units should be assigned the resources they require before funds are allocated to other units. The cardinal principle of a competitively focused strategy is *selectivity*.

Ultimately, this process will reshape the university by moving funds from the least competitive departments to the most competitive ones. Over time, such an approach will change a university's base budget so that it reflects the current competitive environment rather than past practice. Redirecting resources to their most effective use will reduce the constant pressure to find new sources of money for funding new initiatives.

The point of competitive positioning is to challenge the prevailing allocation of resources, developed over time through institutional inertia, and to reexamine periodically the entire academic program to make sure it is designed to strengthen the institution competitively and to maximize the effectiveness with which that institution's scarce resources are deployed.

The proposed competitive positioning approach will not—nor is it intended to—completely change the private university as we know it. Slavishly following a plan developed by considering *only* competitive positioning is as risky as ignoring the competition altogether. The allocation of resources must not only strengthen the university's competitive position, it must also produce a coherent academic program. For this reason, the resource allocation plan should be compared with priorities determined through more traditional academic procedures. Then the final budget becomes an amalgam that reflects a balance between traditional academic concerns and competitive considerations.

Establishing a strategy to strengthen an institution's competitive position is just the first step. An equally essential part of the process is setting up measures of success. In fact, the "scorecard" associated with a budget that is allocated on the basis of competitive resource planning may be the single most important element in bringing about institutional change. Specific, quantifiable goals are indispensable elements in molding institutional behavior.

To track results, Ivy must establish two kinds of criteria:

- *Task criteria*—those that measure whether the school (or unit) did what it said it would do. Did Ivy hire more faculty members in the medical school who could teach, do research, and treat patients?

- *Impact criteria*—those that measure whether actions have the impact Ivy projected. Did the additional faculty members teach as expected and in fact increase research and clinic net revenues as planned?

These criteria provide a basis for evaluating whether the institution is achieving its objectives. In turn, institutional objectives must be translated into a day-to-day operating reality that combines clear objectives with associated rewards for individual administrators. Those running the university's principal units must know just what is expected of them and how their efforts will be judged. They should be asked to develop a personal set of specific objectives and be measured on how well they achieve them.

Other incentives have to be devised to encourage all members of the academic enterprise to achieve agreed-on objectives. If the goal is to increase sponsored research, a more successful investigator should receive greater rewards for his or her work, perhaps in the form of sabbaticals or more desirable research space. An outstanding teacher might get a merit-based salary increase or a leave of absence to develop new course material. The point is simple: if the goal is to change behavior, then individual assignments, compensation, and perquisites must be linked to specific performance.

Introducing the realities of competition, then, is the key to strengthening an organization and to position it in front of the curve of change facing all nonprofit institutions in the years ahead.

NOTES

1. McGeorge Bundy, interview with the author.

2. See William G. Bowen, *The Economics of Major Private Universities* (Carnegie Commission on Higher Education, 1966).

3. William B. Bowen and Neil L. Rudenstine, *In Pursuit of the Ph.D.* (Princeton, NJ: Princeton University Press, 1992).

13

The Merger Option

Mergers and acquisitions—M&A, as they are often called—are commonly thought to be the exclusive province of businesses and investment banks.[1] In comparison with the pace of mergers and acquisitions in business, it is rare for two or more enterprises in the nonprofit world to be consolidated. However, nonprofit mergers have been pulled off successfully.

In the late 1960s, the all-girls preparatory school Rosemary Hall, located in Greenwich, Connecticut, and the all-boys prep school Choate, about an hour away in Wallingford, Connecticut, were threatened by the trend toward coeducation. Standing alone, each of the two schools might have failed in this new environment. But in 1971 the schools merged, and today, situated on a single campus in Wallingford, Choate Rosemary Hall thrives with strong support from the alumni (including those who graduated prior to the merger), a deep, high-quality applicant pool, and a healthy endowment.

The Choate–Rosemary Hall merger overcame the formidable obstacles of physically separate campuses, separate faculties, separate administrations, and intense alumni loyalties to the separate institutions. The merger also had to overcome the fear of some male alumni that women were a threat to male values and bonding.

The Rosemary Hall campus in Greenwich was sold to another school, and a separate set of three dormitories was constructed for women above Choate's existing dorms. In 1971, Rosemary Hall students moved onto the Choate campus, attending the same classes as the male students but retaining their own administration in addition to their separate dorms. This was very much an evolutionary approach to merging the institutions. But today, Choate Rosemary Hall is clearly *one* school, physically and administratively integrated. Walking around the place and visiting with its students, faculty members, and administrators, one would never know that, once, two independent schools existed.

Putting together the two schools was no simple feat. This is hardly surprising when one recalls the controversy that attended efforts by universities such as Tulane and Columbia, years later, to merge already-affiliated women's collegs into the university, long after women students had attended the same classes as men. Graduates from earlier years objected vigorously to these mergers. But Choate and Rosemary Hall did emerge as a single effective institution. This example of a successful merger of two nonprofits shows that a well-planned and well-implemented consolidation is a valid option for nonprofits. Nonprofit organizations might combine for one of the following reasons:

- To consolidate their fundraising programs and to gain efficiencies in administration, or to broaden their joint appeal beyond the reach of either individual enterprise. The goal would be to increase the net take from fundraising through cost reduction or increasing revenue.

- To bring together two organizations operating in the same market, where the market is not large enough to support both institutions (e.g., two hospitals serve the same community), or to avoid duplication of services (e.g., both hospitals build expensive oncology services).[2]

- To expand the resulting organization vertically in order to capture revenues in an allied market by broadening its customer base (e.g., a hospital acquires a nursing home or a health maintenance organization).

- To combine the publicly recognized reputation of one nonprofit with revenue-generating capabilities of a less well known organization (e.g., a television production company with a powerful brand name in the children's market but no computer product combines with a computer software company that has outstanding software programmers but little brand recognition).

- To enable a small organization that is struggling to raise enough funds to support its program, to merge with a larger, more financially stable organization. The two organizations have complementary programs, but the smaller entity operates in a market where the larger enterprise is not present. The larger organization wants a presence in this market, and its entry is eased by capitalizing on the smaller organization's contacts and relationships. In exchange, the larger organization can raise for the smaller entity's programs additional grant funds that the latter lacks the managerial depth to acquire.

- To expand an organization's field of service by acquiring the staff, programs, and funding relationships of an organization in an allied field with the expectation that the insight gained from participation in related activities will enhance the quality of performance of both entities. In effect, their merger will produce a synergy in the programming area (e.g., an organization dedicated to assisting troubled adolescent women combines with an organization serving troubled adolescent men).

Most of the models above represent instances where the act of combining has a potential direct financial benefit. In the last example, there is a reference to the need to achieve a "synergy" in order to gain benefits from a merger. The idea behind the concept of synergy is that the personnel of the merging organizations learn skills from one another and are able to perform in more effective ways than they did acting independently prior to the merger. Based on my personal experience and my studies of for-profit mergers, I am skeptical that such synergy can be achieved in most cases. For example, the Prudential Life Insurance Company is a full-service insurance company that also offers institutions and individuals an array of financial services. In the 1980s, it acquired an old-line Wall Street brokerage firm which, following the acquisition, was named Prudential Bache. One of the hoped-for benefits of the acquisition was that the insurance agents of Prudential and the brokers of Prudential Bache could cross-sell brokerage and insurance products. In fact, however, insurance agents and brokers are motivated by quite different factors, and their training and experience do not equip them to cross-sell each other's products. This and other synergies hoped for from the merger did not materialize.

The Prudential experience of not realizing hoped-for synergies in an acquisition is more common than most businesses that engage in mergers and acquisitions will admit. In addition, there is evidence in the for-profit world that the general expectation that mergers lead to greater profits for the merged enterprise has often not been realized.[3] Thus, prospective mergers require cautious, realistic evaluation and careful due diligence.

If a merger of two nonprofit organizations is to work, a number of things have to be done well:

- Both organizations must think through in advance the strategic, financial, and managerial costs and benefits and must have a clear idea of how the combined entity is going to perform more effectively and efficiently than the separate enterprises.

- The management structure of the combined enterprises must be resolved quickly, diligently, and decisively. Peoples' minds will not be on business while they are waiting to see what job they get or whether they will have a job at all in the combined enterprise. Power struggles, as factions and individuals contest for positions, are counterproductive.

- Both parties must have a good sense, before they merge, of the differences in their respective organizational cultures, whether the two staffs can coexist, and, if so, how to blend them. Unless the cultures are blended, it is unlikely that the two organizations will operate effectively as one enterprise.

- The new senior management must move quickly to meld the two companies at every level, including operations, management, and culture. Unless the combining of the two organizations is done rapidly, not only will performance be undermined during the delay, but employees who feel their interests threatened by the merger may solidify practices that undermine the bringing about of an effective consolidation.

One of the frequent barriers to blending two management teams is figuring out the pecking order of officials in the new entity. Here, a small team of board members from both organizations may be helpful in resolving conflicts, or an outside management consulting firm can be brought in to provide advice. It is best to determine the composition of the board and the CEO of the new enterprise prior to the merger.

Since a nonprofit is not a stock company, it has no shares to exchange in a merger. (This also means that there cannot be an unfriendly takeover of a nonprofit through the acquisition of publicly traded shares.) To effect a merger, the trustees of both organizations have to agree to it, and they have to obtain the approval of the state attorney general (the government office involved in general supervision of charities). It is also prudent to contact the IRS in order to ensure that there are no objections from a federal tax standpoint and that the merged organization, as a new legal entity, will receive the same 501(c)(3) tax status as the predecessor organizations did.

NOTES

1. A "merger" implies combining two equals, whereas an "acquisition" refers to a stronger organization's taking over a weaker enterprise. In most mergers and acquisitions, one party is dominant and calls the shots. Often an "acquisition" is announced as a "merger" in order to save face with customers, employees, and others.

2. The fact that merging organizations are nonprofits does not necessarily give them immunity from antitrust laws. Colleges and universities that shared information on prospective tuition rates and financial aid packages were held to run afoul of the antitrust laws' prohibition of price fixing, notwithstanding their status as 501(c)(3) organizations. However, two enterprises in the same market may merge where other, more powerful entities also exist, so that the merger does not produce market dominance.

3. "The Case against Mergers," *Business Week*, October 30, 1995, pp. 122–130.

14

Converting to a For-Profit Enterprise

The rationale for organizing an enterprise on a nonprofit basis rather than as a for-profit business once seemed fairly simple: If one's basic purpose was to advance a humanitarian, cultural, educational, or scientific goal, then one formed a not-for-profit entity pursuant to the requirements of the Internal Revenue Code. If one's primary purpose was to make money and enjoy the other fruits of ownership, even while serving a public interest, then one organized the entity as a for-profit enterprise. In most circumstances, motive dictated the form of organization.

But today motive alone may no longer be a foolproof guide to the form of organization to create. Moreover, the initial decision to form a nonprofit can be reversed at a later date. Organizations that, instead of depending on gifts and grants, generate substantially more revenue than their overall expenses (i.e., to earn a respectable profit) have the option to convert to a for-profit form.

This chapter examines the range of considerations that shape the initial choice to create a nonprofit organization as well as those that may later influence a nonprofit to convert to a for-profit.

There are a variety of tangible and intangible benefits to organizing a nonprofit. The label "nonprofit" tends to suggest to the public mind a commitment to advancing the public welfare, rather than private gain, and this favorable image enhances access to people and institutions in a position to help the organization. Status as a 501(c)(3) organization also enables such organizations to raise capital through tax-deductible contributions. Assuming an organization is not designed to engage in revenue-producing activities, nonprofit status is the only practical way to raise funds, because nonprofits can access the capital provided to charitable organizations by foundations, corporations, and individuals as well as by government funding targeted for programs of the character nonprofits operate.

Nonprofits, which under IRS rules and regulations qualify for tax exemption, do not pay taxes on the revenues generated by their mainstream activities and activities related to their primary mission. The latter exemption has been interpreted as enabling an organization to be exempt from taxes even on a profit-making activity carried on in a commercial manner in direct competition with for-profit firms (e.g., operation of a museum gift shop).[1]

A nonprofit's favorable image and the public recognition it receives may also enable it to generate income by merchandising products that bear its name. In this era of brand and designer marketing, a well-known name or logo that has a favorable public image can be a valuable marketing asset. The sale of products can be enhanced by the image and name recognition of a powerful brand name. For example, the automobile manufacturer Jeep licensed clothing bearing the Jeep name; similarly, the magazine *House and Garden* licensed Wal-Mart Stores to sell garden furniture bearing its name. And every college in the country sells in its bookstore and athletic stadiums T-shirts and other clothing and merchandise designed not just for its students, but for everyone attracted by its name.

Nonprofit status has certain negative aspects, in the form of constraints imposed by the Internal Revenue Service. These constraints warrant careful review and weighing against the strong positive aspects of the nonprofit form. At the same time, changing conditions in the field in which a nonprofit operates can cause it to revisit its original decision to adopt the nonprofit form of organization. For instance, a number of nonprofit organizations compete in certain industries with for-profit companies and are as vulnerable as for-profits to the trends affecting those industries.

The health care field is one where nonprofit and for-profit institutions compete head-to-head in the same market for the same customers. There has been a sweeping consolidation in the health industry. Nonprofit institutions, like for-profits, are under pressure to acquire or be acquired by other organizations, or else to consolidate operations. In addition, with the staggering growth in the capital costs of operating health care facilities, many nonprofit institutions will have to turn to the capital market for funding, which will entail converting to for-profit status.

One of the by-products of such conversions has been the creation of an array of new foundations, because, under the law as interpreted in many states, a nonprofit that converts to a for-profit organization must contribute to charity the value of its assets in order to compensate for the loss of public benefit provided by the nonprofit form. In some cases, the dollars flowing to charity have been substantial.

An existing nonprofit can change its status to that of a for-profit, but neither the decision to do so nor the process required to obtain approval for the change is easy. Take the historical example of Engineering Information, Inc. (EI).

EI was organized in 1934 as a not-for-profit organization under the laws of the State of New York. The purpose of the organization was to disseminate by various means engineering, scientific, and technical information to libraries, educational institutions, industry, governmental agencies, and the engineering and scientific communities.

For a long time, libraries were the primary consumers of EI's product. Then, with the downsizing embarked on by many institutions, libraries began to scale back their purchases of EI products. Under the leadership of CEO John Regazzi, who joined EI in 1988 from H. W. Wilson, a private for-profit publisher, EI reversed the downward slide in its profitability; but this was a short-term victory brought about by a combination of cost-cutting and the introduction of new products with strong appeal.

In April of 1993, the five-year business plan presented to the board of EI set aside some $500,000 for product development—about enough for the first year of the plan—but contained no provision for further funding of new product development and left open the question of how additional product development funds could be raised. The plan thus put squarely on the table the issue of how to finance future capital needs.

After the presentation of the five-year business plan by Regazzi, I was asked as an outside observer to offer comments to the board. Regazzi had told me beforehand that, a year earlier, the board had sidestepped the issue of converting to a for-profit enterprise, and that there was a lot of understandable resistance within the company to abandoning EI's nonprofit status after nearly 60 years.

In talking with the board, I offered the following observations:

- The challenge facing EI, stated most simply, in the words of the business plan, is to "Transition and diversify EI's products and services to broader-based corporate and end-user markets, while maintaining a market leadership position in existing core markets." Library expenditures and budgets are shrinking. The only way EI can prosper in the library market is to expand its market share. Such a strategy would be difficult for two primary reasons: first, it's expensive; and second, it's an attempt to gain market share in a declining market.

- EI undoubtedly will need to protect its position in its core markets, and it may very well need to expend significant dollars to maintain this position. In the long run, however, EI will be better off to diversify, seeking to reach the mass market of engineers and engineering students who now have the technology to seek information on their own and are increasingly aware of the value of the information they need.

- The plan recognizes that EI must embark on customer-oriented, market research–driven development of new products for new consumers—new both in that they are end users, not libraries, and they are practitioners, not research-oriented engineers in industry and academia.

It was obvious to everyone at the meeting that EI would have to develop a new marketing system aimed at reaching directly the actual consumers of information.

All these actions required more money than EI could expect to generate from its present operations. In addition, most of EI's competitors in providing engineering information were businesses that can and did invest significant funds in equipment and facilities. EI's borrowing capacity was limited, and thus it had to find ways to raise the type of capital that invests in profit-making ventures.

At the time, EI had a number of options available in terms of organizational structure to facilitate the raising of capital for product development and new modes of distribution.

- It could retain its status as a nonprofit and establish for-profit subsidiaries to undertake the development of new products, inviting investors in new ventures to invest capital in exchange for stock.

- It could retain its status as a nonprofit and establish for-profit joint ventures with other for-profit firms that together would develop new products and/or develop a distribution system to market products directly to the consumer. In fact, EI had already entered into a number of such joint development ventures with private companies.

- It could convert its entire organization to a for-profit organization and raise capital in exchange for stock in the new company. Under this scenario, EI would have to donate to a charitable entity the fair market value of its assets.

The first two alternatives contemplated a twofold structure: a nonprofit entity that would carry on EI's basic business but also own an equity position in one or more for-profit corporations. The nonprofit's percentage of ownership could vary from a minority position—entailing giving up management control—to ownership of up to 100 percent of the voting stock (with the outside investors receiving one of several forms of a nonvoting interest—for example, preferred stock, which enjoys a right to participate in profits before payment of a dividend on the voting stock).

While such arrangements have their place, neither of the first two alternatives made sense for EI, for several reasons.

First, the two alternatives required dividing the organization into two classes of personnel—those working on a for-profit basis and those working on a nonprofit basis—when all EI employees were engaged in essentially the same business. This arrangement would have created two cultures and two sets of goals within the same enterprise.

Second, the twofold structure implied different compensation systems, one for those employed by the for-profit subsidiaries and one for those employed by the nonprofit parent, even though the two groups would be engaged in parallel activities. While nonprofits can establish incentive compensation under IRS rules, the incentives cannot be as large or as directly linked to profits as in a for-profit company.

Third, the twofold structure meant that outside partners would share in the control of the for-profit subsidiary and thus could produce a management system at complete variance with the management of the nonprofit parent.

Fourth, the nonprofit status of EI did not appear necessary to the accomplishment of its objectives, nor did it offer to EI any concrete benefits, such as the ability to raise large amounts of funds through contributions.

The establishment of for-profit subsidiaries can be an effective means for a nonprofit to tap into the private capital markets, or to form partnerships with private interests, when the business to be pursued by the for-profit entity is distinct from the mainstream activity of the parent organization. The twofold structure can enable the parent to maintain its access to funding sources that traditionally support nonprofit organizations while also raising for-profit capital. Under such circumstances, having a separate culture, management, and compensation system for a for-profit subsidiary is easier to justify to employees of the nonprofit parent and is thus less likely to prove a divisive factor in the operation of the nonprofit parent.

Moreover, the incentive compensation and, in all likelihood, the higher pay of for-profit employees can be offset by providing other benefits to the nonprofit employees; for example, a better medical plan and a pension plan that—because it is offered by a nonprofit—is the only portable pension plan in the United States.

In deciding on a course of action for EI, Regazzi needed to consider the most effective means of raising capital; but equally important was the fact that Regazzi wanted to shape his organization's culture to be responsive to the changing world in which EI was now competing, and to provide incentives that would motivate his staff to compete effectively with EI's for-profit rivals. Ultimately, the twin considerations of raising capital and restructuring the organization to deal with its competition in a new marketing environment led to the decision to convert all of EI into a for-profit company and to create a foundation to which EI would donate the fair market value of its assets.

Although the board took no formal action that day in 1993, its outlook had changed, and John Regazzi was allowed to go ahead with the preparatory work of establishing a formula that the State of New York would accept for converting EI to a for-profit and locating the capital to fund such a transaction. Obtaining approval of the conversion ultimately required resolving certain tax issues and meeting requirements established by the attorney general and the courts of New York State.

EI knew that it would have to contribute the value of its assets to a new nonprofit entity, but two critical questions arose: What valuation would prove acceptable to New York State authorities, and where would the funds to be transferred to a new for-profit come from? An additional problem was that Regazzi wanted the employees to own the bulk of the new for-profit enterprise through an employee stock ownership plan (ESOP). This meant finding a source willing to put up the capital the new for-profit needed to transfer to the nonprofit foundation, and willing to advance the funds without acquiring an ownership interest in the new business venture. Raising equity directly for EI as a for-profit, with its long track record in the same business, might not have been hard, but channeling the needed capital through financing an ESOP would be no small feat.

The conversion plan also required establishing the fair market value of EI's net assets as a going concern. An early decision was made to leave EI's $2 million in cash and marketable securities with the foundation. The valuation problem was thus limited to EI's publishing assets (including its lease). The appraiser had to be chosen from a list prepared by the New York State attorney general's office.

With respect to the tax issues raised by the possible conversion, EI sought an opinion from the law firm of Sullivan and Cromwell (S&C). As an alternative, EI could have sought a private ruling from the IRS, but such letters can take a long time to obtain. The S&C letter made the following points to the board:

> The Internal Revenue Service has ruled privately that a sale of property by a Section 501(c)(3) organization will not violate the prohibitions against private inurement and private benefit if (i) the property is sold for a price determined on an arms-length basis and at least equal to its fair market value, (ii) the sale is generally in furtherance of the organization's exempt purposes, and (iii) the net proceeds do not inure to the benefit of any private individual.

S&C, in support of this statement, pointed to IRS Private Letter Ruling 8234084 (May 27, 1982) relating to the sale by a nonprofit organization of its hospital and research facility to a limited partnership created by the organization's board of directors. The IRS ruled that the sale did not result in private inurement or benefit because the sale price was set at fair market value, as determined by an independent appraisal, and because no loan abatements or other special concessions were given to the directors in their capacity as the purchasers and operators of the hospital. Negotiations were conducted on an arms-length basis, and the transaction documents were prepared and negotiated by independent counsel for each party. The sale was considered necessary because the charitable entity did not have enough resources to expand the hospital (as required by the growing needs of the community) and also continue its existing research and educational activities. The sale proceeds were used to further the organization's research and educational activities.

Two years later, however, the directors partnership sold the hospital for $21.3 million more than the purchase price. The state attorney general successfully sued the directors for breach of their fiduciary duty, and the IRS recommended that the organization's tax-exempt status be revoked. (See Private Letter Ruling 9130002, March 19, 1991.) S&C pointed out that this later ruling did not attack the transaction per se or the procedures followed by the organization, but instead demonstrated the importance of a good appraisal.

Similarly, S&C told the board that in IRS Private Letter Ruling 8838047 (June 28, 1988), a hospital had sold its real property to a partnership formed by its employees, subsequently leasing the property back from the partnership. The sale-leaseback was necessary to enable the hospital to repay outstanding debt and expand medical services. The IRS ruled that no private inurement or benefit had occurred because the sale price was at fair market value, confirmed by a declaratory judgment action brought by the hospital in state court naming the state attorney general as defendant.

EI would be consistent with the above rulings in selling its assets at their fair market value, as determined by its board of directors on the basis of an appraisal prepared by a qualified independent appraiser using several valuation methods. The sale proceeds would be added to the foundation's investment assets and used to make grants in furtherance of the foundation's charitable purposes.

Payment by a charitable organization of reasonable compensation to "insiders" would not result in private inurement. Whether or not compensation was reasonable must be considered in light of all relevant circumstances. The fee that the foundation proposed paying to the for-profit corporation for providing certain administrative services was substantially less than what the foundation would pay a third party to perform such services.

S&C concluded that, in its opinion, the restructuring would not result in private inurement or private benefit jeopardizing the foundation's tax-exempt status. S&C went on to observe that the restructuring should not result in the foundation's being found to have "excess business holdings." Section 4943 of the Internal Revenue Code imposes an excise tax on private foundations deemed to have excess business holdings. A private foundation, together with disqualified persons, may own no more than 20 percent of the voting stock, profits, interest, or beneficial interest in a business enterprise. If the business is effectively controlled by a third party, the foundation and disqualified persons may own a 35 percent interest in the business [I.R.C. SS 4943(c)(2)].

After the restructuring, the foundation was to own only 10 percent of the voting stock of EI. The only other stockholder, the ESOP, would not be a disqualified person, and thus its holdings would not be aggregated with the foundation's holdings.

On December 30, 1994, Regazzi was ready to act, and a lame-duck deputy attorney general of the State of New York signed off on the transaction just one day before he and his boss—who had lost his bid for reelection—left office. If the transaction had not been ready for signature while the deputy attorney general was still in office, EI would have had to start all over again with educating a new attorney general and his or her deputy and trying to persuade them to approve the transaction.

According to Regazzi, the staff's reaction to the change was very positive. A series of seminars were held with staff members to discuss what kind of an organization EI had been before the restructuring, why the restructuring was being undertaken, and where EI was headed. The seminars proved to be very constructive.

In the minds of EI executives, reshaping the organization's culture was another important reason for the conversion. As one officer commented during the first year after conversion: "We are learning to be a for-profit company." In fact, Regazzi believed the organization benefited from increased employee productivity as a result of its new for-profit orientation, and thus acheived one of the goals of conversion. One senior staff member observed: "Since the conversion, everyone is more conscientious about [his or her] role in the company, and there is a higher level of productivity. No question but people now feel, 'My career is at stake here.'"

Perhaps most significant of all, the EI conversion was carefully structured to protect the public interest. That is, there was an independent appraisal of the assets of the exempt organization and a transfer of equivalent value made to a foundation to serve the original charitable purposes of the nonprofit EI. The foundation didn't function as a back door for supporting the new for-profit enterprise, and the conversion itself did not enrich EI executives. The potential for individual enrichment had to be realized through the performance of the new for-profit entity.

NOTES

1. See Paul Firstenberg, *Managing for Profit in the Nonprofit World* (New York: The Foundation Center, 1986), pp. 162–164.

Section 4.

Operational Issues

15

Performance Management

Profit Motive and Profit Measure

For a business, the level of profit earned and its relationship to capital invested or assets owned provide a ready means of quantifying how well-managed the business is. The inapplicability of such a profit measure to the nonprofit world has been seen as the absence of a profit motive. However, a good many people are motivated by personal financial reward and they serve society in creating the capital and employment necessary for the healthy functioning of an economy, including generating the wealth essential to providing the contributions nonprofits require.

Moreover, nonprofit organizations can embrace certain operations where the profit motive plays a part. For example, a number of university endowments are managed by a separate company whose employees are compensated on a basis comparable to the private sector. Children's Television Workshop compensated the head of its very profitable licensing business on a basis comparable to the private world. (See Chapter 21, which is devoted to discussion of nonprofit organizations generating income to support their programs.)

There is thus a critical constructive role for the profit motive.

In fact, a number of individuals and institutions are now using models of "social investing" that attempt to use the market to create social value. The concept of program-related investment (PRI) can be viewed as the precursor to one of these new models, "mission-related investing" (MRI). PRI remains a distinct category because the tax code requires the rate of return be below market. "Mission-related investing" (MRI), not bound by this constraint, is the logical extension of PRI. It is being practiced by institutions such as the F. B. Heron Foundation, the Annie E. Casey Foundation, and the John D. and Catherine T. MacArthur Foundation, often through intermediaries such as Shorebank Corporation, the Calvert Social Investment Fund, and the Community Investment Corporation.[1]

Absence of a Profit Motive

Certainly, a profit motive is not essential to managing nonprofit institutions efficiently and effectively. Pride in performance and profit are not incompatible but reinforcing. The nonprofit world provides opportunity for entrepreneurial endeavors where the reward for innovation and initiative is the successful creation of a new enterprise, a new program, or additional resources for existing programs devoted to serving a mission that benefits society.

The absence of a profit motive does not mean nonprofits cannot be efficiently run, *provided they devise a system of measuring how effective and efficient their operations are and then rigorously reviewing whether measures were met.*

Years ago, Anthony and Herzlinger, two Harvard Business School professors, clearly stated the dilemma created for nonprofits by the absence of a profit yardstick in this way:

> The absence of a satisfactory, single measure of performance that is comparable to the profit measure is the most serious management control problem in a nonprofit organization. It is incorrect to say that the absence of the profit *motive* is the central problem; rather it is the absence of the profit *measure*.[2]

They were not suggesting that management control cannot be achieved in a nonprofit organization. They argue that, since nonprofits lack the criterion of profitability, they need an effective system of control even more than a business does. They spend most of their 591-page book explaining how to construct such a system. Herzlinger, joined by Denise Nitterhouse of DePaul University, focused on the same topic and expressed the same viewpoint.[3] Their text strives to demonstrate to managers and trustees of nonprofit organizations that they can control the quality and cost of their operations and ought to do so in their own interest. For readers who want to delve into all the nuances of management control in a nonprofit organization, both of these volumes still make excellent reading.

Therefore, it is the absence of appropriate performance *measures* that can undermine nonprofit operations. This complicates the task of judging the performance of nonprofits, for directors and managers as well as potential contributors.

In my career in both the business and nonprofit worlds I have worked for a series of nonprofits that have been artfully managed. In particular, I think that Princeton University is as well-managed an institution as any private company I have worked for. In 1972, I joined Princeton as financial vice president as part of newly elected President William G. Bowen's new administration.

I learned that Princeton was a beautifully run enterprise, sharply focused on its carefully defined educational niche, sensitive to societal changes (it transformed itself from an all-male bastion to a coeducational, diverse institution in the makeup of both its students and its administration), its academic eminence complemented by tight financial control, the expert raising of funds, and superb investment management (outperforming many private investment companies). Princeton is but one of a universe of outstanding nonprofit institutions in education, the arts, social services, medicine, sciences, and other humanitarian endeavors driven by a sense of mission.

We are talking, then, in America of diverse organizations driven by different motivations—profit and mission. The challenge to directors and managers of both for-profit and nonprofit enterprises is to devise appropriate measures of performance and ensure that the organization's reward system is structured to reinforce the motivations of its employees.

The typical brochure or report of a nonprofit organization is filled with descriptions of the programs the organization has implemented and its plans for the future. Little comment, however, is offered on how effective its programs have been. Furthermore, many funders of nonprofits fail to examine the level of management control over performance exercised by their grantees. This is not so much an oversight by nonprofit leaders as a perception on their part that there are few reliable means of measuring programs in objective terms. Nevertheless, assessing the results achieved—and at what cost they were achieved—is essential to the effective management of nonprofit enterprises.

The goal of this chapter is to persuade readers of three basic notions:

- There are processes that can be adapted from the "best practices" of business as well as the work of nonprofits for improving the effectiveness and efficiency of an organization and its programs.

- Establishing verifiable performance objectives and accounting for the degree to which they are achieved is feasible and also essential to gaining public and financial support.

- Grantmaking organizations' review of grantees' management practices is both in the best interests of the grantees and a fiduciary obligation of the grantor.

If the nonprofit sector is to enhance its credibility, documenting the quality of program performance must become a central focus. Appeals for contributions—of all types—are likely to get a better reception if a nonprofit can demonstrate to potential contributors that their support will produce tangible results. With a vast number of organizations seeking tax-deductible contributions, a powerful means of distinguishing an organization is to demonstrate the effectiveness and efficiency with which it performs its mission.

Clearly the issues were first laid out years ago, as were some best practices to address them. Their adoption has been slow. Here I present, in a modified form, a model of oversight from a process I worked with in business. But each nonprofit will want to design the precise system that serves it best in light of its financial and staff resources.

Performance Management Defined

The term *performance management* describes the set of processes for controlling the quality and cost with which programs are delivered. The essence of performance management has a number of elements:

- Identifying up front, in the *preprogramming phase*, in measurable form, the *objectives* an organization intends to achieve, or, where objectives cannot be quantified, identifying the specific *tasks* to be accomplished;

- Establishing a *budget* for achieving these objectives and tasks, and an *action plan* that enumerates the steps that have to be taken by each unit within the organization, including a timetable for accomplishing these steps;

- Tracking actual progress in implementing programs against the *action plan* and the *budget* adopted at the outset; and

- Comparing actual costs, timetable, and results with those set forth at the outset, and, whenever possible, with similar programs mounted by other organizations.

Why Performance Management?

Performance management provides a reasonably objective basis for assessing how well an organization is accomplishing the mission it has defined for itself. Equally important, it also provides a clear sense of direction to the staff as to exactly what is to be done, when.

When I joined Prudential's real estate investment group, it was largely an opportunistic, transaction-driven enterprise. When an attractive opportunity to acquire or develop a property came along, and the deal structure was appealing, the property was snatched up; similarly, if the group received a very attractive offer to buy a property, it was considered, especially if at the moment Prudential needed cash to pay an investor or to invest elsewhere. The strategy worked for years as Prudential was the first major insurance company to undertake large-scale investment in real estate and seek pension funds to coinvest with it, and for a time Prudential was the unchallenged leader in the field. However, as other aggressive players entered the field and the competition for good properties and clients intensified, Prudential began to lose its leadership position.

At that point, the organization was restructured to pursue a set of specific objectives for the group as a whole. In turn, the units in the organization—which heretofore had largely pursued their own agendas—each negotiated with management a set of measurable objectives and supporting action steps. This process, aside from setting a basis for bonuses, established a blueprint of the actions each unit was charged with undertaking and of what it was expected to accomplish, and when. In a complex organization with more than 1,000 people working in various locations across the country and with a wide range of skills and functions, setting specific, measurable objectives and the requisite action steps provided a sense of coherent direction to the organization as a whole. The process was an effective tool in getting everybody to support a common set of purposes and to work in concert to achieve those ends. Under this new approach, "the deal" was no longer paramount; transactions had to fit within the strategies established for each investment fund so that strategy, not deals, became the organization's driving force. As one of my colleagues said, "When you get out of bed in the morning, you don't have any doubt about what you have to do during the day or where you are trying to get to."

The system also provided an effective means for Prudential's top management to track the progress of the organization through the year, and to focus on a unit that might be lagging behind in order to find out why it was lagging and what could be done to speed up progress.

Performance management is also helpful in allocating resources among competing programs. For example, when management is evaluating a request to divert staff members from one program to another, it can get a rough sense of the transfer's impact, positive or negative, on each unit's ability to achieve its measurable objectives. Performance management is not a precise science, but it does equip management with working tools other than pure intuition.

Performance management lies at the heart of the responsibility of officers and trustees of nonprofit organizations. As fiduciaries, they have an obligation to assess the effectiveness of their programs and their organization as a whole and to identify what works and what does not. This is an obligation that the public, the Internal Revenue Service, and federal and state legislatures (which grant tax exemptions to qualified nonprofits), as well as state attorneys general (who have the authority to supervise charities), will increasingly emphasize. Demands for more stringent oversight may be triggered by a high-profile scandal in which funds of an organization are flagrantly used for improper purposes, or by pressure put on legislatures by businesses that resent increasing competition from nonprofit organizations, or by an aggressive public official who senses the vulnerability of nonprofits. In any event, it would be a costly error in judgment to doubt that nonprofits will become subject to more outside scrutiny and that they will be on the defensive if they cannot document the effectiveness and efficiency of their efforts.

Measuring Performance

Of course, not every activity can be measured in quantitative terms. This is also true in business. The point is to measure in objective terms what can be quantified and to obtain qualitative information about other tasks. For instance, an organization may have the goal of improving the lives of young women who grow up in poverty. This goal is a compelling one but it does not lend itself to quantification. However, when the broad goal is broken down into specific objectives, as it must be to create concrete programs, those specific objectives can be quantified. For instance, one objective might be to reduce by a specified percentage the rate of pregnancy among teenage women who participate in the organization's program in a target community, relative to the rate of pregnancy among teenagers who do not join. The extent to which this specific objective is accomplished and the cost of doing so can be calculated and compared to the cost to society of dealing with teenagers who give birth. This comparative cost analysis can be factored into an overall evaluation of the program's effectiveness and efficiency. (Note, however, the caution in the next section about the difficulty of linking causes and effects.)

An organization's performance can also be compared with the performance of organizations that undertake similar tasks and are considered to employ the "best practices" in the field. In business, it is taken for granted that leadership over one's competitors in a given field is the name of the game. Leadership and the reputation that go with it are important in the nonprofit sector as well. The sector is engaged in competition—for funding, for talent, for community support. How an organization performs relative to its "competitors" is therefore relevant. The competition among colleges and universities has long been an acknowledged fact. *U.S. News & World Report*'s annual best colleges survey and *Business Week*'s annual survey of the "best" business schools have capitalized on this reality, and these magazines' rankings of schools have an impact on the market. Other types of nonprofits must deal with the same reality.

Moreover, competitive considerations aside, one of the most effective ways to improve performance is to understand how others who are thought to be outstanding performers accomplish their goals. By comparing the degree to which specific measurable objectives are achieved, and the costs associated with achieving them, one can assess the degree to which another organization is more successful and/or cost-efficient in achieving its objectives. Moreover, the most important aspect of the comparison is not the comparison of numbers; rather, it is the inquiry into what specific actions of the other organization account for its superior performance.

Identifying Best Practices

How does one identify organizations with the best practices in certain areas? First of all, the term "best practices" is a bit of hyperbole, and one shouldn't get trapped by it. What one is really after is an organization from which one can learn how to improve one or more of one's own group's systems. No one, even in the quantified world of business, can say with certainty which company is the best at a particular function. But some companies enjoy a reputation among knowledgeable people as being outstanding at one or more aspects of their business, and their bottom line will very likely show an enviable profitability. Therefore, one need not therefore get caught up in an elusive search for the "best" model as long as the focus is, as it should be, on improving a particular function or functions of one's organization. As Boxwell observes in his book on benchmarking, "The most important criterion in selecting targets is to choose those from which you will be able to learn, learn, learn."[4] For these reasons, I prefer to think in terms of "advanced management practices" rather than "best practices."

Spending some time on library or online research and holding discussions with staff members, board members, grantmakers, and people in the organization's field should easily uncover an organization or organizations from which a nonprofit can learn. This organization may be either a nonprofit or a for-profit enterprise.

For example, if you want to learn how incentive compensation tied to performance objectives operates in a nonprofit environment, visit the Local Initiatives Support Corporation, which employs such a system; if you want to see how in-staff training can be provided by a combination of business school faculty members and the organization's own executives, talk to the UJA-Federation of New York; if you want to understand how a needs analysis and cost-benefit analysis—or other forms of evaluation of a social program—can be done, visit Girls, Inc.; and if you are interested in how an organization adheres to its strategic niche over a period of years while growing its enterprise, talk to the management of Children's Television Workshop.

Many other nonprofit organizations have devoted resources and considerable effort to developing managerial practices worthy of replication. It would be an important contribution to the management of the nonprofit sector if an institution were chosen and funded to establish a database of organizations with advanced management techniques that could be accessed by any exempt organization at a reasonable fee. In the business world, the availability of collections of such data is an asset that firms market. The time, it would seem, is ripe for a clearinghouse of advanced management practices to be established for the benefit of the nonprofit world.

Factors that Can't Be Quantified Still Count

The structured form of performance management does not preclude other considerations from being taken into account. The level of local and national interest in the program is relevant, especially as it relates to the availability of funding. So is the value participants and the community attach to the program. Indeed, feedback from the target consumer is as critical in any assessment of a nonprofit organization's performance as it is to any evaluation of a business. Listening carefully to consumers may open up new, more effective ways of providing the service, or it may spot mistakes that, if allowed to accumulate over time, will undermine the program (e.g., boys in the community won't date girls in the pregnancy prevention program, which, in turn, causes participation by the girls to decline). Analysis of customer feedback may also reveal whether participants' responses are distorted by the very fact of participation in the program (e.g., participants respond differently because they know they are being watched).

The Availability of Comparative Data and Analysis

Of course, one of the handicaps nonprofits often face in assessing performance is the absence in the sector of the equivalent of industry-wide performance data as well as widely applicable financial performance yardsticks. In business, at least in the case of companies whose stock is publicly traded, there is a wealth of information available about companies in any given line of business: reports that must be filed with various government agencies; analyses of companies and their industry by the thousands of Wall Street security analysts who follow American business; and reports in trade journals and general business magazines. But perhaps the most valuable information for evaluating one's own company comes not from published sources but from talking to people who know the business and the company's competitors—customers, bankers, attorneys, accountants, consultants, suppliers, distributors, sales reps, and former employees of competitors. While some of these sources operate under the restriction of confidentiality with respect to a particular client, they can provide useful information about industry practices. Indeed, it is increasingly common today for one company's researchers to call on another company—which may or may not be a competitor—that is known for its skill in a given area, in order to learn what accounts for that company's outstanding performance.[5]

Following are some sources of information about nonprofits and how they operate:

- Form 990, which the IRS requires every nonprofit to file annually, contains a wealth of financial, payroll, and program data and is open to public inspection. Despite its flaws, the form enables any nonprofit to learn a good deal about other organizations, including those with whom it sees itself in direct competition: for example, information about the funds raised for programs, the expenses incurred, the salaries of top officials, and the "outputs" or "products" of major programs. The IRS also maintains two databases, the Exempt Organizations/Business Master File and the files maintained by the Statistics of Income Division of the IRS.

- The amount of research published about nonprofits is steadily increasing, especially as university researchers take an interest in the field. Careful literature and online searches can uncover this information.

- Professionals who service nonprofits, such as lawyers, accountants, consultants, former employees, academic commentators, and trustees, can provide valuable insights.

- Recipients of services provided by one's own organization can be interviewed, and their answers compared with those of recipients of services provided by other similar organizations.

- Field visits can be conducted to other organizations renowned for their outstanding practices.

The Massachusetts Institute of Technology study on industrial productivity noted that a "characteristic of all the best-practice American firms, large or small, is an emphasis on competitive benchmarking; comparing the performance of their products and work processes with those of the world leaders in order to achieve improvement and to measure progress."[6] Boxwell sees field comparisons as the key to benchmarking in business,[7] and Porter sees them as key to analyzing an industry and one's competitors.[8]

Limited Resources for Management Oversight

One obstacle to assessments of performance effectiveness and efficiency is the scarcity of resources that many exempt organizations face along with their need to husband their funds for the support of programs. The real world of many nonprofits involves such a struggle to find the money to run programs, even on a shoestring, that performance management may strike them as an out-of-this-world luxury. When I was teaching a course on nonprofit management at the Yale School of Management, the topic on a particular day was multiyear strategic planning. A student in the class who had worked for several years in a nonprofit stood up and with some exasperation explained that her organization did not know from week to week where the money for continued operation was going to come from, so planning for several years ahead was simply out of the question. Performance management may not be practical for struggling nonprofits, just as many formal business practices don't work in the case of fledgling, entrepreneurial entities. Still, limited resources may call for simpler, less expensive forms of oversight rather than for overlooking performance management altogether.

The Specific Elements of Performance Management

Below is an overview of the principal components of performance management and a discussion of how each part is interrelated with other components of the process. The terminology and detailed pattern of actions set forth here are not intended to imply that there is only one perfect formula. Indeed, each organization should adopt a process that suits its needs, taking into account the resources it has available for this purpose as well as the training and experience of those who will be involved in doing the work.

A system of performance management can be viewed as involving six steps:

1. *Identify goals and objectives.* As part of a planning process prior to the start of a program, identify the *goals* of the program and the specific *objectives* that will achieve those goals. *Goals* are an intended result of the project or program as a whole; they are broad and general.[9] *Objectives* are a specific *measurable* and *time-limited* result of an activity designed to bring about the goal or goals of the program. Staff members as well as selected outsiders should participate in the goal- and objective-setting process.

2. *Formulate action plans.* Assign the specific goals and objectives to the component units of the organization best suited to effect them. Then ask each unit to come up with an action plan consisting of: a) the specific steps required to achieve each assigned objective, including obstacles to be overcome and the extent to which the authorization, cooperation, or support of others is necessary; b) identifying the person or persons responsible for accomplishing each task; and c) a timetable for accomplishing the objectives and the sources of the funds required.

The action plan should be submitted to senior management for review and discussion with staff members and should receive a final blessing from both groups before the program is implemented.

3. ***Identify advanced management practices in the field.*** In setting goals and objectives, and in designing an action plan to achieve them, examine, to the extent feasible, what other organizations have been able to accomplish with similar programs, and especially how they were able to accomplish what they did, the practice is known as *benchmarking.*[10] This exercise is by no means limited to discovering what measurable results other organizations have achieved in similar programs, although that information is worth having in setting your own standards. The most important function of the exercise is to understand the managerial and operational practices that enable outstanding organizations to achieve the results they do.[11] The focus of comparison can be any aspect of your organization's activities that you believe can be improved, even a part of a program.[12] For example, one organization may be renowned for making effective use of volunteers; another organization may be skilled in setting performance objectives for its staff members; a third organization may have a model budgeting process; and a fourth an outstanding strategy for using its management information system to shape its program practices. There is no point in reinventing the wheel if one can simply emulate or even improve on an established practice of another organization.

4. ***Identify necessary data.*** Identify in advance the data that will have to be collected and collated to enable an evaluation of the extent to which program objectives are achieved as well as their overall impact, whether intended or unintended.

5. ***Review progress.*** Once the action plan gets underway, management and staff should periodically compare actual progress with the plan, including cost overruns and other problems, and decide on corrective action.

6. ***Evaluate results.*** When the program is complete, or the funds for it have been exhausted, undertake an evaluation of what has been accomplished, including: a) the degree to which the specific objectives of the program have been achieved; b) the variances between the program as actually implemented and the action plan adopted at the start, with an analysis of reasons for the variation; c) the actual outcomes of the organization's efforts, whether intended or unintended, and the extent to which the outcomes are consistent with the goals of the program;

and d) the cost of the program compared to the value of the benefits achieved. For item c, the specific outcomes achieved in your program should be compared with the outcomes achieved in other programs. The point of this comparison is not only to assess how effective your organization's performance may have been but—also quite important— to develop more insight into what objectives are attainable in a given field and the best means of attaining them.

Critical to the success of this six-step process is *preprogram planning.* Many a laudable program goal has foundered in implementation because the *means* chosen will not work to accomplish the desired end. In many cases, insufficient work has been done prior to starting the program to investigate and analyze what steps will enable an organization to achieve its intended results.

An example of choosing the wrong means is the Ford Foundation's 1967 graduate education initiative. Ford's broad, if highly ambitious, goal was no less than to reform graduate education in the humanities and social sciences. To accomplish this, Ford selected the specific objective of establishing four years as the norm for completing a Ph.D. in these fields. That way, the humanities and social sciences could be as "efficient" in producing Ph.D.s as the "hard" sciences. The means to this end was to provide the same level of financial support to students in the humanities and social sciences as students in the hard sciences received. It was thought that providing students with the wherewithal to remain continually enrolled as full-time students would reduce the number of years needed to acquire the doctorate. It did not. The Ford Foundation program, educators Bill Bowen and Neil Rudenstine observe, "did not succeed either in establishing a new norm for time to degree or [in] reforming graduate education." The Ford program, Bowen and Rudenstine conclude, "was by all accounts a failure in achieving its stated purpose."[13]

In fact, Bowen and Rudenstine point out, providing equivalent amounts of financial support to humanities and social science Ph.D. candidates did not make these disciplines as efficient as the sciences in turning out doctorates. The emphasis on time to degree was misplaced; instead, emphasis should have been placed on finding ways in which attrition, a more serious problem, could be reduced.

Of course, in any pioneering effort, there will be failures, either because the goals are not attainable by any available means, or because there is insufficient experience with the implementation techniques. This does not mean that careful preprogram planning cannot reduce the chance of error.

Another very important aspect of performance management is *postprogram assessment*. In their book on graduate education, Bowen and Rudenstine describe a series of national fellowship programs that have been undertaken in this country for which no postprogram assessment has been made. Their book highlights the importance, wherever feasible, of examining, as part of such assessments, the operation and results of other similar programs. Comparing the results of a range of efforts provides a fuller picture of what goals are attainable in a particular field and what means are the most effective for achieving those ends. Where such an undertaking is beyond the financial resources and personnel capabilities of a particular organization, then the entity that funds the program should consider it part of its funding responsibility to see that such an overall assessment is made at a suitable time by appropriate experts.

A Hypothetical Illustration of Performance Management

Let me amplify on how these elements operate by illustrating their application to a hypothetical organization dedicated to aiding young women who live in conditions of poverty.

The first step in establishing a process for managing performance is to create a set of attainable and measurable performance objectives for the organization as a whole and then to break down those overall objectives into more specific objectives for each component unit of the organization. Our nonprofit, in order to achieve its broad overall goal of aiding certain groups of young women, will identify specific behavioral goals that it seeks to achieve (e.g., a reduction in teenage pregnancy, increased attendance at school, completion of a high school education, reduction of criminal activity) and then zero in on its highest priorities. The first priority is a reduction in the rate of teenage pregnancy in a small number of targeted communities. Next, given its available resources, the organization must determine how large a reduction in pregnancy over what period of time among how large a group of young women in how many target communities is a reasonable specific performance objective.

There is a tendency in the nonprofit world, as well as in government, to attribute value to the size of an organization's program: the bigger the staff, the more participants, and/or the larger the geographical area covered, the better. This kind of outlook is in many ways a product of the fact that performance management is not widely practiced. If it were, the focus would be on the degree to which tangible results were delivered at an efficient cost or, in the economist's jargon, attention would be directed at the quality of outputs rather than the volume of inputs.

Assume that in our target community, prior to the implementation of the program, one-fifth of the women become pregnant in their teens. Our nonprofit can set out to reduce that percentage by a significant degree, in increasing increments each year over, say, a three-year period. It may take some trial and error to establish realistic, quantifiable targets, but the organization will make its best estimate after talking to experts and potential participants. One of the factors that may be taken into account in setting objectives is the experience of other organizations operating similar programs. For simplicity, we will skip the potential input from the experience of others. In the early years, senior management will assess whether a target is missed because the objective is unrealistically high, or because the staff does not execute the program well, or because there is a design flaw in the program.

Assume further that the organization's management sets as an objective reducing pregnancy among women under the age of 18, compared to pregnancy among women who do not participate in the program, by 25 percent. Since change will not happen overnight, a time frame has to be established for accomplishing the performance objective. A useful approach is to establish increasing targets over time—for example, 10 percent in year 1, 15 percent in year 2, 25 percent in year 3.

To achieve this measurable objective, a program has to detail the specific tasks to be performed by the organization's various units. This is each unit's action plan. For instance, the organization's department in charge of recruiting participants may be given the specific objective of recruiting for each program cycle a certain number of participants that takes into account the projected dropout rate of participants in the program.

Assuming the overall goal is to reduce pregnancy among teenage girls in the first year of the program by 10 percent compared to girls in the target community at large, the nonprofit's program department's effort can be broken down into four discrete functions: 1) recruitment of participants and counselors, 2) design of the program's content and its implementation, 3) administrative support, and 4) program assessment. Sub-objectives and action plans are then developed for each unit. The actual counseling of women will be conducted in three-month cycles.

A bottom-up process is employed in which each unit comes up with its own set of proposed objectives and action plans. These proposals are then reviewed with senior management to ensure that they are feasible, and that the objectives and plans of the various units form a cohesive overall program. Management also will make sure that no one is presenting overly low projections in order to increase the odds of achieving them.

The combination of objectives and action plans for year 1 of the program may then look something like this:

RECRUITING UNIT

Objective: Recruit and train five counselors; to be completed by end of second month of program

Action plan:

- Write jobs specs and establish compensation
- Obtain management approval for above
- Contact local schools of social work
- Contact persons who previously worked for organization
- Advertise in social work journals
- Network among social work professionals
- Screen applicants
- Initiate training sessions with accepted applicants

In reality, an action plan would assign dates for completion to virtually all individual steps; for simplicity, I have established one completion date for all steps.

Objective: Recruit 25 participants for each three-month program cycle; recruitment to begin 60 days before start of a cycle and be completed by one week before the cycle commences

Action plan:

- Post notices in high schools and community centers
- Visit homes and hospitals for unwed mothers
- Network among leaders of other community programs
- Interview high school teachers
- Interview welfare officials
- Hold informal meetings with prospects to explain program and encourage them to sign up for it
- Interview potential participants
- Introduce program officials and counselors
- Visit prospective participant's home environment, interview her teachers, and check police records

ADMINISTRATIVE UNIT

Objective: Prepare space for program; to be complete by the end of second month

Action plan:

- Identify suitable space for program sessions, both group and individual counseling sessions
- Make arrangements to secure space
- Obtain computer system for maintaining necessary data base

PROGRAMMING UNIT

Objective: Hold 24 group sessions (2 per week) and 150 individual counseling sessions (3 per participant) over each cycle

Action plan:

- Ensure that teaching materials for counselors and materials for participants are prepared by month 2 and reproduced in quantities necessary for distribution

- Hold training sessions for counselors in month 3
- Assign participants to groups to be led by different counselors in various session formats
- Conduct group and individual sessions

PROGRAM ASSESSMENT

Objective: Deliver program assessments; to be completed within 12 months after cycle ends

Action plan:

- Interview all participants who complete program after end of program and again at later intervals
- Develop comparison with similar programs in at least four other locations
- Draft assessment and review it with program counselors and outside experts in the field

The object of this exercise is to create a blueprint of what is to be accomplished, and how. Forcing staff members in each unit to think through their specific measurable objectives and the actions they must take to achieve those objectives reduces inefficiency once the program gets underway and gives each staff member a clear sense of direction. At the same time, the blueprint is not a straitjacket. If experience during implementation dictates change, then the action plan and even the objectives can be revised.

The degree to which an organization's specific objectives and action plan are being accomplished within the projected time frame should be reviewed regularly by management during the progress of the project and also once the program is completed. Even if unexpected benefits result from a program, management still needs to evaluate whether its staff can consistently achieve the objectives it targets at the outset, and, if not, why not. Does the problem lie in the forecasting process (and, if so, what can be done to improve this process)? Or are there problems in the implementation process that could be corrected with the help of closer oversight by management?

Naturally, experience may dictate modifying the unit performance objectives over time. Some may not prove ambitious enough (e.g., the dropout rate of participants proves higher than expected so the number of recruits has to be increased). Others may prove unrealistically high (e.g., the original target for the maximum number of dropouts). Changes are especially likely to be needed when external conditions change, or when a program is being tried for the first time.

Analyzing the Financial Cost of a Program Relative to Its Achievements

The process described here is analogous to the analysis of a for-profit enterprise's "bottom line." The object is to compare the costs of a program (both direct outlays and indirect administrative and overhead costs) to the total positive measurable outcomes of the program as expressed in quantifiable terms. The focus is not only on the degree to which the specific objectives established at the outset of the program are accomplished but on how other positive outcomes, which may not have been foreseen, are brought about. Not all program outcomes can be expressed in quantifiable terms. For example, in the case of our hypothetical program, young women who delay pregnancy may have the opportunity to choose from a wider range of career options. Self-awareness, pride, and knowledge about contraceptives may also enable participants to establish sounder relationships and make a more informed choice about when to bear children. These positive outcomes cannot be quantified but ought to be included in an evaluation of the cost-effectiveness of a teenage pregnancy prevention program.[14]

Still, a program's cost-effectiveness can be calculated, albeit perhaps not exactly. For instance, in the teenage pregnancy prevention program, the number of pregnancies delayed can be arrived at by 1) calculating the rate of pregnancy among nonparticipants, 2) subtracting from this result the rate of pregnancy among participants, and 3) multiplying the difference by the number of participants.

To see how this works out we don't have to rely on a hypothetical illustration; we can turn to an actual evaluation done for Girls, Inc. This "real-life" evaluation found that 28 of 147 young women between the age of 12 and 20 classified as nonparticipants became pregnant within two years from the start of the program, while 33 of 290 women in the same age range who participated in the program also became pregnant. In other words, 19 percent of nonparticipants became pregnant, compared to 11.4 percent of participants, or a difference of 7.6 percent (22 women).

The value of this benefit can be quantified by estimating the savings to society, based on public investment in Aid to Families with Dependent Children, Medicaid, and food stamps. The Girls, Inc., evaluation consultant estimated the program's savings to society at $8,580 for each participant who did not become pregnant. When this figure is multiplied by 22, the total savings to society is $188,760. The cost of delaying pregnancies in 22 women can also be calculated; in the Girls, Inc. case, the evaluation consultant determined the costs to be about $33,640.[15]

The results of this cost-benefit analysis can now be compared with similar analyses of other programs of the same agency or with figures for other social programs of other agencies, involving goals such as reduction in substance abuse, reduction in recidivism among first-time juvenile offenders, completion of a high school degree, or job training. These quantified comparisons, adjusted for qualitative considerations, can inform a nonprofit's judgment of how effective and efficient a program is, compared to other programs the nonprofit operates and, where data are available, to other similar social programs aimed at the same target population(s).

Again, it would be beneficial if an organization were funded to collect systematically and categorize the results of program evaluations now being done by a wide number of organizations.

Cause and Effect

In all assessments, it is necessary to determine whether the linkage between cause and effect is strong enough to justify the conclusions reached. For instance, in our hypothetical case, there are a number of reasons why pregnancy rates could decline in the program group of young women, other than the content of the program itself. For starters, by joining the program, the participants have shown an interest in avoiding pregnancy (i.e., the group is self-selected). Influences at home or in other facets of the women's lives may influence their decisions to avoid pregnancy. Certainly, if pregnancy rates did not decline over the entire period, the program's effectiveness would be in doubt. Thus, assessments may be more valid in proving the negative than the positive.

The Role of Grantors in Ensuring Grantee Performance

A review of the quality of grantee performance by grantors is in the best interests of improving not only the management of grantees but also the fiduciary responsibility of grantmaking organizations. This view has always had its detractors, who argue that grantor oversight inevitably leads to unwarranted grantor intrusion into the running of grantee organizations.

The UJA-Federation of New York has established a model for striking the appropriate balance between permitting oversight by the grantor and allowing the grantee the appropriate degree of freedom in implementing a grant. The Federation provides annual funding to social agencies in New York City. These agencies, in turn, leverage this funding by raising funds from government and other sources. The Federation's relationship with these agencies has been carefully worked out over time and rests on several critical elements set forth in their strategic plans:

- Determining the most effective mode of service delivery is the responsibility of the agencies.

- The UJA-Federation will periodically determine whether the agencies meet established standards of financial management practice.

- All agencies are expected to assess their own performance periodically. "Those assessments should take into account the *best current practice in the relevant field*, the views of the community served, and especially the views of the recipients and users of services as to the quality, accessibility, and adequacy of the services" [Italics added]. The Federation will provide grant assistance to help agencies conduct such self-assessments.

- The intensity of assessments should vary with the scale and complexity of the agency's functions, but they must be performed.

- Outstanding performance will be rewarded with longer-term and/or larger funding; where performance does not fully measure up, the Federation will provide technical and managerial advice or other assistance that may be needed. But if "poor performance persists" and it is clear that another provider can provide more effective assistance, then funding will be shifted to the other provider.

Another constructive approach to grantor oversight is establishing explicit performance objectives for grantees. The Andrew W. Mellon Foundation, for instance, includes in its grant memoranda to its board detailed "expected outcomes" for each grant it makes. Some outcomes, of course, place more emphasis on quantifiable objectives where the grant program lends itself to such analysis. An expected outcome can be very explicit—spelling out, for example, how many contemporary works a performing arts group must revive in how many forthcoming seasons, and specifying that by the end of the grant period the group must have raised its membership dues sufficiently to be able to continue to revive contemporary works without further funding by the foundation. Other "outcomes"—where quantification of objectives is difficult—focus on the tasks to be completed by the grantee.

NOTES

1. See some of the seminal articles and papers about mission-related investing and social investing in general, such as *Philanthropy's New Passing Gear: Mission-Related Investing, A Policy and Implementation Guide for Foundation Trustees*, written by Steven Godeke with Doug Bauer for Rockefeller Philanthropy Advisors, 2008; and *Investing for Social and Environmental Impact: A Design for Catalyzing an Emerging Industry*, written by Jessica Freireich and Katherine Fulton for the Monitor Institute, 2009.

2. Robert N. Anthony and Regina E. Herzlinger, *Management Control in Nonprofit Organizations* (Homewood, IL: Richard Irwin, 1980), p. 35.

3. Regina E. Herzlinger and Denise Nitterhouse, *Financial Accounting and Managerial Control for Nonprofit Organizations* (Cincinnati: Southwestern Publishing Co., 1994).

4. Robert J. Boxwell, Jr., *Benchmarking for Competitive Advantage* (New York: McGraw Hill, 1994), p. 74.

5. See Robert J. Boxwell, Jr., *Benchmarking for Competitive Advantage* (New York: McGraw Hill, 1994), and Michael E. Porter, *Competitive Strategy: Techniques for Analyzing Industries and Competitors* (New York: Free Press, 1980), pp. 368–382.

6. Michael L. Dertouzos, Richard K. Lester, and Robert M. Solow, *Made in America* (Cambridge: MIT Press, 1989), p. 119. The study emphasizes the need to scan globally to identify the best practices in a company's field.

7. Boxwell, *Benchmarking*, ch. 6.

8. Porter, *Competitive Strategy*, ch. 7.

9. This chapter does not deal with the competitive positioning of an organization to enable it to pursue programs in which it has the opportunity to be a leader because of a comparative advantage it enjoys relative to other organizations in the same field. This topic is covered in Chapter 12 on strategic planning. For the purpose of the analysis of performance management, I assume the organization has found its appropriate niche.

10. Boxwell defines benchmarking as "two things: setting goals by using objective, external standards and learning from others—learning how much and, perhaps more important, learning how.... Benchmarking is not a numbers-only exercise. Setting quantitative goals, often called metrics, through benchmarking is arguably the best way to set goals, but keep in mind that setting goals comparable to or beyond those of the best-in-class without understanding the underlying processes that enable the best-in-class to achieve their results can be useless or worse. Understanding how the companies you study achieve their results is usually more important and valuable than obtaining some precisely quantified metrics" (*Benchmarking*, p. 17).

11. Ibid., p. 35.

12. Boxwell describes the benchmarking process as determining: 1) which value activities in an organization are the activities where improvement will allow the business to gain the most through benchmarking, and 2) the key factors, or drivers, of these value activities, and then identifying the companies with the foremost practices in those value activities. He adds: "These foremost practices may be found at competitors or companies from unrelated industries—any companies that perform the value activities well. For example, Xerox benchmarked L.L. Bean's warehousing and distribution system after determining that Bean's practices were the foremost practices in that particular activity" (ibid., pp. 20–21). The term "value activities" is defined in Porter as the "physically and technologically distinct activities a firm performs." Michael E. Porter, *Competitive Advantage: Creating and Sustaining Superior Performance* (New York: Free Press, 1985), p. 38.

13. William G. Bowen and Neil L. Rudenstine, *In Pursuit of the Ph.D.* (Princeton, NJ: Princeton University Press, 1992), pp. 211-214. Neil Rudenstine is currently the president of Harvard University. He previously served in various deanships and then as provost at Princeton. He and Bowen left Princeton together in 1988 to join the Andrew W. Mellon Foundation, Bowen as president and Rudenstine as executive vice-president.

14. Gerald L. Schmaedick, ed., *Cost-Effectiveness in the Nonprofit Sector: Methods and Examples from Leading Organizations* (Westport: Quorum Books, 1993), p. 36; and Council on Foundations, *Evaluation for Foundations* (San Francisco: Jossey-Bass, 1993), p. 278.

15. Brent C. Miller, Josefina J. Card, Roberta L. Paikoff, and James L. Peterson, *Preventing Adolescent Pregnancy* (Newbury Park, CA: Sage, 1992).

16

Depicting Performance and Financial Condition

Chapter 15 established the fundamental elements of a system for managing the effectiveness and efficiency of a nonprofit's performance. To complement that system, management and the board must receive reports that detail how well the organization is fulfilling its mission and the related issue of the condition of its finances. The fund accounting system that the accounting profession uses to certify the financial condition of nonprofit organizations is not designed to serve as such a management tool, and each enterprise must create its own internal reporting system. The principal components of such an internal system are set forth in this chapter.

Management Information versus Accounting

Statements depicting the performance and financial condition of nonprofits are prepared for a variety of audiences. The nature of that audience, and the message a nonprofit wants to convey to it, shapes the form and content of the documents it receives. External audiences may include the media and the general public, current or prospective funders, lenders, and the Internal Revenue Service; the internal audience consists of the board and management.

The information that management needs to run an enterprise is often different from that which the accounting profession needs in order to prepare the entity's financial statements. Management information must be organized in a way that highlights quickly and easily for executives the key variables that reveal how an enterprise is faring; how well it is meeting the objectives established for it at the outset of the period; and, if it is off track, what factors account for this. In addition, the information has to be available to management at certain crucial time intervals, if corrective action is to be possible. An enterprise must organize its financial information in a format that enables management to oversee the operations of the organization.

Over the years, the accounting profession has worked to make fund accounting more useful in depicting the financial condition of an exempt organization. Fund accounting was conceived, however, to serve the basic purpose of demonstrating whether donated or restricted resources (resources that can be used only for specified purposes) were used in a manner consistent with the instructions of those who gave them. In order to satisfy the grantors of resources to an exempt organization that these resources are being used for the specified purpose, nonprofit accounting entries are classified by funds. Each fund is, in essence, a separate compartment in which resources restricted for a specific purpose are stored. Funds are separated from one another and transactions are treated as transfers between funds. (For example, the expenditure of income from the endowment is treated as a transfer from the endowment fund to the operating fund.)

The difficulty with relying on fund accounting as a management tool is that *the basic reporting unit is not the nonprofit entity itself, but rather the various funds established in connection with the entity.*[1] The result is that fund accounting does not treat a nonprofit as a living, breathing *operating enterprise* but as a composite of a series of separate funds (and funds within funds).

There is no denying that the underlying purpose of fund accounting is appropriate, *but nonprofit organizations do in fact have financial objectives and management needs information that discloses how well these are being met.* The performance and financial results of the exempt organization as an entity must also be elements of a nonprofit financial reporting system.

The accounting profession has limited significantly the number of different types of funds and has made provision for depreciation accounting and cash statements, but fund accounting still does not meet all the needs of the managers of an enterprise. An exempt organization must prepare an informative picture of its program accomplishments and financial condition by designing its own form of financial disclosure to augment the fund accounting statement.

Full Disclosure

The chief failing that I have observed in financial reporting by both for-profit and nonprofit enterprises is a tendency to bury unpleasant realities. Too often, organizations seem to take literally the cynical comment that financial statements are designed to obfuscate rather than to educate. An institution should not kid itself about its true financial condition, but many do. They resort to unjustified optimism about future revenues, understate the vulnerability of their accounts receivable, or underestimate the amount of plant maintenance required or other liabilities for which provision must be made (e.g., severance payments and earned but unused vacation leaves).

Hiding liabilities leaves an organization vulnerable, not only to errant judgments but also to the risk of a sudden, unmanageable jolt to its financial position when a day of reckoning arrives. The appropriate strategy is to make adequate provision for meeting *all foreseeable* obligations in a manner that minimizes their adverse impact. For example, actual outlays for plant maintenance may vary considerably from year to year, according to the nature of the repairs to be made. Instead of simply booking the actual expenditures each year as they occur, an organization can fund the cost of such maintenance over, say, a five-year period by an annual charge to the budget equal to the *average* yearly outlay.

Does a Nonprofit Need a Bottom Line?

In business, the profit measure, or "bottom line," provides a baseline that, when related to other financial markers (e.g., net profit as a percentage of revenues, net profit as a return on assets or as a return on shareholders' equity, earnings per share, and the ratio of share price to earnings per share), illustrates the financial condition of the enterprise. It is these *relationships* between net profit and other financial markers that provide a gauge of a business's performance. Such ratios also permit comparisons with other businesses in the same or different lines of business. In a business, this form of quantification is appropriate because a business's mission is to maximize the financial return to its owners. The aggregation of the varied financial data in a number of earnings-based ratios also aids public investors in choosing among publicly traded securities, thus facilitating the operation of our capital markets.

In addition, a structure to oversee the financial reporting of corporations whose shares are publicly traded has been developed by a group that includes the Securities and Exchange Commission (SEC), institutional shareholders, mutual funds, underwriters of new capital, lenders, thousands of security analysts who follow companies and publish their findings, and trade and general business publications. The financial penalty for publishing misleading financial statements can be quite severe and can be imposed not only on managers but also on the independent auditors who certified the company's financial statements (see Chapter 9, which describes the demise of the Arthur Andersen firm as a result of the Enron scandal).

Historically, being responsive to the needs of the capital markets was not relevant to the functioning of nonprofits. The issue is not whether a nonprofit can calculate operating profit in the same fashion as a business does (it can), but the relevance of such a calculation. Whereas a business's single goal is to maximize the return to its shareholders, an exempt organization has a dual agenda: 1) maximizing the effectiveness and efficiency of its programs, and 2) achieving financial stability. Generating revenues in excess of expenditures—the driving goal of a for-profit enterprise—is not, as a rule, an exempt organization's object; rather, it typically seeks to utilize all its available resources to expand the impact or scope of its programs.[2]

The audience for an exempt organization's financial statements is not public investors but senior management, the board, and lenders or grantors. Accordingly, the aim in the case of a nonprofit is to *disaggregate* the financial data in order to reveal the variables that have the greatest impact on the organization's financial condition. It is unfortunate that grantors often do not undertake a due diligence review of the financial condition of organizations to which they make grants. Since the grants are nonrepayable, grantor organizations feel little motivation to conduct such an examination, and most do not have staff members qualified to perform such an examination. In my view, this is a serious shortcoming, for, if grantors regularly reviewed the financial condition and reporting of grantees, they would impose an important discipline on nonprofits.

Actually, some grantors do review grantee organizations' financial condition—namely, foundations that make "program-related investments." The Ford Foundation originated such investments and remains active in making them. A program-related investment (PRI) is just that: funds are advanced in the form of an equity or debt investment, or a guarantee of another's investment, in an organization important to the foundation's program objectives. The investment is made on more favorable terms than could be obtained from commercial sources. One of the Ford Foundation's objectives in launching a PRI program was to stretch foundation resources by recouping funds advanced under the program. In 1970, I served as the Ford Foundation's second head of PRI, taking over shortly after the program was launched. While the recoupment objective made sense, in my experience the greatest value of the program was that the foundation conducted a due diligence review of potential recipients and imposed conditions on their operation. In addition, PRI staff members often worked with recipients to strengthen their management and financial control systems. Continued monitoring kept the pressure on.

But some of my colleagues at Ford considered it inappropriate, even under a PRI, to impose conditions on the operations of a recipient. In their view, once a grantor selected an organization to fund, it should step back and let the organization act as it deemed best. I did not agree with this view then and do not agree with it now, although it prevails throughout much of the grantmaking world. Only if grantors carefully review the management and finances of organizations they fund will there be widespread improvement in the management of nonprofits.

Multiple Factors Depict Organizational Performance and Finances

In order to depict fully the effectiveness of a nonprofit enterprise, one has to examine a number of critical factors that together provide a fair picture of the organization's productivity and its financial condition.

Examining only the operating statement is not sufficient. For example, the productivity of a nonprofit's programs may—unlike that of a for-profit business—generate no revenue, only expense. Thus, program productivity must be reported and analyzed separately from the operating revenues and expenses of a nonprofit organization.

In addition to the operating statement, one also has to examine a series of factors I group under the heading "capital condition." For example, many nonprofit organizations do not have a planned program of expenditures for major maintenance and often literally wait until the roof caves in before addressing the issue. In contrast, standard hotel accounting requires annual reserves to be set aside to provide for the periodic refurbishment of the hotel. Fund accounting does not, however, require the establishment of a reserve to provide for periodic maintenance of a nonprofit's plant.

For an organization with many buildings, especially if these house extensive science or medical laboratories, failure to take into account the cost of keeping the plant in good physical condition—and also up to the standards set by the Department of Labor's Occupational Safety and Health Act and federal requirements with respect to access by the handicapped—presents a serious financial burden. Any financial report that does not provide for the cost of maintaining an organization's physical plant will present a seriously misleading picture of the entity's financial condition.

It is also important to report on the organization's cash position separately from its statement of revenues and expenses. The latter is not the equivalent of cash. If a building program is underway, substantial outlays of cash may appear on the financial statement as capital expenditures that are not charged to the operating statement. Similarly, repayments of debt principal are not charged against the operating statement but are reflected in a reduction of indebtedness on the balance sheet. Cash actually available to pay current bills *must* be separately identified.

The treatment of gifts also requires care. Some gifts may be payable over a term of years; others may be used only for certain specified purposes (e.g., the hiring of a tenured faculty member to the classics department); still others may be restricted to being added to the university's endowment, so that they can be spent only in accordance with the formula adopted by the school for spending a percentage of the income and capital gains earned by its endowment. The total cash that the university can utilize to meet current needs may thus be only a fraction of the total amount of gifts received in any one year. That figure needs to be separated from the total of gifts received. For these and other reasons, the management information reporting for a nonprofit must cover a range of analyses.

A Reporting System for Management and the Board

The following six critical analyses form the core of an exempt organization's management information report:

1. Program evaluation

2. Annual operating results

3. Sources and uses of cash

4. Capital condition

5. Risk management issues

6. Management report

For each of these analyses, the data must be disaggregated until the factors that have the greatest impact on the organization are identified. In addition, the data should be viewed over a number of years in order to identify trends that may represent a change in the organization's condition.

A Balanced Budget Masks Precarious Financial Condition

The following hypothetical case illustrates the importance of disaggregating data and searching for *trend lines*.

Eastern University proudly announces that it has balanced its operating budget for five years in a row, reporting total revenues equal to total current expenditures, and that during that period it has expanded its educational plant, raised faculty salaries, and increased the size of its professional school faculties (see Table 16.1). But if one breaks down the data further, a very different picture emerges (see Table 16.2). An analysis of trends over this period reveals that Eastern has balanced its budget essentially by raising the cost of undergraduate tuition, room, and board. The percentage of Eastern's revenues accounted for by tuition, room, and board fees has increased over the five years from 45 percent of total revenues to more than half of the school's revenues. The increase in these fees—ranging from 12 to 14 percent a year—significantly outpaces inflation as measured by the consumer price index, as well as the more relevant educational inflation index (more relevant because educational costs do increase faster than the price level in the economy as a whole).

TABLE 16.1: Revenues at Eastern University over a Five-Year Period					
	Year				
	2004	**2005**	**2006**	**2007**	**2008**
REVENUES	$200 million	$216 million	$233.3 million	$252 million	$272.2 million
Tuition, Room and Board Fees	90.0[a]	102.8	116.6	131.6	147.8
Grants and Gifts	80.0[b]	83.2	86.7	90.4	94.4
Auxiliary Revenue	10.0[c]	10.0	10.0	10.0	10.0
Distribution from Endowment	20.0[d]	20.0	20.0	20.0	20.0

a. Tuition, room and board fees in 1990 represent 45% of total revenues and increase at a rate sufficient to fund 80% of the increase in expenses(revenues).

b. Grants from government and private sources and unrestricted gifts from private sources represent 40% of total revenue in 1990 and increase at a rate sufficient to cover 20% of the increase in expenditures (revenues).

c. Auxiliary revenues include principally gross revenues from athletic events, and revenues from the university-owned store, royalties on technology licensed by the university, and miscellaneous other incidental streams of revenue. The dollar volume of such revenues remains constant throughout the period, but a declining percentage of total revenues.

d. Distribution from the total return of the endowment, in accordance with the spending policy approved by Eastern's Board of Trustees, represented 10% of total revenues and continues throughout the period to provide a constant flow of dollars, but a declining percentage of total revenues as endowment returns declined.

TABLE 16.2: Breakdown of Tuition, Room, and Board Fees in Dollars, Percent Increase From Prior Year Fees, and Fees as Percentage of Revenues					
	Year				
	2004	2005	2006	2007	2008
Increase in Dollars from Previous Year	N/A	$12.8 million	$13.6 million	$15.2 million	$16 million
Percent Increase from Previous Year		13.3%	13.4%	12.9%	12.3%
Fees as Percentage of Revenue	45%	47.6%	50%	52%	54%

At the same time, Eastern's fee increases are greater than those of its several principal competitors for undergraduates, as determined by identifying the schools at which a significant proportion of students who reject Eastern actually matriculate. An examination of the percentage of students who choose Eastern over these principal competitors reveals, over the five-year period, a significant decline in the percentage who attend Eastern. Consistent with this pattern, Eastern's admissions "yield"—the percentage of students admitted who chose to attend the admitting school—declines over the five years during which Eastern has a balanced budget. This situation forces Eastern to offer admission to more students in order to meet its revenue goals for tuition, room, and board. The result in Eastern's case is that it is forced to admit students whose qualifications are lower than those of the students it admitted when its yield was higher.

Equally disquieting, the pressure to maintain student quality forces the admissions office to offer admission to a very high percentage of those who do not apply for financial aid, making ability to pay a clear factor in admissions decisions, despite the university's official policy of admitting the most qualified students without regard to whether they need financial aid.

The ultimate negative outcome is that *U.S. News & World Report*, whose ranking of colleges and universities affects students' decisions regarding which schools to apply to, lowers its ranking of Eastern because of the decline in the school's yield and the lower median SAT scores of its student body. The result is a further fall-off in admissions applications, which further shrinks the pool of quality candidates.

The hypothetical case of Eastern University demonstrates the importance of disaggregating gross data to identify critical trends in the factors having the most impact on an exempt organization's financial condition. Eastern, which on the surface appeared to be a growing institution in good financial shape, is in fact in perilous condition, with its financial viability in jeopardy and the quality of its student body declining as it loses ground to its principal competitors.

Following is a more detailed exposition of each of the six analyses I have identified as forming the core of a nonprofit's financial report.

Program Evaluation

The health of a nonprofit institution cannot be measured only in terms of financial data. The vitality of its programs, the care with which these are targeted, and the depth of their impact are at the heart of the organization's strength. The program is the nonprofit's "product"; if the marketplace is not receptive to it, this rejection will soon be reflected in the organization's financial figures, just as the rejection of a commercial product will hurt the financial position of a business.

For each program, factors such as the following need to be evaluated:

Program outcomes versus original objectives (i.e., the extent to which the measurable objectives established at the outset of the program have in fact been achieved). Remember our hypothetical organization dedicated to aiding young women who live in conditions of poverty. The objective in year 1 was to reduce pregnancy in women under age 18 who joined the program by 10 percent compared to pregnancy rates for their peers in the community at large. Assume that 20 of the 100 women who joined the program became pregnant in year 1 and 80 did not. That means the program's output was 80 women who did not become pregnant. If 25 women (who did not participate in the program but served as a control group) out of 100 became pregnant, then the program can be said to have reduced the level of pregnancy by 20 percent in year 1 (25 divided by 5)—well above target.

Program cost versus budget. While our hypothetical organization's output exceeded the targeted objective for year 1, how did the expenditures for the program compare with the budget established at the outset? Did the cost per output, or the cost of deferring pregnancy in 20 cases, fall within the budget? Ratio of inputs of costs to outputs? Did the organization achieve the projected efficiency?

Key factors accounting for variances in outcomes and costs, versus the original plan. Were the variances the result of inaccurate forecasts or of better execution than one could have expected at the outset? Were they the result of factors within the organization's control or of uncontrollable factors? Is there a causal connection between the organization's programs and the objectives achieved, or do factors unrelated to the organization's efforts provide an equally, if not more, likely explanation of the results?

Annual Operating Results

In the case of a nonprofit, the purpose of an operating statement is to determine, on an accrual basis, whether the organization is operating at financial equilibrium. Equilibrium means that the organization does not have to draw on its capital to make up for a deficit, or lacking capital, to cut expenditures or borrow funds. Accrual accounting provides an important perspective because revenues are those earned during the year, whether or not the amounts were received in cash, and expenses are the resources used or consumed during the year (not the resources acquired, as is the standard accounting practice in most nonprofits).

The difference between cash-basis and accrual-basis accounting is principally one of *timing*. Accrual accounting looks at an entity from the perspective of the relationship between revenues and expenditures based on activities during the year. If equilibrium is not achieved on this basis, an inability to pay the bills will eventually occur, even if at a given moment the organization has on hand plenty of cash or its equivalent generated in past years (or has cash allocated to restricted accounts, as in the example above). On the other hand, if activity that produces revenues on an accrual basis is not converted into cash—because fees for services are not paid in full, or because donors default on grant pledges, or because the institution has been spending large amounts of cash for capital construction (which is not included in the operating statement)—the organization can be in a cash bind even though it has a balanced operating statement. In short, both the operating and cash flow statements require examination.

The organization's operating statement of revenues and expenses should be broken down by principal types of revenues (e.g., grants, earned income, fundraising for current operations) and expenses (e.g., management and staff salaries and benefits, office rent, travel, program materials). Some organizations may also find it useful to trace particular revenues and expenses to specific operating and administrative units. For instance, did the expenses of administrative offices exceed the expenditures of the division that ran the programs? If so, why? Did one program unit incur more of a certain form of expense than another unit? If so, why? The aim is not only to examine whether revenues and expenses, as shown on the operating statement, balanced out, but also to identify the variables that most influenced operating results. In addition, it is advisable to pinpoint where expenses can be curtailed without undermining the program, and to review all sources of revenue to see if they can be counted on to increase or at least continue at the same level in the future.

Just how detailed a breakdown of revenues and expenses is useful will depend on the nature of an organization's activities and purposes. Some organizations may find it convenient to follow the expense breakdown called for in part 2 of IRS Form 990. Part 1 of the form's breakout of revenue sources may also be a convenient format as long as one is aware that the IRS form does not distinguish between current revenues and capital contributions, and as long as one takes care not to repeat that error in one's own operating statement.

Sources and Uses of Cash

As noted above, the operating statement is not the same as cash. Cash flow from operations should generally be positive; otherwise the organization will have trouble meeting its operating expenses. Detailing the sources and uses of cash separately is thus critical in determining the liquidity of an organization or, more simply put, its ability to pay its bills. Steven A. Ross and Randolph W. Westerfield, in their leading textbook on corporate finance, maintain that, although there is no official accounting statement for businesses called cash flow, "the most important thing that can be extracted from financial statements is the actual cash flow.[3]

Cash may be generated by programs, fundraising, earned-income activities, the sale of fixed assets, or the incurring of short- or long-term debt. When one is specifying the sources of cash available to a nonprofit, cash that is restricted as to its purpose should be excluded whenever the restriction precludes the use of the cash to meet expenditures in the current year. For instance, gifts to an organization's endowment would be excluded. However, many so-called restrictions are very broad, and each restriction should be carefully examined to determine whether the funds can be used for some current purpose, even a purpose that the organization had intended to finance from general unrestricted funds. Then the restricted fund can be applied to this purpose and the general funds used for another purpose.

Cash outlays may be made for operating expenses or capital expenditures. Thus, cash may be advanced to pay salaries and utility bills as well as to buy computer equipment or repair a building or pay the interest on principal due on a debt. Cash available to the organization contingent on the payment of a penalty (e.g., income from a certificate of deposit if it is cashed in before its maturity date) should be identified along with the amount of the penalty that would have to be paid.

An important issue for the board of trustees to decide is the investment policies that are to govern cash, including how much money should actually be maintained in the form of cash and how much should be held in short-term securities, readily convertible into cash (keeping in mind that the latter earn a return while cash does not).

Sound cash management also requires setting policies relating to the speed with which payables are retired and to how efficient the institution is going to be in collecting cash due. These policies can involve sensitive matters and can have an important financial impact. For example, should a school require all tuition for the year to be paid in full a month before the first day of the term? Should a nonprofit pay its bills exactly when they are due, even if in practice it could drag its feet without incurring a penalty? (It is not uncommon for major corporations to pay their vendors 30 or 60 days late.) At the least, it does not make sense to pay bills before they are due, when there is no discount provided for early payment (as I have found some organizations do to generate goodwill, especially among local vendors).

To appreciate fully the cash position of an organization, one needs to break down cash inflows and outflows into a *month-by-month cash inflow and outflow budget* and then compare actual results with the budget forecast. This breakdown will show whether an organization is temporarily pinched for cash or even in a deficit position because of the timing of inflows and outflows. Depending on the nature of the problem, management may be able to solve it by taking steps to accelerate certain cash payments or defer certain outlays, or it may have to borrow short-term working capital for a brief period. At the same time, analysis of the month-by-month breakdown may show that a cash shortfall is not a temporary problem but that long-term erosion in the organization's cash position is taking place and that more radical reform is required.

In addition, *a detailed aging analysis of accounts receivable* is useful, since it identifies amounts owed to an organization that should ordinarily be paid in cash during the accounting year. If for some reason these accounts are not paid and converted to cash in a timely fashion, the organization's cash inflow will be less than budgeted. For this reason, an organization should prepare, as a supplement to its cash flow statement, a breakdown of accounts receivable that are past due by various numbers of days—30, 60, 90, and 120. Management then needs to evaluate the likelihood of being paid for the receivables that are well past due (e.g., 90 days or more) and, when the prospects are dim indeed, write off the amounts in question.

Capital Condition

For our purpose, the capital of a nonprofit consists of its long-term resources, namely:

- funds set aside for investment;

- long-term debt;

- physical assets; and

- reserves against future liabilities.

A primary responsibility of the board is to determine the investment policies that should govern the investment of funds to be held for the long-term welfare of the organization (i.e., an endowment), particularly the targeted return to be sought and the level of risk to be accepted in pursuit of such a return.[4] In setting investment policy, the board must also establish a "spending policy" that determines what portion of the current appreciation, dividends, and interest should be spent on the current needs of the organization and what portion should be reinvested for the future well-being of the institution. The ideal formula will call for reinvestment at least equal to the anticipated level of inflation, so that the real value of the investment fund is maintained. Restrictions imposed by donors on gifts to the endowment need to be examined to see whether they differ from the spending policy set by the board.

Another important policy issue is how much debt it is reasonable for an institution to assume. A university setting provides a good illustration of some of the questions that can arise. It may be tempting, when the faculty is pressing for a new building or the president wants a visible testimonial to his administration's activity, to borrow a good percentage of the money required for construction, rather than wait until all the money is in hand.

But if a university accumulates debt in this manner, at some point the level of principal and interest payments due may force the university to slash its educational expenditures in order to meet debt service. The total cash flow from tuition and gifts and other sources may be more than enough to cover the debt service—but only if educational programs are cut. Should debt be incurred only where it can be invested to generate sufficient income to service the debt (e.g., enlarging the capacity of the law school so it can accept more applicants), or should debt be used to fund non-income-producing activities (e.g., to refurbish a classroom or replace worn-out roofs) in the hope that future fundraising will service the debt? In the latter case, what percentage of university revenues should be exposed to debt service requirements if new funds to pay the debt are not found? This judgment determines the degree to which the debt will threaten the university's current programs if future revenues do not rise.

The cost of maintaining physical assets in good condition should be planned for and funds set aside over time for this purpose. Most nonprofits do not follow the business practice of depreciating an asset over its useful life, but even this accounting approach may or may not accurately reflect how frequently repairs of physical assets are required. The trustees should create a plan that predicts future major maintenance requirements and provides for a portion of such future requirements to be funded on a current basis. The institution's own history, or that of comparable organizations, coupled with a physical inspection by qualified consulting engineers, should provide ample guidance for drawing up such a plan.

If the organization's financial condition permits it, a funded reserve against future contingencies should be established. Such a reserve can cushion unanticipated expensive damage to the plant (e.g., by a storm) or an unanticipated short-term adverse change in the organization's operating or cash position. Such a reserve can also be used to fund initial work on the development of a new program. This kind of exploration funding is very difficult, if not impossible, to raise, and having even a relatively small amount of money available for such exploration can enable an organization to renew itself continually over time.

Risk Management Issues

Another decision the board must make is to determine what types of insurance, and how much of each, to carry against specified risks. The risks to which an organization is exposed will vary with the nature of its activities and can range from liability incurred by an employee for wrongfully inflicting harm on another party (e.g., medical malpractice) to the damage a storm can cause to buildings. The type and amount of coverage, and how large a deductible (the amount the insured will pay) an organization decides to live with, will affect the size of the insurance premiums it has to pay. Before the issue is decided, bids should be obtained from a series of insurance companies.

Management Report

The chief financial officer of an exempt organization should author, with the chief executive officer, an annual report offering their evaluation of the program performance and financial condition of the organization. Such a report generally centers on the types of analyses outlined in the preceding discussion, with the ultimate objective of informing the board about how well the organization is performing, where it may be vulnerable, and where improvements are possible. The board should insist that the report be candid and realistic. Moreover, the board should be required to adopt a formal resolution accepting the report (as is, or with modifications made by the board) or rejecting it. The report and the board's resolution regarding it should be part of the minutes of the meeting. The object is to create a process that requires the board to make a detailed examination of the exempt organization's program performance and financial condition.

The Role of the Board Audit Committee

The board of trustees bears the ultimate responsibility for ensuring that an organization's financial house is in order.

Today, under pressure from the stock exchanges and the SEC, virtually all public corporations have established audit committees. The conventional role of a corporate audit committee is to meet with the company's outside auditor once a year to hear its report on the company's financial position and control system, as well as the management's response to the auditor's concerns, which the auditor has previously reviewed with the management. At some point, the committee also meets with the auditor without the management present. An effective audit committee is an essential element in the governance of an organization, but the conventional performance of corporate audit committees, while helpful in providing closer financial oversight by the board, in too many instances has not been effective in preventing a breakdown in the corporate control system. Most audit committees simply have not been aggressive enough in scrutinizing the company's financial condition and controls. In an article I wrote in 1994 with Princeton economics professor Burton G. Malkiel, a director of a number of financial and nonfinancial corporations, we concluded that, in the case of corporations, "The 'bottom line' for the audit committee is to shed its reactive mode and become a catalyst in probing for weak spots in the company's internal controls and financial reporting practices."[5]

In the case of exempt organizations, the establishment of a board audit committee is more the exception than the rule. But nonprofits should establish such committees and find one or two trustees with the financial acumen to lead them. Audit committees are especially important for nonprofits, which are not subject to the same kind of external oversight of their financial reporting as businesses whose shares are publicly traded.

As desirable as this step would be, many nonprofits, especially the less prominent ones (which cannot use prestige to attract board members), have a great deal of difficulty enlisting trustees with business and financial skills who have time to play an active leadership role. Thus, boards can help by assuming more responsibility, but instilling increased financial discipline in the nonprofit sector is going to depend heavily on grantors' conducting genuine scrutiny of potential grantees' financial condition and reporting.

The Relationship of the Independent Auditor to the Audit Committee

A change in the typical relationship between the independent auditor and the organization could do more than anything else to make the auditor an effective agent of the board of trustees. At present, the auditor is effectively chosen—and the fee set—by the management, although nominally the board approves the choice. Instead, the audit committee of the board should select and hire the auditor directly, establishing the auditor's direct responsibility to the board. Moreover, the tasks the auditor is to perform as part of the audit should be discussed with the audit committee and progress reports made to the committee. Under current practice, the auditor typically reviews the audit work plan with the management. The establishment of a direct working relationship between the audit committee and the auditor would give the audit a greater independence from the management and thus enhance the board's oversight of the finances of the organization. In fact, in our article, Malkiel and I recommended the same change in the way auditors are retained for businesses.[6]

There are many specific ways in which an independent auditor can assist the board to ascertain that all the policy issues raised by the financial statements have been brought to its attention and that the organization's control system is sound.

1. The independent auditor should certify to the board that the organization has no unfunded liabilities, whether material or not. In the case of one large exempt organization, its administration began a practice of not including in the financial reports certain liabilities where it was expected that funding would be received or that a subsequent surplus would cover the deficit. Over a four-year period, this practice built up $12 million in unfunded liabilities—or, in simple language, $12 million in expenses that had not been charged to the operating statement. Then a new audit partner was put in charge of the account and insisted that the amount was material and that the institution begin writing off the liabilities against revenues. To avoid such situations in the future, the finance committee of the institution insisted that the auditor state in writing whether there were any undisclosed liabilities, material or not. This is a practice all institutions should follow.

2. The independent auditor should identify for the board any significant expenditure that has been capitalized rather than charged to the operating statement. Treating large expenditures this way is a form of abuse that can occur in both business and nonprofit organizations, and the board should review and approve decisions to capitalize large sums.

3. The independent auditor should investigate in depth, on a random, rotating basis, one or more of the organization's control systems. This investigation should be conducted with the same intensity as if a major abuse had been uncovered, but with the aim of preventing even the possibility of any such abuse occurring.

4. The auditor should review the manner in which management has organized financial data for board review and should comment on whether the presentation reveals the most important underlying factors influencing the financial condition of the organization.

Auditors should be persuaded to work with the staff in preparing the management's internal financial report and to advise senior management members and the board, albeit informally, whether the report appears to have been prepared in a professionally sound manner and whether, to the best of the accountants' knowledge, any material fact has been overlooked or omitted. The board, in turn, could expressly declare the auditing firm immune from any liability (except for gross negligence), should the management report contain an error of commission or omission. (The object is not to set up the auditing firm for a lawsuit but to get its best help and advice.)

It would also be constructive if the accounting profession went back to basics and examined anew the forms of financial statements it will certify—and the kinds of audit services it will provide—in order to make a more useful contribution to the management of nonprofits.

Conclusions

The principal components of a management information system should address the following areas:

1. Program evaluation

2. Annual operating results

3. Sources and uses of cash

4. Capital condition

5. Risk management issues.

The data related to each of these areas should be disaggregated to the extent necessary to identify the variables that most affect the performance of the organization.

Analysis of these factors, or critical markers, should form the core of a report by the management to the board (a management report). The board, in a formal resolution, should adopt this report as submitted or as amended by the board, or else reject it.

The boards of all nonprofits should establish audit committees to choose the firm's outside auditor, determine the auditor's fee, and review its scope of work and its findings. In essence, the board, acting through an audit committee, should play an active role in scrutinizing the performance and finances of an exempt organization, not merely react passively to information supplied by the management.

The accounting profession needs to undertake a thorough review of the kinds of services auditors should provide to management and to boards. Accounting firms should review how they can be of more practical value to management and the board than they are today.

NOTES

1. A fund is defined as "an independent fiscal and accounting entity with a self-balancing set of accounts recording cash and/or other resources together with all related liabilities, obligations, reserves, and equities which are segregated for the purpose of carrying on specific activities or attaining certain objectives in accordance with special regulations, restrictions, or limitations." Ronald Braswell, Karen Fortin, and Jerome S. Osteryoung, *Financial Management for Not-for-Profit Organizations* (New York: Wiley, 1984).

2. Some operating nonprofits have from time to time set aside part of their revenues to build an operating reserve fund for future contingencies or to fund new initiatives. Of course, organizations with an endowment do not generally spend all they earn in a year; part of the appreciation and income earned by the endowment fund is reinvested in order to maintain the real value of the fund in the future. But, even with these qualifications, earning a profit is not an objective of an exempt organization and thus is not a useful baseline measure for such organizations.

3. Steven A. Ross and Randolph W. Westerfield, *Corporate Finance* (St. Louis: Times Mirror/Mosby College Publishing, 1988), p. 29.

4. For a review of the role of the board of trustees in overseeing the investment of funds, and the principal options open to it, see Burton Malkiel and Paul Firstenberg, *Managing Risk in an Uncertain Era: An Analysis for Endowed Institutions* (Princeton, NJ: Princeton University Press, 1976).

5. Paul B. Firstenberg and Burton G. Malkiel, "The Twenty-First Century Boardroom: Who Will Be in Charge?" *Sloan Management Review*, Fall 1994, p. 34.

6. Ibid., p. 34.

17

Navigating Economic Downturns

The depth—and potential length—of the recession that became obvious in 2008 created severe challenges for nonprofit organizations. Some organizations face declining revenues as grants and contracts for the services they provide are cut back, especially if they are funded by city and state agencies bound to balance their budgets in light of declining tax and other revenues. Some face the cutoff of essential working capital loans. For others, fundraising may drop off sharply as individual and institutional donors scale back their giving in the face of their own declining resources. Even those institutions with very large endowments may well have some hard decisions to make; endowments at many places lost 20 to 30 percent of their value in 2008 and faced continuing losses in 2009. Institutions with large endowments have typically relied on endowment income to fund a large percentage of their operating budgets—in the case of some universities 30 percent or more—and now face difficult trade-offs between drawing down unrestricted endowment funds and reserves in the face of losses and cutting back their operating and capital expenditures.[1] Thus, even heretofore well-to-do institutions may not escape the negative impact of this severe recession.

There are not a lot of good choices in such a climate. A realistic reassessment of future revenues is a starting point. Ideally the revised forecast will prove prescient enough to permit the organization to go through the cost-cutting exercise but once. However, trying to forecast how long this economy will continue on its downward slide—and when a meaningful recovery might begin to take hold—is an uncertain business. Conditions may prove substantially worse (or better) than are projected. In light of this risk, one may wish to develop several downward forecasts and devise alternative reduced budgets to match the different projections, to be ready to shed costs as actual results dictate.

Some organizations may not want to act on the basis of a worst-case scenario. The degree of flexibility an organization has in adapting to new financial realities will be related to its ability to apply reserves and unrestricted endowment to absorb operating deficits. Absent such capacity, and the unlikely ability to borrow funds, the organization has no alternative but to immediately take whatever steps are necessary to balance its budget.

Some of the options for scaling back costs are:

- Freezing new hires, whether for additions to staff or to fill vacancies

- Freezing all salaries at their present level or reducing the salaries of staff

- Reducing the number of existing staff

- Curtailing travel and conference expenses

- Scaling back communication and public relations expenses

- Deferring new programs and new capital expenditures or eliminating existing programs and halting capital projects

- Negotiating deferred payment terms with suppliers

- Negotiating with donors to modify terms of restricted gifts in order to apply the funds toward the operating deficit

- Tapping the endowment despite the current losses in value

- Eliminating employer contributions to employee 401(k) or other savings plans

- Increasing employee contributions to health insurance

- Reducing the level of pension benefits

- The more drastic option of consolidating the organization with another entity with a similar mission

Each of these options will have pluses and minuses depending on the circumstances the organization faces and the impact of different choices on the morale of its personnel.

For instance, staff may be prepared to forego salary increases to avoid layoffs or to freeze new hires—even ones central to the program—rather than eliminate existing positions. Navigating through a downturn requires the support of board and staff alike if the organization is to retain its cohesion, and thus the budget reduction process should be designed to receive the

18

Activity-Based Cost Reduction

Organizations are learning that they cannot simply reduce expenditures randomly or arbitrarily when the budget is in deficit. First, the costs of an organization's individual activities must be compared with their value to the organization's aims. This approach to reducing expenditures is termed "activity-based cost reduction"; it applies equally to businesses and nonprofit organizations.

However, even activity-based cost reduction must be conducted in the context of a long-term strategy to promote the improved performance of the organization. This requires not simply changing the budgets of individual departments on the basis of activity-based cost reduction, but an examination of processes for delivering products and services that cut across departmental boundaries.

At one time or another, most organizations confront a potential gap between revenues and expenses and are forced to cut back their expenditures in order to restore financial equilibrium. The causes of such a situation can be quite varied. Frequently, senior management, lulled by good times or inertia, allows more and more additions to the budget. Soon, the buildup of expenditures starts to exceed the normal rate of increase in revenues. The inevitable crunch will be worsened if, at the same time, revenue growth slows, sometimes for reasons beyond the organization's control (e.g., because a funding source reduces its support, or because a downturn in the economy adversely affects the flow of contributions, as discussed in the previous chapter). On occasion, some unforeseen adversity (e.g., severe storm damage to a university's campus buildings) strikes either the expenditure or the revenue side of the budget. Even endowed institutions such as foundations may encounter a period during which the securities markets take a nosedive and the total return from investments falls significantly.

Few institutions are wealthy enough to ride out such periods by allowing their capital to absorb operating losses. Since it is often hard to predict how long a period of adversity or disequilibrium may last, the prudent course is either to find new sources of revenue or to scale back expenditures lest the organization find itself in a deep financial hole from which it cannot easily dig itself out.

Unfortunately, organizations often look for cost-cutting measures only after experiencing (in the case of a business) a sharp fall-off in profits, or (in the case of a nonprofit) a looming budget deficit. Such hasty measures are born of an urge to slash expenses and shore up the bottom line or balance the budget as quickly as possible. This can be a costly mistake, for how one goes about curtailing expenditure growth will have a powerful effect on the future character and strength of the enterprise.

Cutting costs in a time of contraction demands as much strategic thinking and careful implementation as the building of new programs in a time of expansion. Examining the "value added" of each activity in an organization, relative to the costs of implementing the activity, is a method of systematically establishing the positive or negative value of each activity in an organization.

The test of an activity's value is whether the organization would be hurt in its ability to carry out its mission effectively—especially relative to other organizations in the same field—and whether its long-term financial strength would be undermined if an activity or function were eliminated. If the answer is no, the decision to eliminate the function is easy. If the function does contribute significantly to the programmatic or financial strength of the organization, then one needs to determine whether its value is worth its cost. For instance, if the budget is in the red, can one eliminate or reduce in size the department that evaluates whether programs achieve their aims? Is it possible to cut back the staff that supports volunteers or creates programs for alumni without hurting the organization's fundraising?

As a rule, the tasks with the least value added should be the first to be scaled back or eliminated. The idea is to anchor a cost-reduction program in the curtailment of the lowest-value-added work, and then to cut staff to reflect the reduced workload, rather than first eliminating people and leaving the surviving staff members to figure out how to get the work done. The evaluation of the value added of activities is a process that I have applied in both a complex for-profit business and a nonprofit institution, and it works equally well in both environments.

Traditional accounting systems break down expenses by category: salaries, fringe benefits, supplies, and fixed costs. In contrast, activity-based accounting views an organization as groups of individuals performing a wide variety of specific activities. Under this system, costs are allocated to what the entity pays for the different tasks its employees perform to produce the product or service. This process can also be used to identify opportunities for outsourcing functions, or to pinpoint functions that can be redesigned for increased productivity.

In the case of service organizations, where personnel costs make up the bulk of expenditures, activity-based cost reduction is likely to be a much more productive approach than simply slashing the costs of various units. Any extensive cost-containment program within such organizations invariably means reducing staff size. Cutting people from a payroll is very different from curtailing capital outlays, reducing inventories, or slashing advertising and promotion budgets.

The turmoil associated with layoffs harms the survivors of the enterprise as well as the people who lose their jobs. Managers will resist such staff cuts if they perceive that the reductions will undermine their ability to get the job done. Unless specific tasks are eliminated first, cutting personnel will leave a unit facing the same workload with a smaller staff, an unappealing prospect for any manager.

Activity-Based Cost Reduction At Work

Let's start with a hypothetical example to illustrate how activity-based cost reduction can work. Assume an organization whose mission is to raise funds from the community and from government sources on behalf of a variety of affiliated social agencies that would not be effective at raising funds if they sought support independently. In our assumed case, the umbrella agency is anticipating a substantial reduction in government funds and has decided to reduce its administrative expenses before cutting funding to its affiliated agencies. Rather than simply announcing an across-the-board cut in the expenses of all departments, it begins to examine the functions performed by its staff. It has a half-dozen program officers and an equal number of assistant program officers. The organization asks each program officer and assistant program officer to describe his or her activities.

The assistant program officers supply the information shown in Table 18.1.

Table 18.1. Activities of Assistant Program Officers in Hypothetical Organization					
Task	End Product	Intended Use	% of Total Time Devoted to Task	Cost of Task	Value Added
Compare grantee's actual use of funds with budget categories approved by agency	Disbursement compliance report	Review by program officers and auditors	75%	75% of salary and benefits = $50,000; plus out of-pocket expenses ($10,000) = Total cost $60,000	Program officers do not make use of reports

The conclusion that can be drawn from this information is that the preparation of grantee disbursement compliance reports is an activity whose scope could be reduced considerably. Instead of each assistant program officer preparing a regular report on all grantees in his or her portfolio, reports could be prepared on grantees selected at random, and the compliance function could continue to be overseen by the auditing staff. By reducing the scope of this function, the agency will be able to eliminate half of the assistant program officers and will save $150,000 in salaries and benefits, plus an estimated $30,000 in out-of-pocket expenses associated with the disbursement compliance report. In addition, the staff reduction will permit the elimination of one secretarial position and will save on space costs. The ultimate savings, on the order of $200,000, will not impair the effectiveness of the agency's program.

A detailed examination of the program officers' activities shows that they spend much of their time reading applications for assistance and writing recommendations for funding approval by the agency board of directors. In fact, the bulk of the agency's funding consists of repeat grants to prior recipients. Few new agencies are funded. Analysis reveals that use of a standard form application and standard form funding request for agencies who have been previously funded would save a substantial amount of time—

258

enough to free up the equivalent of three-quarters of a program officer's time. As a result, one program officer is assigned to work part-time with the agency's shorthanded post-grant evaluation staff.

The reader is likely to protest that real life is not as simple and straightforward as the hypothetical example makes it seem, and that is true; but hopefully it points up a process of analysis that can be applied to a real-world set of facts.

Three Principles of Cost Reduction

Any cost-reduction program must address how the organization is going to maintain the quality of its products or services once expenditures and staff are reduced. Often, top managers simply give up on identifying specific reductions and dictate that each of their subordinates reduce expenditures—meaning any form of expenditure—by a certain percentage or dollar amount. This "blunt instrument" approach fails to meet three principles that should be inherent in any sound cost-reduction program:

1. The cost-reduction program should serve as a method of restructuring and strengthening the enterprise competitively; at a minimum, it should avoid damaging the organization strategically over the long term.

2. The savings identified should be realizable and sustainable over time.

3. The savings should be sufficient to achieve its financial objective, so that everyone is not soon forced to try to cut expenses even further.

Cost reductions need to be made in accordance with a plan for reshaping the enterprise to make it more competitive. Otherwise, cutting expenditures may produce a temporarily balanced budget at the expense of long-term ability to deliver quality services. A long-term perspective is thus as important in reducing expenditures as it is in making outlays for new endeavors. Both are resource investment decisions.

Before scaling back the budget of an organization that is on shaky ground, one needs to give careful thought to the feasibility of reassembling the scarcest resource—talented people who work well together. It may prove wise to underwrite a part of the organization during the down cycle, even at the expense of short-term budget deficits, especially if the employees involved are versatile and, given time and training, may be able to adapt their talents to new work within the organization.

In activity-based cost-reduction analysis, here is what each unit or department is asked to do:

- Identify objectives in order to establish a set of priorities against which to evaluate its activities, staffing levels, and expenditures.

- Break down its staffing and expenditures according to the specific tasks performed by the unit, and then evaluate the importance of such tasks to achievement of the unit's short-term goals. This comparison of the cost of a task to its value is what determines the task's "value added."

- Consider the potential impact of various possible levels of resource availability on the nature and amount of work the unit can perform. This involves detailing what tasks would be curtailed or eliminated if expenditures were reduced by various amounts (e.g., 5 percent, 10 percent) and the consequences of such cuts.

The activity-focused formulation asks management to prioritize its cost reductions in the same manner as it would rank potential areas of expansion—by relating the work currently being performed in an enterprise to the organization's primary objectives. The impact of proposed reductions on strategic priorities can then be assessed and actions taken that are consistent with these aims.

Activity-based cost reduction can lead to expenditure reductions in several ways. Functions that are identified as relatively "low added value" will ultimately translate into the elimination of positions and, generally, related cash and expenditure savings. For instance, when the aggregate of tasks performed by a specific position represents a relatively low overall level of value added, the position becomes a candidate for elimination if expenditures must be cut. The incumbent, if a valuable employee, may be transferred to another position if one is vacant; otherwise, the incumbent must be terminated. When a position is a mixture of low-value and high-value functions, it becomes a candidate for consolidation with another similarly rated position. When this happens, one of the two incumbent employees must be transferred to another post, or terminated.

One of the fruits of activity-based cost reduction is the identification of organizational redundancy—areas of duplicated effort that develop when management fails to define unit responsibilities clearly, or when one unit fails to perform competently, leading others to build their own duplicate systems to fill in the gap. This kind of redundancy is one of the principal sources of organizational fat.

Activity-based cost reduction can also help to identify excess layers of management. For example, in some organizations there is an additional layer of review between frontline executives and senior management. This layer of management collects and repackages information and then transmits it to a higher level. The value of this additional review (or "coordination," in organizational jargon) is questionable in many instances and bears close scrutiny in terms of value added.

Activity-based cost-reduction analysis can also help establish the appropriate range of executive "span of control." The conventional theory is that an executive can only adequately supervise five or six people reporting directly to him or her. Today this concept is being rethought as organizations consider whether staffing subordinate functions with more talented individuals, who are given clear responsibility and authority, will reduce the extent of executive oversight, thus enabling senior officers to exercise control over much larger numbers of staff members.

As Peter Drucker has observed, span of control should be thought of as "span of communication, with control turning out to be the ability to obtain information." This, in turn, means the number of people reporting to a single supervisor is limited only by the subordinates' willingness to take responsibility for their own communication and relationships. Activity-based cost-reduction analysis can help determine whether supervisors are exercising the broadest feasible range of oversight or whether an organization is plagued with too many executives exercising too narrow a span of oversight.

The efficiency of an organization's managerial structure should, of course, be evaluated whether or not the organization is facing the need to cut expenditures. Activity-based cost-reduction analysis serves to illuminate whether an organization is using its staff in the most efficient and effective manner. It also allows an assessment of whether resources are being assigned to the enterprise's highest priorities. Rigorous application of the process can, therefore, avoid the need for more painful cost-reduction programs forced by a suddenly ballooning deficit. Activity-based cost analysis is also an effective way to identify opportunities for outsourcing functions (those with the least added value) and to pinpoint functions that need to be redesigned for increased productivity.

A Managerial Safeguard

Activity-based cost-reduction analysis can also serve as a managerial safeguard against the development of unnecessary expenditures; it can help organizations avoid excessive buildup of staff in good times. At the same time, when cost reductions are needed in order to restore equilibrium, the analysis is the most effective way to pinpoint reductions in the areas of least priority to the organizations. The following specific examples show how activity-based cost-reduction analysis can identify work that can be eliminated without harming the enterprise.

A university established an extensive system for allocating maintenance and office repair costs to business units on the basis of the number of hours and level of skills actually used by particular business units. It kept extensive records of the types of personnel called on to provide service to each department, and of the frequency and length of the service calls. Then it charged each department's budget for the "actual" cost of the services utilized. This careful system for allocating costs does provide a detailed accounting to departments that object to their maintenance bills, but it does not improve the efficiency or quality of maintenance services and the entire system requires elaborate record-keeping by clerical staff. By switching to a system of billing departments on the basis of a predetermined cost-allocation formula, the university can save several hundred thousand dollars a year without in any way affecting the quality of its maintenance.

Other examples of expenditures where the value to the enterprise does not justify the costs of the operation include the following:

- An internal auditing staff whose size and cost substantially exceed the savings the group is able to identify and whose control functions duplicate the work of the firm's outside auditors;

- A weekly financial report that requires the effort of several full-time staff members to prepare but that is rarely used by executives; and

- An item-by-item review of expense accounts by an expense control unit. Testing such reports against formulas requires fewer personnel to perform and is just as effective in keeping expenses within acceptable limits.

In some cases, looking for the value added of the individual tasks actually performed by staff will turn up situations in which personnel are engaged in activities that have outlived their original purpose or that are simply a waste of time. For instance, one organization maintained duplicate systems of financial reports, even though the older system was no longer of value. No one had told the central accounting office that their reports were no longer being utilized by management.

In another case, the central accounting office and operating units did not utilize the same methodology for measuring expenditures and revenues. Thus, they issued reports with conflicting results that, in turn, took additional management time (often at quite senior levels) to reconcile.

Paradoxically, in some cases, activity-based cost reduction may point out areas in which increased internal expenses may actually save the organization money. One entity maintained a very small legal staff, for example, because it felt it was easy to justify the legal fees incurred by outside counsel. In fact, much of the legal work done outside was of a recurring nature and could have been done by competent attorneys in-house at a lower net cost. By adding several attorneys to the in-house staff, the organization was able to save substantial legal fees.

Implementing Reductions

Reducing expenses through activity-based cost-reduction analysis and cutting expenditures through attrition each have their drawbacks. Identifying low-value-added positions as candidates for elimination enables an organization to reduce staff in a manner that is strategic, cutting back in lowest-priority areas. But it is likely to result in more discharges of incumbent personnel than if expenditures are reduced through attrition caused by voluntary departures or retirements. On the other hand, attrition produces openings on a random basis and without regard for strategic priorities. For this reason, attrition may prove to be a more expensive means of cutting staff.

In any case, in order to make significant reductions through attrition—in a manner that does not impair the enterprise—the organization must be able to redeploy personnel and funds to the highest-priority tasks. Whether it is a secretary or a senior executive who chooses to leave, that person may be performing an indispensable function. If that is the case, the organization is faced with one of two choices. It must: 1) hire a replacement, in which case there is no savings (and, in fact, the recruitment procedure will cost the organization additional money); or 2) reassign an existing employee to take over the work of the departing employee. This step demands tight management control at the senior level to overcome any resistance to such redeployment, especially if an employee is transferred across organizational lines. It also requires a flexible and adaptable work force. This, in turn, means designing a staff development system that trains and encourages people to become skilled in a broad range of the organization's operations.

While the process is going on, activity-based cost reduction creates uncertainty for personnel. This uncertainty may hurt morale and may encourage key people to seek jobs elsewhere. Setting a timetable for the changes and briefing key personnel about the timetable as well as their importance to the organization can mitigate some drawbacks.

Just as important, the cost-containment plan—and the reasons behind it—must be carefully explained to the executives charged with carrying it out; indeed, these executives should "own" the plan by participating in its formulation. Without their support, managerial resistance may undermine cost reductions.

In addition, a careful review of the organization's termination policy should precede the process. A sensitive termination plan not only is fair to those who are asked to leave, it also has a positive effect on those who continue working.

An alternate approach is to freeze current salaries. This strategy lowers the increase in base expenditures and slows the growth of costs. It is also a savings that is clearly capturable and has the appeal of equity. Unfortunately, its impact is hard to calculate. It often does not address the root cause of expense increases. It affects the morale of outstanding employees and those who need an increase to make ends meet. As tempting as a salary freeze may seem, it also has many drawbacks.

It is in the organization's self-interest to be considered thoughtful and fair if a downsizing is deemed necessary. A well-planned downsizing can be critical to the success of the organization and will certainly minimize damage and pain to affected employees.

Perhaps most important, the process of expenditure containment must be continuous. Expenses eliminated from the budget during a period of financial stringency tend to creep back as soon as the budgetary heat is off and top management's attention is turned elsewhere. As a precaution, all functions should be reviewed on a rotating basis every three to five years to reassess their ongoing value added to the enterprise. As an organization evolves, certain functions may lose their relative importance, or the organization's financial situation may demand a more rigorous assessment of value added.

Ideally, of course, an organization should avoid hiring unnecessary personnel in the first place. Regrettably, most organizations loosen the reins when revenues are growing and start adding personnel without close scrutiny of the value they add to the enterprise, or consideration of whether the enterprise will be able to afford them in a downturn.

A policy of expanding staff only if the value added is clear can produce an organization that benefits from the cohesion of a stable staff, secure in its sense of the organization's commitment to it, and, in turn, sincerely committed to the organization's progress.

Making Reductions Stick

The same activity-based cost-reduction process serves both for-profit and nonprofit enterprises. In both forms of organization, there is generally little enthusiasm on the part of most managers for controlling or reducing expenses; cost cutting is not a process most managers find satisfying, even in a profit-making organization, where reducing expenses should increase profitability and presumably the baseline for managerial bonuses. I have found that managers reflexively regard cutting their staff as making them more vulnerable. Moreover, despite the fanfare attached to the initiation of the process by the CEO, if, once specific proposals for cuts have been made to him or her, no one comes around to see whether the proposed actions are taken or to tie the unit executive's incentive compensation to the accomplishment of the proffered savings, the whole process will come to naught. As revenues rise again, everyone forgets about eliminating activities that generate little or no added value.

Accordingly, regardless of the process adopted for cutting expenditures, certain principles must be followed if cost reduction is to be effective:

- The organization's top executive must establish a specific dollar level of reduction.

- A system must be established to monitor whether promised cost-saving actions are in fact taken.

- Because an organization will invariably capture fewer than all promised expense reductions, the target established for savings must be higher than necessary to achieve the desired financial goal.

- Organizational unit heads must be held accountable by the CEO for achieving the savings target established for their unit.

- Future proposals to add to expenditures must be separately flagged in the unit's budget submission and must be subject to the value-added test that was applied during the cost-reduction process.

This discussion of activity-based cost reduction covered the basic ways in which an organization can be restructured and retain its independent status. The object is to avoid "expense creep," whereby the expenditure level set during a period of financial stringency is unknowingly allowed to creep back to pre-reduction or even higher levels. The idea is to put the executive spotlight on any proposed increases from the baseline of expenditures produced as a result of the cost-reduction program.

19

The Role of Public Relations

The story appeared on page three of the *Baltimore Sun* under a two-column headline. It was published shortly after the time when a gunman had been shooting innocent residents and related how a number of children in the area were traumatized by fear of being shot. The article included a report how ORT, a network of primary and secondary schools in Israel, provided professional counseling to the students suffering from trauma caused by living in the midst of a war in which children were not immune to the violence. For ORT the story was a way of reaching the paper's readership with a positive image of the organization.

The story was the product of careful planning and the work of professionals in the United States and Israel. Guided by a professional public relations (PR) firm, a representative was hired in Israel to look for stories that might have appeal to the readers of U.S. newspapers. The hiring of a representative in Israel became necessary when it was apparent that school leaders and even ORT's organizational staff had no feel whatsoever for stories that might interest the U.S. press about the work of ORT. The representative in Israel worked from a list of subjects previously identified by the firm's headquarters as types of stories that would both interest U.S. media and convey the picture of the organization that it wanted to get across to readers of the major U.S. media. The established Jewish publications were a secondary target because the idea behind the program was to broaden awareness of ORT in the U.S. in cities where the organization was active at some level. The public relations firm is a specialist in placement—getting stories about its clients in the media, especially the media targeted because their coverage would be respected by a broad audience. These specialists spent time cultivating media representatives so that when they wanted something published, they would not be making a cold approach. The lead time from when the story was identified to be targeted and its appearance in a respected U.S. newspaper was several months. It was the first time ORT had turned to a professional public relations firm instead of relying on its in-house staff, which lacked the experience or contacts to mount a campaign targeting major U.S. media.

Tough budgetary decisions had to be made in reallocating funds from the traditional public relations efforts to the new campaign. Funds also had to be allocated to produce reprints of articles that appeared in the mainstream press for distribution to other outlets and posting on the organization's web site.

The word "campaign" is apt because getting the coverage in the targeted media was going to have to be a long-term effort. One success, such as the *Baltimore Sun* piece, would not create meaningful impact—stories have to be placed several times in target areas to build awareness. Efforts to increase awareness also can be reinforced by having experts in a subject within the scope of the organization's work speak at various forums. In ORT's case, the expertise is located in the countries where the schools are located and so money had to be found to bring the experts to the United States to speak in several of the cities where the media campaign was underway. ORT learned, not surprisingly, that the most effective representatives of the organization were the students attending its schools.

Several U.S. tours of students were arranged and students met with prospective donors, sometimes one-on-one and sometimes at forums arranged by local chapters. Fundraising typically rose in areas in which students appeared. The lesson here: the closer a speaker is to the organization's program, the more actually a participant, the more effective their appearance is likely to be.

In building awareness through public relations, one has to build awareness of the image or nature of the appeal the organization is trying to create for itself. The old adage "I don't care if they use my name in the newspaper as long as they spell it right" no longer applies. Rather, an organization needs to define its appeal and identify the groups who potentially would respond to it. The story about trauma treatment of Israeli children served not only to create sympathy for children, but also to portray ORT as employing modern practices and to present its story at a time when violence against innocents was in the public mind.

In defining its appeal, the organization has to adopt as sharp a definition as is practical. The one thing an organization does not want is to attempt to stand for too many things. One of the functions of PR is to carve out a clear-cut niche for the organization that the public can easily grasp. Carving out such a niche is indeed important to all of the organization's activities, not just public relations.

Recent political campaigns have underscored the importance of staying on message. The lessons learned in political campaigns apply as well to organizational efforts to build awareness. The image of the organization that is put forth must be consistently communicated by all departments.

One of the special roles of PR is "feedback"; learning how various publics— contributors, program recipients, government officials, etc.—perceive the organization, especially its effectiveness in fulfilling its mission at a cost that compares favorably with the work of comparable organizations. Here "candor" is a watchword. It's to be expected that some critics will hold unfavorable views of the organization or some of its programs. These negative views should be brought to the attention of senior management in unvarnished form.

Beyond this, it is the task of public relations to present a full and candid picture of the organization and its activities, and to set a standard of open communication that the staff should adhere to. In a word, public relations has to champion transparency; that is what the times demand.

Because a PR program should express the heart of the organization's appeal to various publics, it is important that the executive director be ultimately responsible for the program and, consistent with this responsibility, become familiar with all aspects of the PR program.

An organization may adopt an ambitious program with many of the same features as the ORT campaign. However, an ambitious public relations program is costly, especially to sustain it over the years, and thus is something that many organizations cannot afford. However, a small organization with limited resources can still apply the principles of a larger effort to its own program.

There is a communications revolution underway that demands public relations campaigns decide upon the most effective media for reaching different audiences. For instance, instead of lengthy letters by the executive director to the board of directors, periodic brief e-mail or text messages to board members may gain more attention. The organization's web site has to be designed to get the organization's message across quickly and then make it easy for users to find the information about the organization that they're looking for. And where the work of the organization develops information of broad interest, that too should be accessible by visitors to the web site. Indeed, one means of building an identity is to become known as a prime source of information about a certain field. The web site can also offer opportunities for the organization and its supporters to exchange views electronically.

One end result of a successful public relations effort is to reach different audiences with a basic message. However, a solid PR program will also help the organization think more clearly about its market niche and what it needs to do to strengthen its appeal. In this way, public relations is an important element in the formulation of organizational strategy.

20

A Marketing Approach to Fundraising

One of the most important challenges to the leadership of nonprofit businesses today is to find innovative ways of expanding revenues. As the introductory chapter pointed out, all exempt organizations, other than endowed foundations, are competing for funds in the face of declining government support and the expectation that private giving will not increase much, at least in the near term. This situation makes the task of raising money more formidable than ever.

A successful solicitation of funds from public and private sources of financial support requires a marketing approach. The foundations of such an approach are 1) careful research and planning by expert, highly motivated professionals to identify the specific needs and interests of financial providers, and 2) a solicitation program that communicates how the organization's specific objectives meet those interests.

This chapter looks at effective ways of raising funds from government, individuals, foundations, and corporations. Chapter 21 encourages nonprofits to examine their potential for earning income through their activities.

The Sesame Street Funding War

In 1973, Casper Weinberger, President Richard Nixon's head of the Bureau of the Budget, sought to cut the Department of Health, Education, and Welfare's (HEW) recommended fiscal year 1974 budget for funding the children's television programs *Sesame Street* and *The Electric Company*. He wanted to slash the show's funding from $9 million to $6 million. It was unclear at the time why these sums, which formed a relatively insignificant part of the federal budget, would draw the attention of anyone in the Bureau of the Budget or why any federal official would want to go after the funding for two of the most popular and acclaimed educational television programs for children in America.

It was particularly unlikely that Casper Weinberger would have done so. He was an astute politician who moved quietly and smoothly along the corridors of executive power, wielding his influence skillfully. He was also a political realist and not in the habit of stirring up publicly visible conflicts that would cast him in a poor light; miscalculation was not part of his style and certainly not useful to a man such as Weinberger, who had clear ambitions to attain even higher positions in the government.

The Bureau of the Budget's proposed reduction in the *Sesame Street/Electric Company* appropriation was eventually defeated by Congress. Children's Television Workshop (CTW) had so many friends on Capitol Hill that Congress overrode the Weinberger cut. However, within a few months after CTW won the battle of the budget with Weinberger, HEW announced that it would audit CTW. In retrospect, it seems obvious that forces within the HEW bureaucracy were intent on getting CTW out of the budget. At issue was the fact that the series were funded by the agency's tiny Office of Technology and consumed a good part of that office's small budget.

As soon as the audit was announced, CTW realized that it needed to reinforce its position with Congress. After CTW had conducted intense lobbying on the Hill, under David Britt's shrewd direction, the House and Senate reports for fiscal year 1975 contained a statement of expectation as to the level of funding to be provided for *Sesame Street* and *The Electric Company*. This event turned out, however, to be merely a temporary advance for CTW in the funding war, not a decisive victory.

One of the special qualities of the permanent government bureaucracy is its ability to pursue an objective over a very long time and despite persistent setbacks. If one avenue is closed off, the bureaucracy will find other routes to pursue its aim. CTW learned this in its 1978 contract negotiations with the Office of Technology. These negotiations, in the byzantine fashion of federal funding, actually related to the reimbursement of CTW for money it had advanced to produce shows that had already been broadcast.

The federal government's fiscal year ends on September 30. Any funds not legally obligated to be spent by this date are lost to the funding agency and revert to the Treasury. By mid-September of 1978, CTW still could not obtain a draft of the fiscal year 1978 contract to reimburse CTW for its funding of *Sesame Street*. Persistent inquiries to the Office of Technology drew the evasive response "We're working on it." Then, on September 19, Representative L.H. Fountain of North Carolina dispatched to HEW Secretary Joseph Califano a letter alleging malfeasance in the use of federal funds by CTW over a long period of time. The letter also questioned the propriety of providing further government funding for *Sesame Street* when, in the representative's view, the series was financially self-sufficient as a result of the revenues it derived from the merchandising of *Sesame Street* products. (The series was not self-sufficient financially if one took into account the administrative costs associated with the show as well as its direct production costs.) In addition, the letter claimed that HEW auditors had taken exception to "financial transactions totaling hundreds of thousands—perhaps millions—of dollars." In fact, the audit had challenged $310,000 in CTW expenditures as not eligible under the terms of the federal grant, but no malfeasance was alleged. Moreover, at the time of the Fountain letter, HEW auditors had not responded to CTW's sharp rebuttal. Eventually, the dispute was settled for $171,000. Since the audit report had not been released publicly, it was obvious that its contents had been leaked, undoubtedly in exaggerated form, to Fountain's staff.

Indeed, it was evident that certain HEW staff members had plotted the whole carefully timed scenario. Fountain admitted to Representative Lindy Boggs, one of the numerous friends of *Sesame Street* on the Hill, that he was not at all familiar with the contents of the letter. He had no animosity toward *Sesame Street*; coming from tobacco-growing country, he was after Secretary Califano because of the latter's antismoking campaign.

CTW mounted a fierce counterattack, knowing it had fewer than 10 days to get a signed contract, or the funding would be lost. The Workshop roused its friends in Congress and in Jimmy Carter's White House, and it pressed its case with two high-level executives in HEW with whom it had prior relationships, Califano's chief deputy and his executive secretary. In addition, CTW tapped public broadcasting representatives in Fountain's home state as well as community groups that it worked with in North Carolina as part of its ongoing national effort to encourage children of low-income families to view the program.

Once again, CTW won a pitched political battle to preserve *Sesame Street* funding. Califano gave the go-ahead, and the contract was signed a few hours before midnight on September 30. However, as a notice to CTW that the war was still not over, in December of 1978, the allegations in the Fountain letter were published by Washington columnist Jack Anderson, who ignored CTW's rebuttal.

After the dust had settled on the fiscal year 1978 contract, Fred Bohen, Califano's executive secretary, took me aside and said, "Look, you won this one but you had everything going for you. Next time you are not likely to have so many friends in the right place."

"You are implying, Fred, that there will be a next time?"

"More than implying," he responded. "The technicians in the bowels of this place don't like *Sesame Street*. They don't get any public credit for the show—that all goes to their bosses—and they are tired of having so much of their budget locked up in one show. Sooner or later they will get you."

I recognized that Bohen was describing the reality of CTW's situation with HEW, so I proposed that the agency phase out our funding over a four-year period, which would give us ample time to adjust to the loss of government support for the show. Bohen liked the idea, and in due course an agreement was reached. Over the next four years, our funding was phased out in a smooth transition without further incident.

The ultimate loss of federal funding by an enterprise with all the political clout and public stature of *Sesame Street* shows the dangers of relying on institutional support, whether from the government, a private foundation, or a corporation. Institutions have a way of changing their agendas. Unless an exempt organization has diversified its sources of revenue, it is very vulnerable to such shifts.

Assessing the Potential to Raise Money

The starting point in any effort to raise funds from any source is to recognize that funding sources are typically inundated with appeals for support, and that getting their attention takes skilled planning and execution.

In fact, such a profusion of messages is unleashed on the public today that it is hard for any single enterprise to be heard. A torrent of advertisements for commercial products and services, campaigns for political candidates and issues, and appeals for worthy causes flood the communication channels. To be noticed at all, one has to create a sharply differentiated and powerfully delivered message.

A marketing approach to fundraising will be premised on a realistic assessment of the potential of the organization to raise money. Past efforts of the organization, results achieved by comparable organizations, and sounding out of prospects will inform the judgment as to how successful a campaign is going to be. Fundraising goals will not be defined solely by the cost of the programs the organization wishes to conduct. Rather, program aspirations must be tempered by a realistic assessment of the market potential for raising support.

Fundraising, whether directed at individuals or at institutions, must also be seen as involving an exchange: value is given by a donor in exchange for value received from the fundraising organization. For instance, government agencies look to advance programs that further their political interests; foundations seek organizations that implement their objectives; businesses give research grants because university-based researchers can often do the work less expensively than the company's own staff; corporations want to advance their public relations goals or even get help with sales promotions; and private donors tend to seek enhancement of their self-esteem.

While not every gift involves such motives, an organization seeking money has to think about—*and carefully research*—what will motivate a funding source to contribute, as well as the right time and place to make the pitch. As Philip Kotler writes in *Marketing for Nonprofit Organizations*, "Donations should not be viewed as a transfer but as a *transaction*."[1]

Positioning Your Appeal

A marketing approach begins, then, with a conscious calculation of an organization's potential appeal to various possible fund providers ("market segmentation"). This analysis will seek to identify a particular segment of fund providers to whom the organization may have a stronger appeal than those of other fund seekers. The single most important decision in devising a marketing campaign is this positioning.

Edward L. Nash asserts in his book *Direct Marketing: Strategy, Planning, Execution*:

> The essence of strategic product planning requires . . . a commitment about what your product or service is and how you want it perceived. You can't have it be all things to all people. It can be the best or the cheapest, traditional or innovative, entertaining or educational. To try to be everything at once is to be nothing.[2]

To position an organization in the fundraising market, then, a careful definition of the organization's appeal is required. Often, the organization's internal description of its services has to be recast in broader, more basic terms to appeal to potential contributors. For example, the American Film Institute's campaign to preserve old film negatives from physical deterioration is presented to potential donors as a program to preserve an essential element of America's cultural heritage.

Communicating Your Appeal

In a well-conceived marketing effort, careful research is conducted into the motives that prompt funding sources to give, as well as their stated criteria for gifts. The form and content of appeals is then tailored to the interests and nature of specific funding targets. In every case, the form and manner in which the appeal is communicated to the donor are as crucial as the content of the message.

For instance, if alumni loyalty to a school is seen as the primary motivator of giving, an educational institution will organize a system whereby selected alumni raise funds from their peers. In other words, an alumnus or alumna of each class (i.e., a class agent) is appointed to conduct a mail solicitation of funds from classmates. This effort is backed up by phone calls from the agent and other volunteer alumni or, occasionally, by current students. Cultivation of very wealthy alumni for major gifts is handled by personal visits from university officers, generally the president.

Nonprofit institutions without a core of loyal supporters may solicit funds from targeted segments of the public by using volunteer door-to-door canvassers; this method usually requires publicity in order to succeed. Appeals may also be cast in the form of invitations to expensive theater benefits or dinners honoring a well-known figure, both of which require a reliable list of upscale potential ticket buyers in order to attain their goals.

If the best potential fund providers are foundations or government agencies, a skillfully written grant application is usually required. But carefully planned personal contact with officials is also important in helping the nonprofit organization to become familiar with the funding source's interests as well as its criteria and process for making awards.

Coordination and Diversification

The fundraising effort should be centrally coordinated in order to avoid solicitation of the same potential donor by more than one department. An attempt should also be made to diversify the sources of support so that an organization is not beholden to one or even a handful of powerful benefactors. Wherever possible, vulnerability to the inevitable volatility of government and foundation funding should be minimized by the solicitation of private support. Indeed, a prudent nonprofit institution that obtains foundation or government support will anticipate from the outset that such aid will be phased out someday and will plan for alternative sources of funds.

Market Feedback

A marketing approach to fundraising is a two-way system. It involves planning and formulating the institution's appeal for funds to potential donors, but it is also an important source of information as to how well the institution's product is being received in the marketplace and to changes in that marketplace. A marketing network thus serves as an intelligence system.

Tom Peters and Robert Waterman, Jr. pointed out in their *In Search of Excellence*:

> Excellent companies are better listeners. They get a benefit from market closeness that for us was truly unexpected, that is, until you think about it. Most of their real innovation comes from the market.[3]

In sum, marketing is a deliberate and conceptual approach to raising funds; it is a disciplined managerial process involving analysis, planning, and execution. It is an *assertive* process; it sees a nonprofit organization as *earning* the support it receives by conferring important benefits on funding sources rather than simply appealing to the goodwill of benefactors. The four major sources of funding are government, foundations, corporations, and individuals. Each of these sources can be regarded as a separate donor market with its own special characteristics and requirements.

Government: A Special Relationship in Jeopardy

In today's economy, it is a way of life for private organizations, whether for-profit or not-for-profit, to seek contracts from the government. Exempt organizations are providers of social goods, and government is by far the largest purchaser of such goods. The government is thus a natural partner for many nonprofit institutions in their efforts to carry out their social missions.

Indeed, for some nonprofit activities or projects, there is no alternative except to seek government support. The scale or nature of a particular project, for example, may dictate government funding as the only available resource. For example, take the case of a research project like Princeton University's Plasma Physics Laboratory, where the practical payoff, if any, in harnessing hydrogen fusion to provide energy won't come until more than 30 years after the start of the project. The annual cost of this basic research is close to $100 million. Industry won't pick up the tab. The only realistic source is the federal government.

Historically, the government has been perceived as a natural ally of nonprofit organizations, not only funding many of them but also sharing their concerns and policy agendas. The advice of nonprofit leaders and professionals was regularly sought by government agencies and legislative committees in dealing with issues and in the design of new programs.

Fundamentally, the special rapport between the government and nonprofit sectors may fracture, and changing political agendas can provoke a more generalized negative attitude toward nonprofits on the part of government. Government regulations in various areas can be applied to nonprofits with increasing vigor, adding significantly to the organization's expenses. Nonprofits are going to have to work both "harder" and "smarter" than ever before to maintain their traditional special relationship with the government sector.

The following discussion refers not to maintaining the special relationship between the government and nonprofit sectors but to the ordinary day-to-day hazards of seeking government support.

Government Funding: Special Costs and Risks

As the "*Sesame Street* Funding War" illustrated, the continued availability of any form of government support is inherently uncertain as political priorities change over time.

Another drawback of government funding is the frequent need to obtain funds from a variety of government agencies with conflicting program priorities and requirements in order to raise enough money to support a single program. A classic illustration of this is the way public broadcasting is funded by the federal government. The Corporation for Public Broadcasting (CPB), the government institution charged with channeling funds to public television stations and helping them to develop programs, has nowhere near the amount of funds required to finance programming for the system. The stations, even with their own efforts to tap public support, must marshal additional sources of funding in order to pay for programming.

In contrast, the commercial television networks in the country provide "one-stop shopping" for program producers: if a network wants a program, it can and will pay the costs of its development. (Commercial television budgets are traditionally much larger than those in public broadcasting.) The result is that producers for public television must not only sell a show to the stations, but they must work very hard to find some combination of government agencies and private corporations willing to help fund the program. This kind of search is not only frustrating and expensive to conduct, but, even when it is successful, it often involves trying to balance the conflicting goals of the various funders, shaping and twisting a concept to please diverse interests. The wonder of the public broadcasting system is that somehow so many quality programs are produced in spite of it.

The difficulties and costs of raising public money for television are by no means unique; rather, the cited problems plague a wide range of social efforts dependent on government support.

Success in obtaining government money also poses its problems. There are subtle and not-so-subtle dangers in living on government funding. Government funding poses the following risks:

- Distortion of the institution's true interests to conform to government objectives.

- The creation of "have" (government-funded) and "have-not" (non-government-funded) departments in the same organization.

- The establishment of a special class of personnel whose only connection to the institution is their work on a government contract. For instance, for many years the Plasma Physics Lab at Princeton University, with more than 200 employees, had only two university departmental faculty members associated with the project. The vast bulk of lab employees became a special class of employees who sought salary arrangements different from those of other university employees, creating all kinds of problems and tensions.

- Detailed, far-ranging government audits that threaten the heart of an institution's freedom and are expensive to respond to, even if the organization can eventually refute all claims. For example, the 1974 audit by the Department of Health, Education, and Welfare (HEW) of Children's Television Workshop's *Sesame Street* series recommended government review of CTW executive compensation policies even though no salaries higher than $30,000 a year were charged to the government grant. The 1974 audit also recommended greater reuse of show segments to reduce costs, which constituted government influence on programming decisions. In the same audit, HEW staff members also recommended that CTW submit to competitive bidding the segments of the *Sesame Street* series performed by the famous Muppet characters Big Bird, Ernie, and Burt! To government auditors, these marvelous and unique puppets were as replaceable as nuts and bolts.

- The imposition of requirements that are unrelated to the substance of the funded project but further the funding sources' collateral aims. For instance, HEW required CTW to caption *Sesame Street* for the deaf, at a cost to CTW of $150,000.

- Voluminous reporting and review requirements that absorb so much of a nonprofit organization's time and energy as to distract it from its main tasks.

The frustration of dealing with a stream of red tape is often compounded by the efforts of many bureaucracies to cloak their staffs in anonymity, precluding grant recipients from identifying the individuals who are responsible for adverse actions.

The moral here is not that government funding inevitably poses unacceptable risks, but rather that government funding is not for the unwary and unsophisticated. A nonprofit's management must therefore assess the extent to which the operation of an institution is vulnerable to the reduction or cutoff of the flow of government funds. In particular, it should examine in advance whether a potential reduction or cutoff would affect:

- Core programs;

- Critical, hard-to-replace personnel; or

- Indirect costs that have been allocated to government projects and that can not be eliminated even if funding is lost.

If it is at all possible, such program commitments and costs should be funded, at least in part, with nongovernmental money so as to minimize the damage that would occur to an institution if its government funding were curtailed.

Building an Organization to Seek Government Funds

An entity that must regularly approach government sources for significant support needs a professional staff with experience in dealing with public agencies. This staff should process applications for funds; coordinate different departments' search for funding; maintain contacts with officials of key funding agencies, and with the legislators who play decisive roles in controlling such agencies' funding or overseeing their operations; ensure compliance with government regulations; and stay abreast of shifting government priorities and interests. Where necessary, the staff must also learn how to pierce a bureaucracy's veil of anonymity and find ways of making the agency more responsive. A nonprofit organization must be as professional in seeking government funding as large corporations are in raising capital from Wall Street.

In particular, the staff must master the nature of the government appropriation process. An understanding of the process—and the key players in it—is required in order to support the efforts of a friendly executive department or set of legislators in securing funding from the legislature, and to plan for when the actual funds are going to be available. The risk of delay in getting funds from the government has to be taken into account in planning the cash flow of an organization.

Nonprofit institutions playing the government funding game must be prepared, on occasion, to mount a political campaign to protect their interests. In order to be able to mount such a campaign, an organization has to develop over a period of time a political base it can call on. It has to cultivate relationships with the legislature and within the executive branch, as well as with public constituencies, in order to be able to bring them into play when necessary. The 1970s saw a move in the U.S. House of Representatives to eliminate or curtail the tax deduction for charitable contributions. In the end, the movement was defeated—not by presenting neatly argued position papers (although these were prepared) or by lobbying members of Congress on the bill (although this was done), but by developing grassroots support for the deduction in every representative's home district. The organizers of this effort received their highest accolade when one member of Congress told them, "You guys are as tough as the unions!"

Foundation Grants

There are some 90,000 foundations in this country, but foundation resources and activity are concentrated in a small percentage of the nation's total foundations. The 2009 edition of *The Foundation Directory*, published by the Foundation Center, lists 10,000 foundations that account for approximately $588 billion in assets, or 86 percent of all the assets of active grantmaking foundations in the United States. These foundations made a total of almost $40 billion in grants.[4]

Foundations vary widely not only in size but also in character and in operating style. A good number of foundations are family foundations set up by a wealthy individual to support activities that are especially meaningful to the donor. Such foundations are typically administered by family members or legal counsel. At the other extreme are the professional foundations that support a wide range of activities according to priorities set by their boards of trustees; these foundations are administered by full-time professional staffs.

Corporations sometimes organize foundations to give away up to 5 percent of adjusted net income, the contribution of which they are allowed to deduct against corporate taxes. Some corporate foundations are administered casually on a part-time basis by a member of the corporate staff, or in some cases by a full-time staff member specially hired for the purpose. In addition to the foundations that make grants to others, there are operating foundations, which use their resources to conduct their own research or to provide a direct service. (Obviously, this type of foundation is of little interest to an organization seeking funds for its own programs.

Many people assume that foundations are interested in any good work they hear about. In fact, almost all foundations of any size now have very well-defined program objectives; certainly this is the case for professionally staffed organizations.

Historically, foundations have not liked to provide general institutional support; they prefer to back specific new programs that would not be undertaken but for the foundation's help, and that mesh with the institution's defined program objectives. Most foundations are hesitant to make grants for endowment or for buildings. They prefer to fund operational programs. Today, some foundations are championing general support and longer-range funding as strategic practices.[5]

Foundations like to make grants that they are convinced will have an "impact," by which they mean inducing others to emulate the program they have financed. They also tend to favor "leveraging" their funds, by which they mean attracting others to contribute to the financing of the program in which they invest.

As one might expect, the degree of precision with which foundations express their objectives varies widely from institution to institution. For instance, three foundations may all be similarly concerned with helping higher education, but one will announce its goals as "aiding higher education," another as "helping colleges and universities deal with their management and financial problems," and a third as "improving instructional methodology and content, especially projects that cross traditional lines between disciplines." Without specifically inquiring of each foundation, it would be impossible to tell from a simple reading of these statements whether they would all support similar specific programs or have very different aims in mind.

To illuminate how a foundation's program goals can shape its grantmaking, let me review how one foundation developed its program. Lloyd Morrisett, head of the Markle Foundation, explained to me in an interview the rationale he had presented to his trustees in 1969 that led to the redirection of the foundation's program from support of medical school professionals to communications. In our conversation, Morrisett recalled having recommended that the foundation center its efforts on communications because:

1. The communications industry was an area of great importance but had been largely ignored by philanthropic institutions. The Ford Foundation was active in supporting public broadcasting, but the entire terrain of commercial broadcasting was largely unexplored.

2. Even a small foundation like Markle could have an impact since the target audience, senior officials in the fields of publishing and broadcast communications, was quite small, numbering perhaps no more than 10,000. The number of people and institutions one had to influence was thus relatively small in comparison to, say, the number of people involved with public schools in this country. Lloyd was convinced that the principal reason for the failure of the foundation project is "undercapitalization financially or intellectually." Thus, finding a universe small enough for Markle to fund adequately with its budget was critical.

3. Government regulation of broadcasting as well as of copyrights, and the Supreme Court's interest in First Amendment issues, would inevitably raise significant public policy issues. Such issues represent an area where it is relatively feasible for a foundation to fund useful efforts. Moreover, the scope of such issues is more readily definable in broadcasting than in such broad fields as education.

4. Morrisett's own experience before coming to Markle indicated that broadcasting was a good field in which to leverage funds. As a vice president at the Carnegie Corporation, he had initiated the idea of creating Children's Television Workshop and had spearheaded the assembling of a consortium of foundations and the federal Office of Education in order to provide $8 million to launch the workshop in 1969.

5. The people skills needed for grantmaking in communications involve an analytic orientation; an understanding of economic, social, and legal issues; and an appreciation of the impact of public policy on an industry. These skills are general enough for many people to acquire them relatively quickly, especially in comparison to a specialized area such as, say, pediatric endocrinology.

6. The timing was right. If a foundation's efforts are to succeed, there has to be a receptivity in the larger public, as well as in important institutions, to the foundation's aims. The resources that even the largest foundation can marshal will not have an impact unless the climate is hospitable. As an example, Morrisett cited Children's Television Workshop's initiation of the *Sesame Street* programs in 1969

as a case of "perfect timing." The public was focused on preschool education, and potential friends of such a program were in the right places in government and foundations.

Many foundations, once they have identified an area of general interest, such as communications, will develop a set of more specific objectives. For instance, they may try to foster more effective "children's educational programming" and "informational" programming within the field of communications. Under Morrisett, however, Markle resisted this approach. In Morrisett's view, "If an area is important, I'm not sure I would place many limits on decisions to grant support in the field ... beyond the limits of imagination and available resources."[6]

Many foundations today have as clearly articulated a rationale for their choice of program interests as Markle did back then. Accordingly, a nonprofit's focus in seeking a foundation grant has to be on matching an organization's program goals with those of a specific foundation.

Since even the most narrowly focused descriptions of foundation interests are likely to be somewhat elastic, a fund-seeking organization should go beyond published descriptions and study what types of grant awards a foundation has in fact made. The foundation's annual report is a good source for this information.

Even with this research, informal contact with the foundations an organization thinks offer potential will save time in the long run. A good application takes effort to prepare; if filed blindly, it may sit for weeks at a foundation that has no interest in it. A phone call, even in a case where no one in the organization knows an official at the foundation, can produce helpful hints as to whether a particular activity is likely to be of interest. A brief letter may elicit enough information to preclude the preparation of a full-blown application that is of no interest to a foundation.

If a preliminary inquiry is encouraging, try to arrange a visit to talk with a foundation official before filing a formal application. Find out what the foundation's internal process is for awarding grants and what criteria it applies in making awards. Learn the timing of its funding cycle and try to ascertain what kinds of things really interest the staff member who will review the grant proposal.

For example, would it help to invite the person to visit your organization? Is there something compelling you could show a foundation representative that would give life and power to what could otherwise be dry words on paper? Is the staff member interested only in the content of an organization's program, or is the overall quality of its management, especially its financial administration, also crucial? Can you distinguish your program in some fashion from those of your competitors? What kind of demonstration might show the officials that a grant will have impact beyond the boundaries of your organization? Is leveraging funds important to this particular foundation?

Finally, nonprofit organizations, if they can afford to, should cultivate potentially supportive foundations on a regular basis, not just when they want to put in a grant proposal. Larger institutions, such as major private universities, will typically assign a development staff officer (an "account executive") to make regular calls on a list of target foundations, partly to keep up contacts and partly to learn of new directions or interests developing at the foundation. The account executive sometimes arranges for a senior officer of the university or a distinguished faculty member to accompany him or her to talk about some aspect of the university, not necessarily one for which funding will be sought.

The point is that success at grantseeking has less to do with the altruism of an organization's aims than the skill with which it identifies a foundation with matching interests and then cultivates this interest.

Corporate Support

Many corporations provide support for charitable activities, as the federal tax code permits such businesses to deduct up to 5 percent of their adjusted gross income for gifts to charities. Some corporations, as I noted earlier, organize their charitable activities in the form of a foundation; some operate quite informally. But some programs of nonprofit organizations may also be funded out of a corporation's regular operating budget, if the programs further a specific business purpose of the company. For instance, the underwriting of a public television series may be charged to the corporation's public relations or advertising budget, while counseling services for chemically dependent employees or job training may be funded by the personnel budget. In considering the potential for corporate support, therefore, nonprofit institutions should begin by analyzing how their program can serve the interests of specific business entities. Initially, in the attempt to narrow the universe of corporations to a prospect list that can be explored in depth, the following criteria may be useful:

1. *Geographic proximity.* Corporations tend to favor supporting nonprofit organizations located in the same geographical area, especially where it can be shown that the service provides some benefits to the corporation's employees (e.g., a local health care facility or cultural activity).

2. *Specific benefit to the corporation.* Corporations will favor supporting a necessary service provided by the nonprofit enterprise directly to a company, such as counseling the corporation's chemically dependent employees. Other services may be attractive to companies because they have a general need for them, although the benefit to the company from any particular nonprofit organization may be only indirect. For example, engineering schools might seek support from companies that hire large numbers of engineers.

3. *Personal relationships with key officials.* Personally knowing someone in the right corporate department, or at least someone senior enough to steer a nonprofit institution to the right person in the corporate structure, is an obvious advantage. Board members of a nonprofit organization, as well as professional staff members, should always review their corporate contacts as part of a fundraising search.

4. *An image fit.* A corporation's advertising and public relations efforts may suggest themes or objectives for which the nonprofit institution's program can provide support. An example is provided in the discussion, later in the chapter, of how Children's Television Workshop gained the support of United Technologies Corporation for a new children's television series.

5. *An existing area of interest.* A corporation may have previously supported similar programs. For example, the Mobil, Exxon, and Atlantic Richfield corporations were known for their interest in underwriting public television series, so a nonprofit entity with a public television project could have considered them as possible prospects. Other companies will be known for their active support of the performing arts, museums, hospitals, and so forth.

These criteria, however, are just a starting point in approaching a corporation for funding. In preparing to approach specific companies, a nonprofit organization must keep in mind that corporate support for nonprofits is prompted by a pragmatic interest in enhancing some aspect of the corporation's goals. Hence, in seeking corporate funds, a nonprofit should be able to explain how supporting its program will in turn further a particular corporate objective.

For example, take United Technologies' $2 million grant in 1979 to Children's Television Workshop to help fund *3-2-1 Contact*, a public television series on science and technology for children between the ages of eight and twelve. At the time, United Technologies was a conglomerate spending substantial sums on trying to build a corporate identity as a leader in the technology field. Its public relations department had just added two executives who had been at Mobil Corporation and had worked on that oil giant's active underwriting of public television series. CTW contacted the UT public relations staff informally to see whether UT might be interested in being the sole corporate sponsor of the show. When UT expressed interest, CTW made a presentation first to the public relations department and eventually to Harry Gray, UT's chief executive officer, and his key aides. In pitching its proposal, CTW was aware that in public television an underwriter of a show receives only a brief oral and visual mention of its name at the end of the show, after the production credits are shown. This exposure is minimal, especially compared to the scope of commercials for the much larger audiences attracted by commercial television. How, then, did CTV induce UT to contribute $2 million to *3-2-1 Contact*?

In all its presentations to UT, Children's Television Workshop stressed that underwriting *3-2-1 Contact* could give UT substantial public relations benefits, provided that it vigorously promoted its association with the show through advertising in newspapers and other mass media. Of course, in order to do this, UT would have to spend a good deal of money on advertising in addition to what it would spend underwriting the show. But such advertising would bring wide attention to UT's underwriting, regardless of how many viewers actually watched the series on public television and noticed the brief underwriting credit at the end of each show. United Technologies bought CTW's concept.

Just before *3-2-1 Contact* went on the air, United Technologies placed ads in selected major U.S. newspapers and national magazines with the headline, "Will there ever be another show as worthwhile as *Sesame Street*?" That gave United Technologies the double benefit of underwriting a show for children on science and technology and acquiring an association with *Sesame Street*, the most widely known educational children's television show in history.

Tie-in promotions with vendors of commercial products or services are another means of tapping corporations to support nonprofit causes. A tie-in promotion involves a commercial vendor linking its product to a charitable cause.

In business, this is known as "affinity marketing." Long-distance telephone carriers and credit card companies assign a percentage of customers' expenditures to a charity they select. In a twist on the routine, a phone company might assign 1 percent of its annual sales to 30 nonprofit organizations chosen by its customers in an annual poll. Today more and more businesses are utilizing this technique.

Individual Contributors

The vast majority of funds provided to 501(c)(3) organizations entitled by the IRS to solicit tax-deductible contributions are contributed by individuals rather than by foundations and corporations; over 80 percent of the estimated $308 billion Americans gave to charity in 2008 came from individuals.[7]

Successful fundraising from individuals (including solicitation of gifts from entities they control) is in the first instance a product of an appealing cause, persuasively advocated by senior representatives of the exempt organization who have a gift for donor cultivation and the ability to close a transaction. Like every type of fundraising, it is also very much the result of careful planning and investigation by an expert staff.

Campaigns Aimed at a Cohesive Constituency

Cohesive constituencies consist of individuals who share membership in an institution of civic prestige (e.g., a museum), or in a religious congregation,[8] or have attended the same school, or have shared an experience (e.g., having been treated in the same hospital), or share a special personal affinity with the exempt organization. If a group is large enough, its size may justify the cost of organizing a campaign specifically targeted at the group and capitalizing on group members' affinity with the exempt organization.

However, as the competition for what is at best a slowly growing pool of private contribution dollars intensifies, more and more individual organizations have to consider whether they can raise more money by appealing on their own for contributions or by joining forces in an umbrella campaign by organizations in the same field. Organizations with a very distinctive and sharply defined mission with which their patrons particularly identify can have a special identity—a brand name, if you will. Such organizations, if located in a large enough community, may well find that maintaining their own campaign pays off. Philharmonic orchestras, operas, and ballets in the country's major cities obviously tend to believe they fall into this category.

At the same time, there are individuals who give generally to the performing arts for public relations or other reasons, and there will thus be a substantial number of common contributors to the performing arts. Would a consolidated campaign—with the potential to gain efficiencies in its administration and thus put more dollars into a broader, more visible, and more effective cultivation of donors—yield more net funds for the participating organizations? Such consolidated campaigns are particularly productive when each of the participants is too small to achieve strong name recognition on its own among contributors. The United Way and the United Jewish Communities annual campaigns on behalf of hundreds of smaller agencies are examples of how a consolidated campaign can pay off for smaller entities.

I was engaged in raising funds for such an organization, built around chapters in different cities. This presented challenges in coordinating the efforts of these diverse groups and the national leadership. In particular, the lay leadership in these different cities may differ from the national leadership and consequently have its own agenda and ambitions, and may not readily accept funding goals or the funding message set at the national level. Indeed, the culture of these diverse cities may well differ from each other depending on the attitudes and outlook of the local leadership. There can also be a tension between the national fundraising message, addressing the organization's overall aims and goals, and a local community's focus on how it is perceived within the local community. Fundraising strategies can also differ, with the national organization seeking to raise funds through direct solicitation of contributors and local organizations hosting fundraising events centered on honoring a well-known local figure.

How then to best to manage an organization with both local fundraising chapters and a staff focused on creating a national campaign? One essential step is for the national staff to spend considerable time and energy courting the chapters, seeking to persuade them, to the extent practical, to buy into the goals and strategies set at the national level. The national organization ought to find ways to provide support to the chapters, such as providing materials for events and a flow of information about the work of the organization. It is also important to have representatives of each local chapter who also serve as part of the national leadership and to find occasions to bring together the lay leaders of the local chapters with the national leadership. One effective strategy is to organize missions to the organization's programs, combining local and national leaders in the same trip. One also should seek to have a visible national presence at local events to convey the message and aims of the organization as a whole. Finally, it makes a difference in motivating chapters to raise their sights if the national staff and leadership sets its own ambitious fundraising goals and achieves them.

The Characteristics of a Successful Fundraising Campaign

Certain intangible qualities make for a successful fundraising campaign. I call them the *Ten Fundamentals of Constituency Fundraising*.

1. Dynamic and Well-Informed Leadership is Essential. Before I left for New Orleans and Tulane University in the late summer of 1989 to head, among other duties, Tulane's forthcoming major fundraising campaign, I decided to talk to some people in the East who had been successful at the task. My favorite among those I spoke with was George Hyman, a Wall Street investment banker who was chairman of New York University's highly successful campaign. He had a strong, forceful personality and obviously enjoyed his fundraising role. I still remember his observations on the art of successful fundraising from individuals:

> I love raising money. It's a good cause, and I make people feel good by asking them, because that tells them I think they have accomplished something in this life.

> I never worry about asking for too much; I'm just flattering the prospects by suggesting I think [they are] worth more than they actually are.

> I never call on a prospect unless I know everything about the person—not just what he or she does for a living or his or her probable net worth, but what [the person's] interests are and, in the end, what is likely to motivate [the person] to act.[9]

I didn't quite realize it at the time, but Hyman had captured the essence of a campaign:

• Be proud of the cause you represent and of asking others to contribute to it. It's good work.

- Do meticulous homework not just to identify prospects but to know all that you can about them. This kind of previsit preparation is the key to successful cultivation.

- Know what will motivate prospects to give—for example, access to someone they value but could not meet on their own, a leading faculty scientist or economist; or a chance to offer advice or to have their name on a building. *Do not equate capacity to give with a willingness or readiness to give.*

- Above all, the leaders of the campaign must be well known among the organization's constituency or enjoy a strong reputation with the group. They must come across as personally committed, focused, persuasive, and visibly confident in the success of the cause they represent. Certainly, this was the impression George Hyman conveyed from the moment one entered his presence.

2. Not Every Gift Can Be Accepted. Early in my work at Tulane, I learned another indispensable ingredient to successful fundraising: learning when to say "no" to a gift, hopefully without antagonizing a potential donor.

At Tulane, a leading board member and his wife very much wanted their name on a new building the university was planning. They offered what they considered a substantial gift, but the building's naming was one of the university's best opportunities to raise a very large gift. The offered gift fell short of this standard. Since the largest share of any campaign's contributions comes from a relatively small number of very large gifts, the university could not afford to give away the building name for what, in terms of the campaign's needs, was a modest gift.

Moreover, since this donation would have been one of the campaign's firsts—and by a major figure in the Tulane community—it would have sent the wrong signal. As I learned in studying other university campaigns, if a drive is to start off on the right note, it is critical that the first gifts come from important figures in the community and in amounts that represent a "stretch" on their part. The gifts need not be among the largest of the campaign, but the leaders of the university have to demonstrate that they have gone the extra mile, relative to their own resources, because of the campaign's importance. The goal is to send out a signal to other leaders that this campaign is so important that they are going to be called upon to dig deeper into their pockets than usual.

Since I had been the one to point out within the administration that we could not afford to accept the proposed gift, the president assigned me the task of informing the trustee that his gift had been rejected. The trustee was not at all pleased when I delivered the response, but I went to some pains to explain the logic of the university's position and to stress that the university was very pleased with being offered the gift and would be happy to provide a naming opportunity in a prominent place *within* the building. The prospective donor rejected the alternative, but a few years later he and his wife offered a much larger gift, and the building was named after them.

3. The Majority of Funds Will Be Contributed by a Few Individuals.
Peter Edles, a veteran campaign consultant, makes the following observations in his book *Fundraising: Hands-On Tactics for Nonprofit Groups*:

1. Ten percent of the goal comes from a single gift.

2. Approximately 80 to 90 percent of incoming funds are donated by 10 to 20 percent of the membership or constituency.[10]

A similar picture was painted for us at Tulane by our campaign consultant, Marts & Lundy; the initial Tulane Campaign Plan projected that half of the target $300 million would come from 49 donors who gave a $1 million or more, including one gift that would account for 8 percent of the total and nine gifts that accounted for nearly 30 percent of funds raised. (See Table 20.1 later in the chapter for the complete projection.)

4. The Campaign Must Have a Sense of Urgency.
Fundraising has a way of taking much longer than one expects unless the campaign staff and leadership are driven from the outset by a strong sense of urgency. When one embarks on a multiyear campaign, it is easy to think there is plenty of time to get things done. But time has a funny way of slipping by if the campaign staff and leadership become overly absorbed in internal meetings and don't "get out on the road." My point is simple: you are not going to raise money by talking to each other; the potential donors are "out there," and you have to start the cultivation process as early as possible.

Prospects can also sense the pulse of a campaign. If they get the feeling that the fundraising organization does not believe its needs are urgent, they are not going to be in a hurry to open their wallets. It's hard for an organization to convince prospective donors that it has a compelling cause if it proceeds to make its case at a leisurely pace.

You also never know when some change in external and internal circumstances will upset a well-planned campaign. For example, stock market crashes not only seriously reduce the wealth of some key prospects, they unnerve even people who were not as affected and make them less disposed to part with their personal resources. So, if conditions favor your campaign, don't assume life will always be thus; get going while the circumstances are right.

By the way, in business sales there is nothing like the prospect of getting a sharply reduced bonus because one has fallen behind on one's call schedule to keep a sales force on its toes. I can't see why an incentive system would not similarly motivate the development staff of an exempt organization.

5. Paradoxically, You Can't Rush the Cultivation Process. Even when one is dealing with prospects who have previously made capital gifts and are active in the leadership of the organization, one must be prepared to spend time soliciting their views on the organization. This means listening carefully to them, responding candidly to difficult questions they may raise, taking them into one's confidence to explain the state of the organization and its plans, inviting them to special organizational events, exploring their gift-giving ideas, and offering a range of possible purposes for their gift. It's rare to make a first call on a prospect and have them whip out their checkbook and make the hoped-for gift. Getting a donation from a first-time prospect customarily takes quite some time, just as in business it may take a while to persuade a new customer to buy a product, especially if the product is a new one.

At Tulane, an alumnus who was prominent in the community told me one day about one of the city's wealthiest and most successful entrepreneurs, who was not a graduate of Tulane—or of any university—and whom the city as a whole had largely overlooked. This man wanted help from the university with a small matter: he wanted a hotel belonging to him and located near the campus to be listed by university departments as a place to send guests and hold meetings. The university arranged a luncheon with him, and within a week his hotel was listed as he wished. Shortly thereafter, the hotel's business from university guests improved substantially. My wife and I then spent months getting to know the man and his family (and, indeed, became good friends).

The next step came six months after the initial meeting, when we asked the entrepreneur to help mobilize some of the people in the city's hotel and restaurant business to support the university's effort to become a member of a regional athletic conference. Our friend did this with great enthusiasm. Still later, he was asked to become a member of a new committee just established by the board of trustees to oversee one of the university's new business ventures. At no time during this process was the idea of his making a gift to the university broached; our goal was to get him involved with the university in areas in which he could contribute, so that eventually he might be receptive to the idea of making a significant gift.

6. A Well-Managed Organization Is a Prerequisite. The rules and realities of fundraising closely resemble those of raising capital for a business. A fundraising effort should be premised on the idea that contributors will be more receptive to an organization whose track record shows that the organization is well managed and can project and then deliver *specific* results. Donors, as a rule, go for "winners," not failing organizations. If an organization is newly formed, then its leaders need to have a record of experience and expertise, and they must produce a solid plan for both the management of the organization and its campaign.

Donors also want to be told just how their money is going to be used and what concrete results they can expect to see. Once, the dean of Tulane's business school and the chancellor of the medical school were fighting over whose priority it was to cultivate a prominent and very successful graduate of Tulane's business school. To try to settle the dispute, I visited the donor and asked him whether he wanted to make his major gifts to the medical school or the business school. He replied that he and his family preferred to make their contributions to the medical school to support specific research projects by particular physicians, because they could see the outcome that resulted from their support. The donor was thus designated a medical school prospect, and the school was given a year to demonstrate that it could cultivate him to contribute in line with his means.

7. The Cultivation of Contributors Does Not End When Their Money Comes In. The results of a fundraising campaign should be measurable, and the organization should report to contributors how their money was used and what results were achieved. There is, in fact, no more effective way to stay in touch with contributors and to sustain their loyalty than to report to them regularly on the progress being made with the use of their funds. This kind of communication is particularly effective if it comes from the person or team employing the donor's funds. In the case of major gifts, an appropriate ceremony honoring the donor is in order.

Perhaps most important of all is the organization head's readiness to spend time with a major giver *after* the gift is in hand. The president of a private research university and his wife, for example, spend a long weekend every year visiting the home of the university's largest benefactor, and they regularly accompanied another significant benefactor on a trip. Both of these occasions provided an opportunity for easy conversation about the university and other topics. Note that the subject of further giving by the donor is never raised on these occasions.

8. Keep Broadening the Prospect Base. It is risky to keep mining the same limited group of donors for large gifts. Some major donors are not financially able to keep giving on the same scale; others may develop new interests for their charitable giving (since the odds are that many of your major donors are being wooed by other organizations). Some may hold back until they see others step forward, not wanting to be looked to for yet another leadership gift. Indeed, at Tulane, one of the largest donors to the capital campaign told us that he wanted to see if the university could find others who could give in the way that he had because, unless we did, the university could not expect to increase significantly the amount it raised. Finding new major prospects has to be a top priority of the precampaign planning, and especially of the research staff.

9. A Customer-Focused Culture is Key. It is a formidable management challenge to educate personnel to rethink the way they view their jobs and the people to whom they should direct most of their energy. To do so amounts to changing the organization's culture. But this is precisely the challenge that leaders of many nonprofit organizations must meet if they want to increase the funds they raise from private contributors. Nonprofit employees, like their counterparts in many business organizations, are typically absorbed in accomplishing the tasks assigned to them by their immediate supervisors, and in their supervisors' reaction to their work. After all, it is those supervisors who determine employees' raises and promotions.

Even within development staffs, it is not unusual for employees to focus on gaining exposure to senior officers of the organizations, particularly the head of the organization, rather than on cultivating prospective contributors. Following the familiar routine of pushing papers and attending internal meetings on fundraising issues is less demanding than leaving one's home terrain and addressing the concerns—and attracting the interests—of potential prospects.

A fundraising staff that is too internally focused is the result of an organizational ethos that confers status according to how often one meets with the president or his or her chief deputies, as if one were working in a government bureau where the perception that a person has access to higher-ranking officers is itself a source of power. Such organizations are *bureaucratic* in character.

Changing this kind of culture requires a revamping of both the financial and psychological compensation system so that cultivation of prospects is rewarded. In addition to changing the reward system, senior management—starting at the top—must promulgate for each organizational unit a very clear set of objectives. One universal objective should be that developing the goodwill of prospective donors is part of everyone's job. New values have to be established through clear and consistent communication.

Within every organization, there are numerous opportunities to get across messages as to what the basic values of the organization are. I can remember Bill Bowen, as president of Princeton, emphasizing at every opportunity—in large meetings and in personal conversations—his conviction that a commitment to excellence in every phase of university activity was to be Princeton's hallmark. No one could fail to be aware of the standard of performance expected of them by Bowen.

Part of bringing about a change in an organization's culture is making all employees aware of what is involved in cultivating prospects. Effective cultivation involves more than a call on a prospect; it relates to all the dimensions of potential interaction between an institution and a prospect. It certainly includes getting out fast, accurate, and thoughtful responses to routine inquiries by prospects, as well as listening carefully to issues raised by a prospect and treating the prospect as someone with ideas as well as money to contribute. The countless daily interactions between an organization's staff and prospective supporters need to reflect the priority to be given to these supporters. Nothing infuriates a donor or prospect more than a curt or inaccurate response to an inquiry about the status of his or her past gifts, particularly if the response reveals that the staff has not kept accurate records of how much a donor has contributed, or how much of such a contribution has actually been used for the purpose for which the funds were raised. An employee who, rather than providing an explanation, reacts as if the donor's question were intrusive, can obviously have a negative effect.

Cultivation of donors ideally takes place separately in time and place from the actual campaign. As an undergraduate at Princeton, for four years I heard over and over again how important alumni were. Days were set aside to bring the alumni back to the campus in a visible and prominent way, to honor many of them, and to express appreciation for their financial support. To top it off, before graduation, the senior class raised money for a class gift to the university. In marketing terms, the university took advantage of the four-year period during which it had potential future givers as a captive audience, and it drove home its message, albeit in a positive and not heavy-handed way. Princeton today has one of the highest percentages of alumni who contribute to the university. In contrast, Tulane made virtually no effort to convey to its undergraduates the importance of the role that alumni could play in the life of the university after graduation, or to communicate the expectation that alumni should give of their resources to the university. Tulane's percentage of alumni contributors was much lower than that of Princeton and a good many other schools.

It is also very important for the organization's head officer to model the behavior he or she expects of others; word about what is important to the president travels quickly through an office network. If the president never leaves the office, this fact is noted. But the organization will also notice if the president or executive director devotes a substantial amount of time to seeing prospects and listening carefully to the comments of people outside the organization, and shows, by his or her personal priorities, that cultivation matters.

10. A Campaign Never Ends. Labeling a fundraising effort a "campaign" is typically associated with an organization's attempt to raise money for specific projects, programs, and facilities, as distinct from gifts that are not restricted in their use. Both capital or purpose-specific gifts and unrestricted gifts should be part of an organization's fundraising strategy. To heighten interest in capital or purpose-specific gifts, a numeric goal for such giving is announced and a deadline for raising such funds set. The program thus becomes a campaign. But if an organization is able to raise capital gifts, it should do so on a continuing basis, whether or not the effort is publicly labeled a campaign. The staff and resources required to raise the targeted funds should be maintained, and not disbanded simply because the public phase of the effort is over.

The Importance of Planning

To these ten fundamentals of fundraising, one more essential ingredient should be added: *careful planning*. Such planning entails a meticulous process covering a series of steps that build up to actually asking prospects for money.

Before solicitation of donors begins, the following elements must be in place:

1. A carefully crafted *strategic plan* specifying concrete objectives and a year-to-year projection of the amount and type of giving required to implement the plan.

2. A carefully *researched projection* of the level of funds the organization can expect to raise that relates to the cash flow assumptions of the strategic plan.

3. A *specific plan* for raising the targeted amount, including campaign strategies, themes, and organization.

4. A *table of needs* listing specific needs and assigning a target amount to be raised for each need.

5. A well-trained, well-organized, and *highly motivated* team—including an expert research staff—to conduct the campaign.

6. A campaign *leadership group* made up of board members and other prominent people with strong ties to the organization.

Let's break down these elements in more detail.

Balancing Strategic Plan Objectives with Donor Preferences. The strategic plan should identify the basic priorities of the organization and provide a year-by-year forecast of the amount and types of funds to be raised. Often, projections of funds to be raised do not differentiate between gifts that match basic priorities and those that will not; the forecast is done as one overall figure. The plan, however, should project the level of giving that will be consistent with the organization's needs as well as the amount of giving that will fall outside of its priorities because of donor preferences. In the end, a balance has to be struck between strategic plan objectives and the types of funding it is feasible to raise. For instance, Tulane University's strategic plan gave top priority to a very limited number of objectives; it was understood that convincing grantmakers, corporations, and individual donors to shift their contributions to one of the university's priorities would not be easy or always successful. But the university believed it worthwhile to emphasize its priorities with prospects.

A donor's ideas for a project may be far more grandiose than an organization's. This conflict may represent a difference not only in philosophies, but also in perceptions of what the organization can afford. For example, a museum may envision only a modest improvement of its building, whereas key donors may want to create an entire new complex. Such a complex not only will cost more to maintain over the years but will require a far larger expansion of the curatorial staff and acquisitions budget than the museum's plans call for. Since potential conflicts cannot always be anticipated, a mechanism has to be established to resolve such issues when they arise.

Arriving at a Researched Projection of How Much Funding Can Be Raised. The organization's lists of needs cannot by itself determine the expectations of the campaign. A number of research techniques need to be employed to come up with a reasoned estimate of the amount and types of funding that can be raised, year by year.

Among the available means of developing a forecast are:

1. *An examination of past campaigns.* Certain rules of thumb can be applied to project the growth in giving that can be expected compared to past efforts; however, one needs to be aware of relevant changes in circumstances relating to the organization or the fundraising environment. It is especially important to determine whether the major contributors to past campaigns can be expected to match or even exceed their past level of contribution. Informal conversations with such contributors or people who know them well can be helpful here.

2. *An examination of the amounts organizations in the same field have raised in the past and/or are planning to raise in the future.* For example, if the state cancer society has in the past raised twice as much money as the state heart association, then the heart association ought to look at the cancer society's campaign tactics to see if better execution could improve the heart association's fundraising. An examination of the cancer society's past campaigns may show that the campaign results are distorted by one or two unusually large gifts and that thus the cancer society's fundraising record does not provide a fair basis for setting expectations for the heart association's campaign.

3. *A demographic comparison of the organization's constituency with that of another exempt organization.* A market research firm can undertake such a comparison and, basing income projections on zip code analysis, draw a comparison of the fundraising potential of the two organizations.

Tulane employed Marts & Lundy to do such an analysis. Interestingly, the analysis showed that Tulane's constituency had more giving potential than those of a number of competitive schools that, in fact, raised more funds.

4. *A screening and rating program* in which the organization's fundraisers talk to people in each community to get their opinion of the giving potential of people they know in the community.

5. *Focus-group interviews* in which a carefully selected cross section of the organization's constituency in a community is interviewed by a professional experienced in conducting such research. The object of such focus-group work is not to pinpoint fundraising targets, but to learn more about the attitudes and outlooks of the individuals the campaign will approach, in order to develop appropriate campaign tactics and themes.

At Tulane, I resisted the idea of commissioning a feasibility study, over the objections of the development staff and against the advice of our outside consultant. Such a study employs a consultant to interview actual prospects in order to develop a sense of the level of giving an organization can expect and the issues it needs to address in the campaign. The use of feasibility studies assumes that prospects will be more candid with a third party than with an organization's executives and staff. This may well be true. However, in Tulane's case, I did not want our prime prospects to be approached until the university had had time to organize and disseminate to this select group the university's strategic plan and its message for the campaign. We knew that prospects' enthusiasm for what would be a challenging effort had to be developed over time.

Moreover, the university was in regular contact with its major givers; the president was meticulous about staying in touch and was very well informed about donors' attitudes. I concluded that a feasibility study, although a staple of most campaign planning, was not going to provide enough insights to justify the cost in this instance. Whether I was right or wrong in this particular case can be debated; my point is that an organization needs to make a careful cost-benefit analysis of all proposed expenditures, regardless of how customary those expenditures may be in campaigns.

All these forms of inquiry should provide the basis for preparing a gift range table. This table shows: 1) an estimate of the number and sizes of gifts to be solicited in various ranges (e.g., $1–5 million, $250–500 thousand), and the number of gifts in each range that are projected to be raised; and 2) the number of prospects that, based on past experience or the experience of other organizations, typically have to be solicited in order to obtain the targeted number of gifts in each range. Table 20.1 is an example of a gift range table from the Tulane University Campaign Plan.

Table 20.1. Gift Range Table from Tulane University Campaign Plan							
Range	Prospects	Cumulative Prospects	Expected	Donors*	Average Gift*	Total Dollars*	Cumulative Dollars
$25 million	3	3	1	$25,000	$25,000	$25,000	8%
$10–25 million	6	9	2	12,500	25,000	50,000	8%
$5–10 million	18	27	6	6,667	40,000	90,000	13%
$1–5 million	120	147	40	1,500	60,000	150,000	20%
Subtotal	147		49		150,000		50%
$500,000–$1 million	90	237	30	667	20,000	170,000	7%
$250,000–$500,000	195	432	65	308	20,000	190,000	7%
$100,000–$250,000	450	882	150	187	28,000	218,000	9%
Subtotal	735		245		68,000		23%
$50,000–$100,000	750	1,632	250	60	15,000	233,000	5%
$25,000–$50,000	1,500	3,132	500	30	15,000	248,000	5%
$10,000–$25,000	2,240	5,532	800	13	10,000	258,000	3%
Subtotal	4,650		1,500		40,000		13%
$10,000	many	many			30,000	288,000	10%
Rec'd Bequests					12,000	$300,000	4%
Grand Total					$300,000		100%

*Dollars in thousands.
Because of rounding, percentages may not add up to totals.

Outlining a Campaign Plan. The campaign plan has to deal with a series of elements:

1. The organization and functions of the fundraising staff.

2. A gift table projecting the number of gifts of specified sizes that must be raised and the number of prospects the organization is likely to have to approach in order to raise such funds (see Table 20.1).

3. The role of the board of trustees in the campaign and the identity of the trustees, or others closely associated with the organization, who are going to form the campaign leadership committee. This committee

oversees the management of the campaign by the staff, sets major policies governing the campaign, and resolves conflicts or issues that arise during the campaign. Customarily, members of this committee share in the work of cultivating major gift prospects.

4. The essential steps in the campaign and principal tactics to be employed:

   a) *When to label a fundraising program a "campaign."* The term "campaign" can be misleading to the extent it that implies a one-time effort; exempt organizations, as a rule, raise money every year. Some of their efforts may be directed toward raising grants from foundations and government, and gifts from individuals, that are unrestricted in the purpose for which they may be used. This unrestricted giving—generally termed "annual giving"—tends to be broad-based in the number of contributors, and to be made up of smaller gifts than capital gifts. Annual giving money is very valuable because the organization is not restricted to using the funds for specific purposes, giving it flexibility in deploying the money. Annual grantseeking and unrestricted giving efforts are typically supplemented by an effort to raise "capital gifts"—gifts raised for a specific purpose, program, or project of an organization as set forth in the table of needs (described later in this chapter). In essence, annual giving and capital giving are different modes of appealing to donors. The term "campaign" is often used to refer to both, but in this text the terms "campaign" and "capital campaign" refer to a program to raise gifts for a designated purpose. Paradoxically, such an effort is sometimes conducted without publicly labeling the effort a campaign—at least for a time. Or the label may be applied only as a device to build interest among potential donors of capital gifts. Whether and when to apply publicly the label "campaign" is thus a tactical choice.

   b) *The character of the campaign buildup.* No institution simply announces one day to its constituency that it would like to launch a capital campaign. First, the groundwork has to be laid to motivate the constituency to support the campaign once it is announced. Precampaign programs usually include communication with the constituency as to where the institution stands with regard to programming and finances, and why it is considering a capital campaign. When I began my tenure at Tulane, for example, a systematic effort to build ongoing ties between alumni and the university was little more than a decade old, and in many cases alumni's memories were linked to the city of New Orleans, rather than to the university. In fact, for many years, alumni who came back to visit the university did not visit the campus, but returned to the New Orleans haunts they had enjoyed as students. Only in the 1980s did the university recognize the importance of alumni reunions and begin to stage campus programs, built around faculty and outstanding graduates, to attract alumni back to the campus.

We recognized that in these circumstances alumni, especially those living outside Louisiana who had lost touch with Tulane, had to have their affinity with the university rekindled. Many such alumni had little current information about the university and were unaware of the significant progress the university had made in the last decade in gaining stature among American universities. Furthermore, many of these alumni had graduated before the school began seeking significant support from alumni, and thus most alumni could not be approached to contribute to a capital campaign without some prior education. This situation also explained why, in the 1980s, only slightly more than 20 percent of the alumni provided financial support to the university, a far lower figure than those reported by the universities that Tulane regarded as its competitors for students, faculty, grants, and other forms of support.

To deal with this situation, the university launched a *multifaceted "identity" campaign* to reach out to "lost" alumni and bring them up to date on the "new" Tulane. This effort included a series of presentations about the strategic plan to audiences across the country; improved alumni education programs on campus and in cities around the country;[11] mailings (to 15,000 alumni identified as the best prospects) of both a specially edited, colorful version of the strategic plan and a series of letters from the president about various university issues; a redesign of Tulane's alumni magazine, which was mailed to all alumni, to make it visually and editorially more appealing; and invitation of small groups of special prospects to the campus for a weekend.

c) *The nucleus campaign.* This is the part of the capital gift campaign that is conducted before any formal announcement is made that a campaign is underway. The object is to approach the prospects who are expected to make the leadership gifts and see how much money can be raised from this prime prospect list. Here leadership by the full board in making gifts is very important. As a rule of thumb, an institution can expect to raise about three times the amount raised in the nucleus effort. Sometimes the nucleus campaign goes so well that the ultimate campaign target is raised; conversely, the target may be scaled back if the nucleus gifts do not meet expectations. Ultimately, the size and character of the total campaign are determined by the success of the nucleus campaign.

The University of Pennsylvania campaign is worth examining for a moment because it illustrates the importance of setting the campaign target at a level consistent with the image of the university that its leaders wish to convey. Sheldon Hackney, who was president of Penn throughout the campaign, made this point in a conversation: in his view, the university was on the upswing in terms of its perceived stature at the time the campaign was being planned, and it was important psychologically to set a campaign goal that was in line with the level of funds raised by the nation's best universities. Since Stanford University had just successfully raised $1 billion, Hackney believed that Penn could seek to do no less. All the preplanning research and conventional analysis indicated that this level was very ambitious and that $800,000,000 was a more prudent goal. But when alumnus Saul Steinberg kicked in a $25 million gift during the nucleus phase, other major gifts followed, and the goal was set at $1 billion over five years. In the end, the university raised $1.4 billion as alumni, pleased with the growing recognition of their alma mater's stature, got behind the fund campaign.

d) *Integrity and campaign counting policies.* Like many entities involved in sales efforts, exempt organizations sometimes inflate the results of their capital campaigns to encourage further giving and to build organizational morale. But the last thing any organization should do is kid its own management and board; indeed, I would argue that exaggerating results to any constituency will prove a mistake in the long run, for sooner or later the truth will come out and the entity's credibility will be damaged. At a time when misleading figures have been supplied to publications that rate colleges, charities need to sharpen the accuracy of their reporting, whether to their own leadership, to the Internal Revenue Service and state authorities, or to the public. Thus, policies governing how contributions to the campaign will be counted must be set at the outset.

In the case of an entity that raises capital gifts every year, which year is designated as the first year of the campaign? Do pledges of future contributions, which are not always honored, get counted? (Counting them is a bad idea because the institution, in setting its budget, has to know what money can be expended.) Is there any justification for including money that is to be left to the organization as a bequest at a (still living) donor's death? (Since a will can be revised at any time, the answer is no.) What value should be placed on a gift of real property or art transferred in kind?

The answers to these and similar questions must be decided in light of the obligation of nonprofits to assume leadership in accounting for their performance and integrity in their reporting to various constituencies.

e) *Preparation of campaign themes and materials.* The principal themes of a campaign are usually embodied in the *case statement.* The themes provide the overriding rationale for the campaign, in contrast to the appeal of specific projects listed in the table of needs. A case statement is an externally focused document and has to be shaped to elicit a positive response from the audience to whom it is addressed—the potential contributors to the campaign. Seeking funds to enable an already successful organization to reach a new level of excellence is a familiar theme; another is enabling an organization to expand its program to a broader audience or to enter allied fields. An example of a potentially less appealing cause was Yale University's plea—among other things— for money to restore campus buildings that it had for years neglected to maintain properly. Focus-group research can be helpful in determining what kind of case statement is going to have the strongest appeal to an organization's constituency. A capital campaign requires all kinds of multimedia presentations; a decision should be made as to how much the campaign can afford to spend on these and which ones to produce. Work should then begin on their preparation and, to the extent feasible, the presentations should have a common visual identity as a way of reinforcing the message that a campaign is in progress.

f) *Campaign budget.* Regardless of whether an organization is engaged in a campaign or a noncampaign, a fundraising budget must be established that is affordable and, ideally, that is in line with corresponding expenditures by similar institutions that have successful fundraising programs. A study made in the late 1980s by the Association of Governing Boards of Colleges and Universities showed that member institutions, on average, spend 21.8 percent of total dollars raised on running the campaign. More relevant, of course, are the fundraising expenditures of the institutions that Tulane regarded as its competitors: Tulane found that its expenditures trailed those of its competitors who were more successful in raising funds. The old maxim "You have to spend money to make money" does apply to fundraising.

Some organizations make the mistake of cutting back on their fundraising and staff expenditures as soon as the public campaign goal has been met, only to find that the flow of capital gifts then drops well below the level the organization continues to require. The raising of gifts for special programs, projects, and other identifiable objectives of an organization should be a continuous process, whether or not it is publicly labeled a capital campaign. The level of funds sought may vary from year to year depending on the general environment, constituencies' ability to provide such gifts, and the organization's needs, but there is no inherent reason why seeking capital gifts—those targeted for specific purposes—should cease once a publicly announced campaign has reached its target.

g) *Campaign procedures and organization.* Procedures have to be established to deal with a variety of issues that will arise during the campaign. For example, in a multidivisional organization, in the case of a prospect whom more than one division wishes to pursue, which unit gets first crack at the prospect, and for how long a time period does it have the exclusive "right" to pursue the prospect before releasing him or her to another unit? If a gift falls outside the table of needs, should the organization accept it? If strings are attached to a gift by a donor, are the conditions acceptable to the organization? If early courtship of a prospect by development staff members or divisional officers yields promising results, when should the president of the organization or a trustee be called in to meet with the prospect? It is also important to compare the campaign's progress regularly with projections, and to share information about which approaches and themes are proving to be effective or ineffective and what problems or criticisms fund solicitors are encountering from prospects. It is essential that the key people in the campaign meet regularly to review its progress, as well as the policy issues that arise, and that a clear line of decision making be established. Ambiguity as to who can decide what can prove as deadly in fundraising as in other managerial functions.

Creating a Table of Needs. A table of needs is a summary of all the purposes for which funding is being sought. The list of needs can be limited to the organization's strategic plan priorities or, to inject an element of flexibility into the campaign, it can go beyond the parameters of the strategic plan. Obviously, the more appealing the list of projects is to donor interests, the more funds the organization can expect to raise. Since it is impossible to define every potential donor's specific interests in advance, providing a diversified list of needs can help draw in the broadest range of contributors.

At the same time, an organization cannot simply let donor interests determine its programs; hence the bulk of the projects for which funds are sought ought to be consistent with the organization's priorities. In essence, then, a table of needs is a well-crafted list of specific funding needs, weighted in favor of the organization's highest priorities but including some projects that investigation or experience shows donors like.

Still, it is likely that some donor will want to support a project that is not included in the list. The donor's interests should not be rejected out of hand; they may make good sense and have been overlooked in the planning process, or they may be relevant as a result of a change in the organization's circumstances since the list was drawn up. Also, it may be possible to negotiate with the donor to frame the terms of the gift so that the donor is satisfied but the funds can be applied in a way that the organization's leadership believes will serve the institution's interests. But in the end the purpose for which the funds are offered may be so far off base, or the terms on which they are offered may so directly violate the organization's principles (e.g., allowing a donor to select, or have a voice in the selection of, a school's faculty) that the organization has to refuse the gift.

Organizing and Training an Expert Staff. In the early days of systematic fundraising, many institutions showed a tendency to staff the fundraising unit—or development group, as it is now called—with employees who were not productive in other departments or, in the case of schools, alumni who were not progressing well outside the academy. It quickly became evident, however, that fundraising was a professional business, requiring experienced and expert staff. Over the years, as development has become recognized as a professional occupation, the number of competent development officers has substantially increased, although most administrators of exempt organizations would still agree the pool of talent is not as deep as they would like. The situation will change as exempt organizations continue to emphasize that they want their development office personnel to have the training and experience needed for the level of responsibility assigned to them, and to be paid accordingly.

Fundraising has become too important to be left to "good old alums" or one of the organization's not-quite-so-talented executives; it requires the most expert personnel that can be found. In some organizations there is little difference between the salaries of the executive director and the chief fundraiser. Organizations are now looking in new places for development expertise. Princeton University turned to a business executive, and the

University of Pennsylvania chose as head of its capital campaign Rick Nahm, who had been a very successful fundraiser at a small Kentucky school, Center College. Nahm turned out to be as able and well-organized a campaign head as I ever encountered on the college scene. Now, having waged a campaign that exceeded its ambitious goal, he has moved on to become president of Knox College in Ohio.

In fact, as mentioned earlier in Chapter 8, exempt organizations should give serious consideration to establishing a form of incentive compensation for development staffs. Virtually every sales force in the business world is compensated based on individual productivity. Why won't the equivalent staff in a nonprofit setting respond to similar incentives? In the university world, I've heard the counter-argument that deans who raise money for their programs don't get bonuses, so why should the development staff? There are two answers to this argument. First, deans do in fact receive salary increases if they are successful in raising a good deal of money for their programs. Second, a dean's goal is to improve the overall quality of a program, and raising money is only part of what is required to achieve that objective. In contrast, raising money is a development staff's only task, and experience shows that most people in this line of work perform more effectively when their productivity is financially rewarded.

I've also heard the counter-argument that donors will not want to see part of their gift going to the person who cultivated them. Maybe so, but in fact, part of every campaign's receipts goes to pay the expenses of the campaign. This means that the real challenge is to convince donors that the overall expenses of the campaign are reasonable, not to debate how much of funds raised are assigned to paying incentive compensation to the most productive members of the development staff.

If exempt organizations want the quality of people who enter development work as a career to continue to improve, then they need to adopt reasonable incentive formulas.

One other innovation in the organization of a development staff is critically important: building an expert research group. Increasingly, well-organized development units have a research staff, but the practice is by no means universal yet. The basic function of a research staff is twofold:

- To identify prime prospects from a wide range of data sources. This information may uncover potential donors already known to the organization, but whose wealth has recently increased as a result of business success or an inheritance. Research may also turn up altogether new prospects whom the organization has lost touch with or is simply unaware of.

- To develop a profile of such prime prospects that helps the fundraiser successfully solicit their help. The anecdote earlier in this chapter about the preparation undertaken by George Hyman, the chairman of a New York University campaign, shows how useful a well-crafted donor profile can be.

In addition, a research unit, if staffed to do so, can conduct useful research into the funding potential of the organization and the themes that the organization needs to stress in order to motivate its constituency. These services can also be purchased from consultants, and so the costs and benefits of insourcing and outsourcing such work have to be evaluated. However, at the least, the research unit should be aware of what kinds of market research are available and which outside firms are the best providers of such work.

A research staff can also be charged with keeping abreast of tactics employed in other organizations' fundraising campaigns that can be adopted in some form by the organization, as well as of the introduction of new and potentially lucrative gift products by other institutions. This is another form of looking at the "best practices" of other organizations advocated in an earlier chapter. Again, good campaign consulting firms can provide this kind of information, drawing on the knowledge they have gained in working on other campaigns, and so the question of whether to perform this function internally or ask a consultant to undertake it has to be examined. Again, the research unit should at least be able to make informed recommendations as to the best providers of such services.

Another aspect of building a solid development organization is to provide better, more extensive staff training than is customary in many nonprofits, including training that goes beyond the narrow focus of a staff member's current assignment and gives all development staff members a broad understanding of the field. Most development personnel I've worked with know what they know only from their previous work experience. Priority should be given to training the development staff in all aspects of fundraising and particularly to acquainting them with modern methods of market research and the legal and tax considerations that affect contributions.

Parts of this training, at least in the area of market research techniques, can be provided through executive programs offered by business schools. Another feasible and cost-effective approach may be to have a school produce and present, under contract, a curriculum tailored to the needs of the organization, or to develop a joint program between organization executives and a business school faculty. Experts from the field or related fields can also be invited to make presentations to the staff. For example, I brought a skilled marketer and banker to wealthy individuals to Tulane to explain to the entire development staff techniques for cultivating prospects, especially ones already converted to customers. One could see the staffers' looks of astonishment as the banker detailed how she had turned out more than 200 personal notes a week to clients and prospects and how she had used all of her activities to expand her network of contacts. Her presentation gave the staff a whole new context in which to think about cultivation. Whatever the formula, educating development staff in its profession and enlarging its skills beyond its particular experience are essential.

Forming a Campaign Leadership Group. Any trustees of an organization have to make a commitment not just to write a check but to involve themselves actively in the running of the campaign. Such trustee presence is necessary to demonstrate the board's commitment to the campaign, to bring to bear the experience of board members in how best to approach their peers, and to enlist trustees to call on certain prospects in situations where they can exert more influence than anyone else (perhaps because a trustee has supported a prospect's charity, or because the two are peers in the business world, or because of the "stretch" gift the trustee has made). Trustees should also contribute the benefit of experiences they may have had in other similar campaigns.

In choosing a leadership committee, one needs to look for the qualities required by the role such a committee is to play: members should have stature in the community and prior experience in fundraising; they should be major contributors in their own right; and they should have a network of personal associations and a knack for persuading others to follow their example. Committee membership need not be confined to board members; others with the right combination of talents and an interest in the campaign who are affiliated with the organization or its cause (e.g., alumni or volunteers) may make excellent committee members. The head of the capital campaign at Princeton during the time I served as vice president of finance was not a board member but an alumnus who had been active in raising funds for the university's annual giving drives. As the result of the fine work he did as campaign chair, he was later made a charter member of the university's board of trustees.

NOTES

1. Philip Kotler, *Marketing for Nonprofit Organizations* (Englewood Cliffs, NJ: Prentice Hall, 1982), p. 427.

2. Edward J. Nash, *Direct Marketing: Strategy, Planning, Execution* (New York; McGraw-Hill, 1982), p. 215.

3. Thomas J. Peters and Robert H. Waterman, Jr., *In Search of Excellence* (New York: Harper & Row, 1982), p. 193.

4. *The Foundation Directory* (New York: The Foundation Center, 1996).

5. See "The Importance of Strategy" on the William and Flora Hewlett web site (hewlettfoundation. org/what-we-re-learning/our-approach-to-philanthropy/hewlett-foundation-president-s-statements)

6. All comments by Lloyd Morrisett are from an interview with the author.

7. *Giving USA 2009*, published by the Giving USA Foundation™.

8. United Jewish Communities in New York is an organization that raises funds for more than one hundred social agencies serving the Jewish population in New York and for various organizations in Israel.

9. George Hyman, interview with the author.

10. Peter Edles, *Fundraising: Hands-On Tactics for Nonprofit Groups* (New York: McGraw-Hill, 1993), p. 11.

11. Many colleges have found strong alumni interest in presentations by outstanding faculty on professional topics or other areas of interest to adults. Some schools have even held weekend sessions on professional subjects or "alumni colleges" on themes of general interest. All organizations should think about how the areas in which they are expert can be communicated to adults in such a way that listeners feel they are learning something, not being asked for money.

21

Generating Earned Income

The first book I wrote, back in 1986, was titled *Managing For Profit in the Nonprofit World*. The title was inspired by my experience at Children's Television Workshop (CTW), producers of the *Sesame Street* television series. The Workshop, building on the success of the television program, deliberately set out to make a "profit" by licensing the *Sesame Street* name and characters to makers of books, records, toys, and other products for children. The goal was to invest such "profits" in the production of *Sesame Street* and other educational programs of the Workshop with a view to reducing the show's production costs and the Workshop's dependence on foundation and government grants. The licensing program has proved to be very successful— what you would expect given the power of the *Sesame Street* name and appeal of its characters. And when one day the federal government stopped funding the show, the Workshop could absorb the cutback because of its stream of earnings from licensing.[1] Diversification of funding sources is thus a prime motive for pursuing earned income opportunities.

The Workshop is not the only nonprofit to be successful at generating earned income. The Roundabout Theatre moved from near bankruptcy to being one of the leading producers of plays on Broadway, complete with its own theaters. In part, its ability to pull itself up from rock bottom was a function of the appeal of the shows it produced, some of which were aimed at audiences seeking popular commercial productions with the potential to generate profits. Todd Haimes, the company's artistic director, who guided it to its present success, was quoted in an interview in the *New York Times* that, "I have no problem producing something that I think is popular or commercial to make money, as long as the money goes to the not-for-profit purpose."[2]

The income earned by a public charity from business endeavors may or may not be subject to tax.[3] If the business is considered to further the mission of the nonprofit organization, it is deemed related income and is exempt from income taxation. If the business is considered unrelated it is subject to an unrelated business income tax (UBIT), unless the income is in the form of a passive royalty, dividends, or rents, in which case it is also exempt from taxation.[4]

The Need for New Revenue Sources

Consideration of how to cope with rapidly increasing costs is driving many nonprofit organizations to consider a range of options for building revenues. An aggressive and professional fundraising effort makes sense for organizations in a position to undertake one. But not all nonprofit institutions have a constituency that can provide significant financial support. Moreover, more than a few nonprofit institutions have mounted imaginative and aggressive fund drives only to find they still were not able to offset their rapidly escalating expenses. Cyclical or extraordinary inflations and recessions create a difficult climate for raising increased sums from contributors.

Generating income is not inherently alien to nonprofit organizations. Museums operate gift shops; universities, museums, and other institutions invest endowment funds in the securities markets; other nonprofits publish information to earn income; etc. But, historically, this income is seen as a byproduct of the organization's efforts, rather than as the result of a deliberate focus on how the organization can market its services.

The "bottom line" here is that there may well be opportunities for organizations to generate earned income that they have overlooked. Many nonprofit entities do not consider this revenue-generating option, thinking it impossible or inappropriate, and for some it is not a feasible strategy. But a good number have been successful at developing new sources of earned income.

The operating style and values of business and nonprofits are not *necessarily* diametrically opposed systems; there is a way to merge the very best practices of both the for-profit and nonprofit worlds. Such a model may very well become more widespread in the future. The bottom-line discipline and "time is of the essence" drive of business to make a profit can combine with the nonprofits' passionate commitment to its purpose, and its socially alert values. The result can be a highly motivated and sharply focused enterprise driving hard to achieve its objectives, with full awareness of its mission and the social consequences of its operations. In addition, the sophisticated management techniques, technology, and unforgiving discipline of business will lead to a more advanced, efficient operating methodology for nonprofits. In turn, the mission-driven focus and values of nonprofits will motivate businesses to systematically assess the social consequences of their actions. This is not to say that our best businesses and nonprofits do not already exhibit these qualities, but many do not. Converting them to this hybrid model may be blue-sky thinking, but it is a goal worthy of pursuit and, increasingly, many people are doing just that.[5]

Opportunities for Earned Income

Creating a successful stream of earned income is a challenging task for many nonprofits. Few have the power of the *Sesame Street* brand name or the commercial opportunities of a New York City theater company. Nevertheless, there are opportunities if the goal of generating such income is approached systematically. Before looking into specific opportunities, there should be an internal analysis of: 1) an organization's special strengths; 2) the size and character of its membership base (for membership organizations) or base of contributors; 3) the appeal of its brand name (one may have to consult people in the business of promoting brand names, hopefully on a *pro bono* basis); and 4) whether the organization's management team has the experience and expertise to develop such income or whether the organization needs to obtain help from a consulting firm, at least to start up the activity, or to hire a full-time professional to exploit the opportunities. Children's Television Workshop found that to build a successful licensing program it needed to hire on a full-time basis an executive with substantial experience in licensing, especially for the category of products the Workshop would be marketing.

There are a number of factors that will increase the likelihood that an earned income venture will be successful:

- Compelling business opportunity
- Compatibility with mission
- Knowledge of or research into the market
- Strong, savvy entrepreneurial team

- Solid business plan

- Strong support by the board and CEO

- Adequate financing

Since even the best-laid plans may not work out, it is wise to establish limits to the resources and time the nonprofit will devote to generating earned income, and to devise an exit strategy should the organization wish to withdraw from a venture. At the very least, the potential advantages of having a stream of earned income warrant organizations taking a careful look at the possibilities.

Starting Point: Part of the Value Scheme

How does a nonprofit organization, long dependent on the charity of others, set about finding ways to make money on its own? The starting point is the organization's system of values and its attitudes toward itself and its customers.

An organization that incorporates financial independence into its central value scheme will seek systematically and aggressively to identify and develop opportunities for revenue diversification. An organization that falls prey to the psychology of dependence will miss opportunities to improve its financial future.

There are at least four categories of opportunities that should be examined.

NEW MARKETS FOR TRADITIONAL SERVICES

While the primary focus of this chapter is on ways and means of earning income from commercial activities, more aggressive marketing of traditional services to new clients is no less important a way of earning new revenues. New income may be generated by finding new customers for an organization's traditional services. For example, community mental health organizations can offer corporate employee assistance programs that utilize their staff health counselors. Public television enterprises can extend their work to the audiences that use new multimedia communications technologies. A university may offer programs of interest to adults well past the college age, especially retirees looking for stimulation. A university with a strong nonprofit program may offer advisory services or training programs to nonprofit organizations. (Baruch's School of Public Affairs has been quite successful in creating such programs.)

A decline in undergraduate enrollments (when the country produces fewer 18-year-olds) may be offset by the appetite of older adults for education or by offering distance learning. The University of Phoenix has been cited as an exemplar of this approach. Many universities also have realized that their scientific and engineering discoveries have commercial potential and have initiated programs to capitalize on this potential. (These programs, however, have not been free from concerns over faculty conflicts of interest and disputes between university and faculty over ownership rights.)

Sometimes the potential to generate income from the activities a nonprofit already undertakes is overlooked because the organization fails to examine the possibility, being locked into its conception of itself as a charitable enterprise. For example, an organization with 20 years of experience arranging and managing student and adult international exchange programs became pressed to find new funds. Its fees for arranging such programs had been declining and a recession in Japan caused a drop in the number of programs it arranged. Forced to look elsewhere for funds, the organization realized for the first time that it had acquired skills and experience that could be marketed for fee income—namely, the ability to attract students from foreign countries to education and training programs in the United States run by American universities hungry for applicants, and the preparation of business executives (both outbound U.S. executives and inbound foreign executives) to cope in a new culture. The organization had never before thought of marketing the skills and experience it had acquired in its own field to other fields. It had simply overlooked the opportunity to generate new sources of income from its core activities.

COMMERCIAL SALES

Everyone is familiar with clothing that bears a school's logo. Such sales are driven by the appeal of the institution's brand name. Hospitals offer gift shops for visitors seeking to bring something to a patient. Nontraditional sources of income can also be derived from the marketing of products or services related to an organization's principal activities. For example, New York City's Metropolitan Museum of Art nets substantial revenues from its restaurants and from the sale of art reproductions, gift items, greeting cards, and other publications in its shops and bookstores.

LEVERAGING THE BRAND NAME

A number of organizations have found that their name can help sell commercial products or services. For instance, an organization with a broad membership can enter into an arrangement with a commercial provider to market its products with the nonprofit's brand name on everything from health, life, and auto insurance to travel packages. To be successful at this game requires an identifiable constituency of considerable size (since the response rate to any mailing is very low), highly effective materials, and the financial ability to afford the up-front costs of preparing and mailing the materials. The cost of such mailings can be reduced if they can be "stuffed" into a mailing the organization is otherwise undertaking (as credit card companies regularly do).

FURTHER UTILIZATION OF ASSETS

Imaginative use of underutilized assets can be a source of increased revenue. For example, Stanford University, and later Princeton University, saw that their vast campus land holdings were far greater than what they could ever use for educational purposes. Both schools initiated large-scale office park developments on some of their excess acreage, appealing to companies that wanted to be located close to a university's unique resources. These universities have now earned handsome sums from what would otherwise be idle, non-income-producing land. In the same vein, a good number of universities whose campus facilities would normally be idle in the summer now produce added income through summer semesters and the hosting of conferences and other special events, including sports camps for youngsters.

New York City's Museum of Modern Art has demonstrated that an institution may have "underutilized land" even though it appears to take up 100 percent of the land on which it is located. In this case, the museum sold the air rights above its quarter-acre building site to commercial developers for $17 million.7 Other museums, have been creative in selling or developing the air rights above their properties for commercial development. Renting space to commercial tenants may also be feasible for some organization's whose office capacity exceeds their needs, especially where it is feasible to consolidate some of the space occupied by the nonprofit, as some organizations have done successfully.

Invest or License?

In creating a business venture, one of the trade-offs is between licensing and investing capital. There may be a readiness on the part of organizations that have capital to invest in a business opportunity that they have identified. By risking capital, if the business succeeds, it should provide a greater flow of income than if the organization issued a license. Of course, the return should also be more attractive than the return that can be earned by investing in the capital markets. (Otherwise why invest in a business that provides a lesser return than a portfolio of securities?) Advancing capital, however, is a risk; the business could prove to be disappointing or there may be a call for additional capital.

One may exercise greater control of a business enterprise as an owner rather than as a licensor. The degree of control depends on whether one is the sole owner or a part-owner (with a partner well versed in the business, for example) and on the share of the business one owns (e.g., an equal share versus a minority position). A licensor can exercise some degree of control, however. For instance, Children's Television Workshop always insisted on the right to review the quality of the licensed product and banned television advertising before nine at night so it would not be directed at young children.

Developing Marketing Orientation

To find new revenues today, nonprofit enterprises must consciously adopt a "marketing orientation" in the same way they apply this outlook to their traditional means of raising revenues (as described in the prior chapter).[6] Philip Kotler, in his text on nonprofit marketing, characterizes a marketing orientation for nonprofit institutions as "customer centeredness," meaning that the focus of the entire organization is not on developing products or making sales, but on satisfying "customers' changing needs and wants."[7] Indeed, with respect to their entire program, nonprofit organizations need to be in touch with what the marketplace wants, not just their own ideas of what the public ought to want.

Kotler argues that organizations that move toward a marketing orientation take on characteristics vital to their survival, becoming "more responsive, adaptive, and entrepreneurial."[8] The nonprofit organization that consciously seeks to expand its revenues develops, as a business does, a realistic feel for its competitive environment. It recognizes that nonprofit entities compete against each other, not only for paying customers and a share of grants and contributions, but also for public attention and support. Tom Peters and Robert Waterman, Jr., writing in *In Search of Excellence* about profit-making corporations, describe "customer orientation" as a "way of 'tailoring'—a way of finding a particular niche where you are better at something than anybody else."[9]

As I observed in Chapter 12 about carving out a market niche during strategic planning, a nonprofit enterprise needs a sharp sense of what is distinctive or special about the services it offers, its "comparative advantage."

Capitalizing on Comparative Advantage

A comparative advantage is the edge an organization gains by concentrating its activities in those fields in which it has greater expertise than its competitors. Peters and Waterman refer to comparative advantage as "sticking to your knitting." They assert, "Our principal finding is clear and simple. Organizations that do branch out (whether by acquisition or internal diversification) but stick very close to their knitting outperform the others. The most successful of all are those diversified around a single skill...." The authors add that there is overwhelming evidence that successful companies "have strategies of entering only those businesses that build on, draw strength from and enlarge some central strength or competence."[10]

Fears of Commercialism

Efforts by a nonprofit organization to generate revenues from its own activities or programs may run into objections that they are inappropriate. In the public mind, nonprofit institutions are devoted to worthy causes and lose money regularly. Their very existence is perceived as dependent on charity rather than vigorous self-reliance. Earning income is seen by some as incompatible with a charitable posture.

To some extent, this tin-cup image is encouraged by the nonprofit sector itself. Many nonprofit organizations hold to the view that to be businesslike—to seek ways to generate funds internally, to diversify sources of income, to stick to a financial plan—is to succumb to a commercialism incompatible with the pursuit of high artistic, scholarly, or social goals. Contrary to such fears, however, nonprofit institutions have been able to carry on commercial activities in ways that are not incompatible with their basic mission or image. Institutions have successfully imposed high standards of quality, as well as conditions designed to protect their image with consumers, without impeding the financial success of commercial efforts.

However, any effort to persuade a not-for-profit institution to seek revenues from a commercial source, and to do so on a businesslike basis, may run into an unexpressed but strongly felt organizational ambivalence about the appropriateness of entering into the commercial arena. Frequently, nonprofit organizations are staffed with people who, for a whole variety of deeply felt personal reasons, have chosen to work in the not-for-profit world rather than the commercial world. In many ways, they are uncomfortable with the environment and culture of commercial endeavors. It is not unusual for such professionals to be quite self-conscious about establishing that they are different from the people who populate the commercial world. Accordingly, the proposed entry into commercial activities may cut against the grain of deeply held feelings.

Typically, the people who run not-for-profit organizations are unfamiliar with how businesses are run, although this is less so today than in the past. For the most part, nonprofit professionals have concentrated their careers on social issues and have little training or experience in business. This makes them, appropriately enough, wary of becoming involved in such endeavors. Moreover, in seeking to move a nonprofit entity toward a commercial enterprise, one is dealing with what is still a much-debated notion—that not-for-profit organizations can be successful at commercially oriented activities.

Beyond these environmental barriers to commercial activities, there are some genuinely tough policy and operating issues regarding how to mesh nonprofit activities and commercial endeavors within the same organization. These substantive issues are complex and not always susceptible to clear-cut resolution.

Most of the expressed reservations boil down to a fear that the values inherent in pursuing commercial success are at variance with the values underlying a nonprofit social mission. Profit, rather than product or service quality, is seen as the primary objective of the commercial sector. Therefore, in the minds of some, pursuit of commercial gain inevitably means relegating the organization's mission to a lesser place in the scheme of things, or that program quality will be compromised. This line of reasoning is pressed vociferously by institutions that are especially image-conscious, such as colleges and universities, but a good number of businesses are also built upon the delivery of very high-quality products or services. The high end of the market is their niche. Thus, superior quality can be as important to commercial success as it is to the mission of a nonprofit enterprise.

Often masked by the debate over quality is the underlying reluctance of nonprofit personnel to accept, as constraints on their actions, financial limits designed to preserve a profit element. People whose driving motivation is linked to the content of their work, rather than its profitability, may find it difficult to balance profitability and artistry. This is true not only of nonprofit staff but also of artisans in many fields. In their minds, art simply should not have to yield to finances. But the balance between returning a profit and maintaining product quality is one that both nonprofit institutions and profit-making businesses can achieve.

A related reservation is that the pursuit of commercial gain will be carried on in a way that is insensitive to important social and ethical considerations. In particular, very real concerns are often expressed about the use of a nonprofit organization's name to endorse a commercial product. On one hand, such endorsements can present good opportunities to earn income where the organization's name carries weight with consumers. On the other hand, the integrity of the organization can be jeopardized if people perceive that it is lending its name to products that do not measure up to the standard the public associates with the institution, or that it is allowing its name to be inappropriately exploited. Case-by-case determinations are, by and large, the most practical approach to resolving such issues.

For instance, Children's Television Workshop's entry into the licensing of commercial children's products was initially opposed by some because of concern about product quality and fears that "hard-sell" television advertising techniques might be used to pitch products to young children. The Workshop's solution was to insist on stiff quality review by its own staff and to prohibit television advertising of licensed products during hours when young children were watching.

As the CTW experience illustrates, a nonprofit institution's concern for its values can often be made an explicit part of the commercial enterprise, and not necessarily at the cost of profitability. In fact, protecting the organization's image can be important to the success of a commercial venture. For instance, television advertising of CTW's products to preschool and young children might have alienated parents who, after all, are the real market for such products.

Or take the case of Princeton University's development of the Princeton Forrestal Center, the 1,600-acre commercial real estate venture on land adjacent to the school's campus. As part of its development plan, Princeton dedicated significantly more land to the preservation of open space and environmental protection than was required under the then-applicable zoning ordinances for the area. The university adopted stricter standards because of its environmental concerns, but these tougher specifications also enhanced the value of the land dedicated to development. Thus, social commitment and pursuit of profit were by no means incompatible.

Another typical reservation is that profit-making endeavors will lead to a focus on making money rather than on the program of the organization. The corollary to this argument is that commercial activities will bring into the organization a breed of employee who will not share fellow employees' dedication to its mission.

In fact, employees bent on making profits (and reaping the personal rewards of such success) may initially have less understanding of a nonprofit institution's program interests than those hired to administer the program. In some instances this will prove to be the case; in others attitudes may be more a matter of exposure and education than irreversible bias. In any case, the experience of CTW and other nonprofit organizations is that it is possible to find business executives who share the organization's social objectives.

Another frequently raised concern is that commercial success may undercut the willingness of government funding sources and private donors to support a nonprofit enterprise. The argument is advanced that the flow of income from business ventures will make government and charitable support seem unnecessary. The risk of this happening does exist, but there are two countervailing arguments.

First, it is desirable to substitute business income for inherently volatile and uncertain government aid. Second, the fact that a nonprofit organization is earning part of its revenues from commercial endeavors may well encourage private donors, and even government agencies, to think more highly of the organization. At Princeton, much was made of the university's skillful management of its endowment and its successful development of the Princeton Forrestal Center real estate project when cultivating potential alumni donors.

Nevertheless, there is a series of well-taken concerns regarding the competence of nonprofit organizations to participate in commercial endeavors. Typically, the most formidable practical barrier to a nonprofit institution's successful entry into the commercial arena is its inexperience in business ventures. As noted earlier, nonprofit staffers tend not to be trained or experienced in business endeavors, and so they have only a limited sense of how to evaluate commercial opportunities or begin to exploit them. To overcome this deficiency, nonprofit organizations that are neophytes in commercial matters had best turn to board members versed in business and to their contacts for advice and assistance. Professional consultants can also be helpful in examining an organization's potential to generate income from commercial sources.

Once a nonprofit institution is determined to participate in a commercial venture, it can hire staff members experienced in the business, and a good number of organizations have done so successfully. But this type of hiring is not a simple task. Often business personnel fear that working in the nonprofit world will stigmatize them if they later seek employment again in private business. (Fair or not, a good many in the business community see the nonprofit arena as a "soft" world lacking the drive and discipline of the profit-making sector.) At the same time, nonprofit organizations tend to be reluctant to provide the type of compensation, especially incentive compensation, that attracts able business talent.

Of course, seeking to meet the financial expectations of profit-making business executives is not without potential complications for a nonprofit organization (see Chapter 5, "Maxamizing Your Human Resources"). If the compensation offered profit-making personnel engaged in commercial undertakings is higher than that of nonprofit program staff members, there is the potential for internal conflict, especially if the program staffers believe that their efforts are being exploited commercially. Nevertheless, nonprofit institutions can provide, and have provided, compensation arrangements that are reasonably competitive with comparable undertakings in the profit-making world, without tearing their organizations apart.

The potential resentment of higher salaries for commercial personnel can be minimized if the organization carefully examines the compensation offered for comparable positions by business enterprises and also engages in a process of evaluating, from the standpoint of internal equity, the salaries attached to various positions in the organization (again, see Chapter 5, "Maximizing Your Human Resources"). In addition, the organization can tie these higher rewards for commercial staff members, in part at least, to the success of the business venture on which they are working. At the same time, resentment of the compensation paid to profit-making personnel will be lessened if it is made clear to the other staff members that the success of the commercial venture is helping to pay their salaries.

I recall, one summer day at Princeton, being stopped by a faculty member as I walked across the campus. The professor objected strenuously to the prospect of renting the university's otherwise empty facilities to "outsiders" during the summer. I replied, "Well, we don't have to, but the income we will earn this year will support about a dozen junior faculty members." The professor expressed surprise that the rental program meant so much to the university and wished me luck with it.

Finally, there is the danger that a nonprofit will fail to make clear the ground rules under which it operates a profit-making enterprise, the consequence being lack of clarity as to whether the venture's goal is to make a profit or to advance the organization's social mission. But clarity of objectives can be achieved, especially if the commercial venture is sufficiently separated from the nonprofit organization in terms of policies, personnel, and even location.

In sum, to enter the commercial arena, a nonprofit's management must attract and appropriately motivate competent business professionals, balance and clarify its competing social and profit-making interests, and ensure that all employees, whatever their tasks, are sensitive to the organization's crucial values. In this way, able nonprofit institutions can tap existing business opportunities.

Tax Considerations

Engaging in business activities need not jeopardize the exempt status of public charity organizations, although private foundations are not permitted to own more than 20 percent of a business. The tax law does not bar nonprofit enterprises (other than private foundations) from actively engaging in business activities and even earning a profit, provided the profit is used to support the organization's exempt purposes and does not inure to the benefit of private individuals. In general, as long as the generation of income is a means of promoting the organization's social aims rather than an end in itself, it is an appropriate activity for a nonprofit institution.

However, the fact that an organization (other than a private foundation) may freely engage in business activities without jeopardizing its exempt status does not mean that the income from such endeavors will necessarily escape taxation. As the following discussion shows, certain kinds of income earned by nonprofit organizations may be subject to taxation.

Legal Forms of Profit-Making Activities

The structure of the profit-making component of a nonprofit organization can take varied forms: a working group, a division, or a separately incorporated subsidiary, which can be either nonprofit or profit-making in form. Of course, by definition, the separately incorporated profit-making subsidiary will pay corporate income tax on any net profit it earns.

In the case of a group or division organized within the not-for-profit corporation or a nonprofit subsidiary, the excess of the component's revenues over its expenses—that is, its profits—may or may not constitute taxable income. If the revenues are generated by an activity that is *related* to the organization's exempt purpose, they will be exempt. (For example, Children's Television Workshop, producer of *Sesame Street* and other educational television series for children, also publishes an educational magazine for children. Income from this endeavor is tax-exempt.) If the income is generated in a manner that is *unrelated* to the organization's purposes (e.g., if a university owns a factory), the income will be subject to federal income taxes with certain classes of exceptions—generally passive income in the form of dividends, interest, rents, and royalties. This holds true whether the component is organized as a working group within the nonprofit division or as a nonprofit subsidiary.

The determination of whether to classify a profitable activity as unrelated (and therefore subject to federal income taxation) or related (and therefore exempt) should *not* be made solely on the basis of tax regulations. Such determinations rarely involve black-and-white situations. The financial gain from claiming tax exemption needs to be compared with certain intangible benefits of profit-making status. Establishing an activity as profit-making may be very important in setting the tone for the enterprise. Moreover, a nonprofit enterprise that engages in a highly visible commercial endeavor but claims that the income is exempt from taxation can generate criticism from for-profit businesses in the same field.

These risks are much greater if the enterprise is competing with tax-paying business firms. In numerous instances, such firms have complained that they are facing "unfair competition" and have triggered investigations by the Internal Revenue Service or provoked the concern of legislators. Simply put, an exempt organization must consider carefully the real potential for public criticism if it generates significant income from active participation in profit-making enterprises, yet pays no tax at all on such income.

Operational Considerations in Organizing Profit-Making Activities

More aggressive marketing of traditional services to new customers should not, as a rule, present formidable problems for a nonprofit, but the operation of a business enterprise by a nonprofit institution is a complex managerial challenge. In the first place, as noted earlier, it is difficult to attract and appropriately compensate people with the skill and mindset required to run a business enterprise for a nonprofit institution. People who care about making money in their work tend to be drawn to profit-making organizations. Moreover, people who can generate profits want to be rewarded for their success. This means paying them additional compensation over their base salary if they meet their financial goals. The tax law does permit nonprofits to pay incentive compensation if it is reasonable and normal for the position. However, what the IRS may consider "reasonable and normal" may not be enough to attract top-notch business professionals. A way around the problem is to form a for-profit subsidiary.

Perhaps more serious than the problem of staffing, profit-making activities present the subtle but clear risk of confusion of purpose. The cultural values of nonprofit and profit-making enterprises are quite different. Typically, profit maximization is the overriding goal of a business venture. The single-minded clarity of this objective is an important force in guiding business operations; the value structure of nonprofit enterprise is more diffuse. At its center is the nonprofit organization's mission, which is the chief value that attracts personnel to work for the institution and external sources to give it support. The mission also shapes the enterprise's priorities. But financial survival is also important. Thus, a not-for-profit entity is an organization with fundamental duality of purpose—social mission and financial well-being (the latter being, of course, a far more limited objective than the goal of profit maximization that drives profit-making enterprises).

This duality of objective makes it difficult for a nonprofit institution to manage a commercial business well. Simply put, it is not likely to have the clarity of *business* purpose essential to an effective profit-making operation.

For example, assume that an activity, closely related to an organization's main purposes and offering the potential of producing income, fails to turn a profit. Should it be discontinued, or does its social value justify its continuation?

The mere possibility that such an activity may be continued, even though it is running at a loss, can undermine the necessary focus on creating profits. If profit making is not central to an enterprise, then even those working on a profit-making venture may excuse themselves from the pressures of trying to produce a profit. If earning a profit is not the supreme value, then one can be more relaxed about meeting the budgets and timetables that are necessary to produce a profit, but that impinge on the effort to turn out the highest possible quality product. In a nonprofit environment, perfectionism may indeed substitute for a bottom-line orientation.

Accordingly, where both nonprofit and profit-making activities coexist within the same enterprise, there is a strong risk of confusion of objectives and operating style between the two components. This is not to say that nonprofit institutions cannot insulate profit-making activities from those nonprofit values and operating styles considered inimical to the success of a profit-making venture, but special care has to be taken in organizational design to achieve such insulation.

The Princeton Forrestal Center of Princeton University provides a model of a successful profit-making enterprise undertaken by a nonprofit organization; the reasons for its success within a nonprofit environment now, in retrospect, seem fairly apparent. The center was launched in 1973 with twin objectives. They were:

- To convert idle university-owned land into income-producing property with a rate of return at least comparable to that of the successful return earned by the university's endowment; and

- To upgrade the quality of development rapidly taking place in the vicinity of the campus.

It is clear that the center achieved both of these objectives. In fact, the project significantly exceeded its financial goal, and a series of factors may be isolated that account for the success of the center's development.

First, the concept of developing university-owned land commercially was initiated only after exhaustive consideration of various alternatives in a series of wide-ranging discussions with the administration, key faculty members, local community leaders, and the board of trustees.

Second, university officials with pertinent skills teamed up with outside real estate professionals to organize and lead these inquiries. The team did its homework, and its presentations were thoroughly professional.

Third, during the formative stage of the development, a senior university officer close to the president was actively involved in overseeing the development and ensuring that it had the necessary support within the university and the local community. The project was staffed with outside professionals experienced in real estate development, but they were not burdened with the task of winning the ongoing support of the university. That role was played by the senior officer, who was specifically designated by the president to handle the assignment. The senior officer was involved in oversight of the project's management but continued to play his regular institutional role within the life of the university. He served as a knowledgeable champion of the development, dealing with the politics, anxieties, and nonprofit mindset of the university community.

Fourth, the president fully comprehended the financial and institutional risks involved in the development. He understood particularly the pressures such risks might create for him (e.g., external or internal complaints about the concept of the venture or its manner of execution).

Fifth, the day-to-day development work was carried out by the cadre of professionals from the commercial real estate world. They not only provided the needed skills but also established a profit-oriented environment for the project's management.

Sixth, the university's officials and its outside professional team limited their development efforts to planning the site, obtaining government approval of the plan, and then finding, and leasing land to, companies wishing to build offices or to develop the hotel/conference facilities or housing units planned for the site. By restricting its development role, Princeton avoided the complexities and risks of building and leasing finished space, and thus limited its business efforts to areas in which the university team had clear competence and experience.

Seventh, at the outset a contract was established with the outside professionals that tied the bulk of their compensation to the financial success of the development, and that provided them with the opportunity to earn a profit on their efforts comparable to what they could earn in a similar development launched by a profit-making enterprise.

Eighth, it was established from the outset that policy decisions about the development, including whether to initiate it, were to be made by the board of trustees and, within the board, by a committee made up entirely of trustees with relevant business backgrounds. The committee quickly established that the development was to be treated as a business: it understood the risks involved in the development, did not flinch from backing the venture with university funds during the start-up phase, and at critical moments provided active personal assistance to the project team.

Ninth, the project team was housed away from the university campus and in its day-to-day activities rarely mingled with the university community outside of meetings specifically related to the project.

Tenth, the center's financial goal was quite explicit: to provide a better return on the assets utilized in the development than was being received from the university's endowment. While the center was also charged with attaining a high level of quality that would influence the caliber of development in the region, there was no ambiguity about the priority of its profit-making goal.

The Princeton Forrestal Center is not unique in the nonprofit world. For instance, Harvard University's endowment funds and real estate assets are managed by a university-owned corporation of full-time professionals located in Boston, rather than at the university campus in Cambridge; this unit works under compensation arrangements comparable to those of similar professionals in the profit-making world. The group reports to the treasurer of the university, who is a fellow of the Harvard Corporation. (The treasurer is a part-time official drawn from the professional investment world.)

The point here is that the creation of a successful profit-making component within a not-for-profit environment—the building of a culture within a culture, so to speak—is a difficult business. The chances of successfully doing so will be enhanced if:

- The for-profit component is, from the outset, clearly labeled as such, and its different objectives and need for a different operating style are recognized from the start;

- The profit-making component employs its own set of professionals from the profit-making world;

- Separate compensation policies are adopted for the component that provide appropriate incentives for profit-minded professionals;

- The relationship between the component and the institution is managed by a senior executive of the nonprofit who is charged specifically with championing the project and insulating it from inappropriate interference by the institution's staff;

- Ultimate responsibility for the project is vested unequivocally in a group of the institution's trustees, who themselves are experienced participants in the profit-making world; and

- The component is physically separated from the institution.

In short, the greater the separation in terms of format, staffing, oversight, and location, the greater are the chances that the profit-making component will be able to function with the clarity of purpose and operating style appropriate and necessary to its objectives.

Financing Self-Generated Revenues

When it comes to financing a new business activity, a variety of financing options are available for nonprofit organizations. The real art is to understand exactly what role financing can play in furthering that business. Each financing option can make a different contribution to a business beyond simply providing money. A nonprofit organization needs to establish what it wants from a financial source beyond money before it can really determine where to go in search of financing.

Financing Options

A nonprofit organization may raise financing:

- From funds generated by existing revenue-producing activities. Unfortunately, few nonprofit enterprises have sufficient resources available to fund a new endeavor.

- From venture capital or other conventional public and private financing sources available to fund qualified new businesses. Such financing may take the form of either equity or debt, or some combination of the two, depending on the business's needs and financial condition. If the new business is not strong enough to attract funding in its own right, the nonprofit organization may put its credit on the line to secure capital. The terms of financing would be the same as those granted to a profit-making organization of similar resources launching a similar venture.

- By licensing a commercial profit-making company to develop the business in exchange for a royalty based on sales, net profits, or some in-between standard. Under a licensing arrangement, the commercial firm typically provides all the capital and oversees the active management of the business. The nonprofit organization confines its role primarily to exercising quality control over the licensed product. Where the nonprofit organization receives a royalty based on sales revenues rather than on a share of profits, the income will be exempt from federal income taxation. Moreover, most alert nonprofit institutions avoid royalties based on anything other than gross revenues in order to avoid getting involved in the morass of another company's accounting practices. To be in a position to negotiate a royalty arrangement, the nonprofit organization must have a name or other property elements that can enhance the sale of a product.

- By forming a joint venture with a commercial company to develop the business. The joint venture can take the form of a partnership, a stock corporation, or a contract between two entities to develop a business jointly without forming a new legal entity to operate it. The relative amounts of capital and know-how contributed by the nonprofit organization and the commercial company will vary from case to case. If the organization's name or other intangible assets are of enough value to the business, the organization may be able to negotiate for an ownership share without having to invest its own funds in the venture.

Each of these options offers a different combination of control and risk. For instance, the nonprofit institution will have the greatest control over a venture financed entirely with its own funds, but it will also bear the complete financial and management risk. The least risk exposure is offered by the licensing route, but this route provides the nonprofit organization with the least degree of control over the business.

At the same time, each of the options offers a different range of support for a new undertaking. To determine the kind of support that will be most valuable, an analysis should be made of: 1) the skills and resources the nonprofit organization brings and does not bring to the proposed venture, 2) the availability within the proposed commercial financing source of the particular skills and experience necessary to execute the proposed business, and 3) the goals the nonprofit organization is seeking to achieve through the venture.

Such an analysis will help to determine what type of financing and financing source make the most sense for the intended business. Failing to undertake this analysis seriously increases the risk of seeking the wrong type of money from the wrong source.

For instance, a nonprofit organization may have an opportunity to generate revenues from a commercial venture, and the organization's name, trademark, or affiliation with the business may be important to the exploitation of the opportunity. But the organization may not wish to expose itself to the financial or managerial risks of undertaking a business venture. It may also have few skills to bring to the development of the business. In such cases, the appropriate strategy is probably for the organization to license another firm to exploit the particular commercial opportunity in exchange for a royalty based on the revenues generated. Note, too, that the tax law treats passive royalty income as tax-free to the organization. Active involvement in a business thus has to offer a handsome return in order to provide more net after-tax income than tax-free royalties.

Licensing

Children's Television Workshop decided years ago to license a series of established commercial firms to produce toys, games, clothing, and other items under the *Sesame Street* trademark. CTW wanted to earn nonbroadcast revenues from this uniquely valuable trademark. But the Workshop did not have the capital or desire to invest in manufacturing and distribution businesses, nor did it wish to generate taxable income. Moreover, it was concerned that active involvement in an intensely competitive nonbroadcast business would divert management attention and focus from CTW's primary mission of producing educational television shows for children. Accordingly, licensing others to produce and market *Sesame Street* toys, books, and clothing made the most overall sense for CTW, even though the Workshop's control over the manufacture of products bearing its name was limited. When a product is licensed, the nonprofit licenser retains the right to approve the quality of the product (CTW also had rights to approve advertising and marketing plans), but a right to approve quality does not provide the same power over the shape of the ultimate product as an active role in its creation.

Joint Ventures

Of course, licensing may not always be feasible or desirable. A nonprofit organization may find that the product or service it wants to market commercially is so new that creating the product will require a genuine act of invention, or that the organization's reputation will be so closely linked to the product or service that it cannot delegate responsibility for its production to others. It is one thing to license the use of a nonprofit institution's name or properties to help market a product whose characteristics are known; it is another thing to do so where the product must first be invented. In such cases, the institution may well decide to play an active role in the development of the product or service. This can lead to the institution's either undertaking the venture on its own, with a combination of its own capital for equity and conventional lending sources for debt financing, or entering into a joint venture with an established commercial firm. The joint venture can allow the nonprofit institution to play a strong role in product development. At the same time, such an arrangement can give the institution access to the expertise of a commercial partner that complements the institution's own talents, as well as make available the commercial firm's equity capital and credit resources.

For instance, using its own funds over the period of a year, CTW conceived of an educational play park attraction for children (which ultimately came to be known as Sesame Place), in which children play with a unique set of play elements, science exhibits, and computers. The park was projected to cost some $10 million. The park is different from the ride-oriented, passive entertainment of traditional theme parks, and CTW wanted to be an active participant in the creation of this new concept. It also believed that a series of parks would be built and would, in the aggregate, offer a very attractive return to an equity participant, especially compared to a royalty. At the same time, the Workshop recognized that experience in park construction and in the operation and marketing of amusement parks would be crucial to success. Furthermore, CTW was in a position to invest only a small part of the total equity capital required to build a series of parks, and it lacked the needed credit to obtain the debt financing necessary for multiple parks.

CTW decided to reject offers of funding from venture capital groups and turned instead to the theme park division of Anheuser Busch to form a combined venture to own, build, and operate jointly proposed parks. CTW looked to Anheuser Busch to provide not only the bulk of the equity capital for the parks and the credit for the necessary borrowing but, just as important, the personnel required to construct, operate, and market the project in conjunction with CTW's creative team. Anheuser Busch thus played a role in the development of the parks that no purely financial institution would have been willing or equipped to undertake.

However, despite the array of complementary talents provided by the joint venture—and the strong appeal of the attraction to young children—it never attained the hoped-for financial success. Construction cost overruns in the case of the initial park and a poor location choice in the case of the second facility are among the reasons for the financial shortfall. However, none of these failings can be attributed to the form of the enterprise; they were errors in execution, in which I was a full participant. I also advocated the joint venture format over the objections of some senior staff members who wanted a royalty arrangement with Anheuser Busch to avoid risking CTW's limited capital on an untested concept. Their judgment proved correct when the actual cost of building a park skyrocketed beyond our estimates. When it became evident that the cost of building the parks would be higher than expected, CTW renegotiated the contract with Anheuser Busch to provide for royalty payments.

The Business Skills of Financing Sources

As part of the process of determining what contributions are needed from a financial source, a realistic assessment needs to be made of the limits on a nonprofit organization's ability to implement a business. Organizations— profit-making as well as nonprofit—tend to overestimate the transferability of their competence from one field to another, and thus they often forego the opportunity to find a partner that can supply the skills and assets they may lack.

In contrast, Princeton University recognized from the outset its limitations in developing the 1,600-acre mixed-use real estate development on holdings adjacent to its main campus. The university determined that it had expertise in planning and developing the uses of land, processes in which it was regularly engaged with respect to its campus and adjacent holdings, but not in designing, building, or financing commercial structures, which it had never done. Hence, the university decided to sell or lease land to developers and private companies, enabling them to build their own office, research, and housing facilities, and to limit its role to land planning and development and to design and quality review. This strategy not only confined the university's role to its area of knowledge, it also reduced the capital the school had to advance and limited its financial exposure.

Shared Values

As part of the process of defining what contributions a financial source can make to a venture, it is useful to compile as specific as possible a list of the characteristics desired in a financial partner (e.g., expertise in managing construction, operations, marketing). The list should also detail the less tangible characteristics wanted in a partner—for example, an appreciation for the values and culture of the nonprofit institution, a shared commitment to producing a quality product (even at the expense of foregoing some short-run profitability), and recognition of the importance of the public's perception of the quality and integrity of the organization.

In short, it is necessary to determine whether the partners share a common set of values. If they do not, they will eventually become antagonists, however much both may want to realize a profit from the venture.

In the end, whatever financial approach or internal structure it adopts to develop a business, the nonprofit organization will have to acclimate itself to the culture of the commercial world. This is never easy for organizations driven primarily by the desire to advance social goals rather than by the profit motive. However, to achieve its diverse aims, a modern not-for-profit must be a hybrid: a classic charitable organization in purpose, and a successful business in raising revenues. Where these two values coexist in proper balance, one can expect to find a viable, vibrant not-for-profit organization.

NOTES

1. For the story how *Sesame Street* fought the initial cutback but eventually over time absorbed the funding reduction, see the first edition of *The 21st Century Nonprofit*, pp.118–120.

2. Quoted in Jeremy McCarter, "One Cheer for Roundabout," *New York Times*, October 29, 2007.

3. A public charity is an organization that normally receives a substantial part of its support from governmental units or from direct or indirect contributions from the general public.

4. For amplification of these rules, see Paul Firstenberg, *Managing for Profit in the Nonprofit World* (New York: The Foundation Center, 1986), pp. 166–169.

5. One excellent jumping-off point for discussion of these considerations is http://www.blendedvalue. org/. There you will find links to a number of publications exploring the idea of "hybrid" organizations, whether nonprofit or for-profit.

6. Philip Kotler and Sidney J. Levy, "Broadening the Concept of Marketing," in Philip Kotler, O. C. Ferrell, and Charles Lamb, eds., *Cases and Readings for Marketing for Nonprofit Organizations* (Englewood Cliffs, NJ: Prentice Hall, 1983), pp. 3–4.

7. Philip Kotler, *Marketing for Nonprofit Organizations* (Englewood Cliffs, NJ: Prentice Hall, 1982), p. 22. Thomas J. Peters and Robert H. Waterman, Jr. (in *In Search of Excellence*, New York: Harper & Row, 1982, p. 14) characterize a marketing orientation in private companies as being "close to the customer" with a focus on providing "unparalleled quality, service, and reliability."

8. Kotler, *Marketing for Nonprofit Organizations*, pp. 24–27.

9. Peters and Waterman, *In Search of Excellence*, p. 182.

10. Ibid., pp. 293–294.

11. *Nonprofit Times*, November 1995, pp. 33–55.

12. "Real Estate Transaction," in *The Buck Starts Here: Enterprise on the Arts*, A Conference for Nonprofit Organizations on the Legal Aspects of Making Money (New York: Volunteer Lawyers for the Arts, 1984), p. 65.

A Postscript—Looking Ahead

This book has been written, for the most part, in the present tense, discussing largely the issues extant today without venturing to offer a vision of the future. This postscript seeks to compensate for this shortcoming by engaging in some degree of speculation as to the trends and conditions most likely to prevail in the years ahead. This exercise is always problematic, but at least the analysis of the future trends is rooted in the previous chapters. To keep the forecasting simple and straightforward, there follow twelve points in bold relief without supporting argumentation.

1. American nonprofits will continue their historic role in fostering educational, scientific, cultural, and humanitarian advances. However, the degree of public and governmental support for such work will, in good measure, be dependent on greater vigilance in preventing abuses in the form of individual enrichment or the application of resources to blatantly noncharitable purposes.

2. Pressure will grow for detailed accountability of the effectiveness of an organization's programs, especially more insightful outcome analysis, and for detailed explanation of the methodology used to measure results.

3. Organizations will become more transparent, providing greater insights into how effective their programs are and how critical decisions are made.

4. Despite fears of a talent shortage, waves of able people will come forward to meet the vacancies in the nonprofit world, both corporate executives caught up in a downsizing and graduates of master's programs; the nonprofit sector will continue to attract socially-minded entrepreneurs bent on finding remedies for the globe's ills.

5. There will be increasing movement of personnel between the for-profit and nonprofit sectors as well as between government and nonprofits.

6. Board members will become more active and their selection will be a product of a carefully considered search process.

7. Boards will become dedicated to establishing their own sense of cohesion as a board, meeting regularly without management present.

8. The entire board will have a clear grasp of the organization's financial condition and compensation practices.

9. Recruiting top-flight directors will continue to be a challenge.

10. Nonprofit enterprises will increasingly be international in character.

11. Funding sources will increasingly address how recipients can grow their capabilities.

12. Blurring of the line between nonprofit and for-profit enterprises will continue as nonprofits strive to generate earned income.

The foregoing projected developments may not prove out, but I am quite confident that we are on the cusp of significant change in the environment and rules of the game for nonprofits. The change may be stimulated by government, the pressure to emulate the reforms adopted by public corporations, directors intent on complying with best practices, the leadership of industry consortia, and demands made by funding sources. Whatever the source, the nonprofit sector will face new expectations of how the organizations are to be run and the performance they are to achieve.

Index

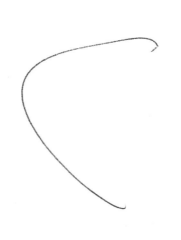